GOOD APPLES

BEHIND EVERY BITE

Susan Futrell

UNIVERSITY OF IOWA PRESS, IOWA CITY

University of Iowa Press, Iowa City 52242
Copyright © 2017 by Susan Futrell
www.uipress.uiowa.edu
Printed in the United States of America

Design by April Leidig

The University of Iowa Press is a member of Green Press Initiative
and is committed to preserving natural resources.

An earlier version of the description of pruning in chapter 4 was
originally published as an essay, "Winter Apples," and is reprinted
with permission from *Vermont's Local Banquet,* Winter 2008.

Printed on acid-free paper

Library of Congress Cataloging-in-Publication Data
Names: Futrell, Susan, 1955– author.
Title: Good apples : behind every bite / Susan Futrell.
Description: Iowa City : University of Iowa Press, [2017] |
Includes bibliographical references.
Identifiers: LCCN 2017005563 | ISBN 978-1-60938-482-1 (pbk) |
ISBN 978-1-60938-483-8 (ebk)
Subjects: LCSH: Apples. | Apples—Marketing.
Classification: LCC SB363 .F88 2017 | DDC 634/.11—dc23

LC record available at https://lccn.loc.gov/2017005563

*To the caretakers of
apple trees everywhere*

In nature nothing exists alone.
—Rachel Carson, biologist, writer,
and ecologist (1907–1964)

I think [the apple], above all others,
may be called the true democratic fruit.
—Henry Ward Beecher, clergyman, essayist,
and social reformer (1813–1887)

CONTENTS

ACKNOWLEDGMENTS

I DON'T KNOW IF it is all the time they spend around apple trees that makes so many apple growers such humble, lovely people, or if those qualities are why they've chosen to grow apples, but they seem to go together. The growers, scientists, crop consultants, and others I've met who work with apples represent some of the most creative, dedicated, smart, and skillful fruit experts in the country. I am especially grateful to:

Growers in the Eco Apple program past and present, including Aaron, Dana, and Naomi Clark, Clark Brothers Orchards; John Lyman, Lyman Orchards; Peter Ten Eyck, Laura Ten Eyck, and Joe Nuciforo, Indian Ladder Farms; Barney and Christiana Hodges, Sunrise Orchards; Zeke Goodband, Scott Farm; Eric Henry, Blue Hills Orchard; John Rogers, Peter Rogers, and Greg Parzych, Rogers Orchards; Elizabeth Ryan, Breezy Hill and Stone Ridge Orchards; Andy Orbaker, Orbaker's Fruit Farm; Josh Morgenthau, Fishkill Farms; Chuck Mead, Mead Orchards; Karl and Betsy Schlegel, K. Schlegel Fruit Farm; Glen Schreiter, Saxtons River Orchards; Ed Davidian, Davidian Brothers Farm; Homer Dunn, Alyson's Orchard; Adam Sullivan, Champlain Valley Apple; Bill Suhr, Champlain Orchards; Joel, Bill, and Vito Truncali, Truncali Farms; Calvin Beekman, Beekman Orchards; Brien and Emily Davis, Hope Orchards; Steve and Marilyn Meyerhans, The Apple Farm; and all the others who have been part of the network over the years.

Thanks to apple growers across the country who generously gave me their time and the permission to tell their stories, especially the late Wynne Weinreb, Scott Beaton, Mark Gores, Kevin Stennes, Harold Linder, and Jessica Welch. And to everyone who recommended apple growers to talk to, orchards to visit, experts to consult, and apples to try, so many of whom gave me time and information and stories that I wasn't able to include: Maury Wills, Sacia Morris, and many others.

An assignment from Rich Pirog, then head of the marketing program at Leopold Center for Sustainable Agriculture at Iowa State University, first sent me to Harold Linder's orchard in southeast Iowa, which led to a project on heirloom apples, which led me to Red Tomato and ultimately to this book. So thanks, Rich, for everything.

Michael Rozyne, change maker, teacher, friend for life, gave my obsession with apples a useful purpose.

My colleagues at Red Tomato, Laura Edwards-Orr, Angel Mendez, Diane Rast, Gideon Burdick, Maria Mastanduno, and everyone I've worked with there over the past ten years, my thanks for your patience, flexibility, and forbearance in giving me the time and encouragement that made it possible to write this book. Chris Loughlin and Barb Harrington at Crystal Spring lifted me up with prayers and spirit. Thank you all for doing the work you do; it matters and I'm honored to do it with you.

Thank you to Tom Green, Peter Werts, and their colleagues at IPM Institute of North America for tireless work on behalf of a more ecologically sustainable world. Thanks to Dan Cooley, University of Massachusetts, who contributed some elegant explanations of apple science; Jon Clements, University of Massachusetts Cold Spring Orchard; Tracy Leskey, Appalachian Fruit Research Station; David Granatstein, Washington State University; Patrick O'Malley, extension horticulturist, Johnson County, Iowa; Ken Meter, Crossroads Resource Center; Rob Koch and Mike Biltonen, Apple Leaf; Art Agnello, Harvey Reissig, David Rosenberger, and Abby Seaman, Cornell University; Peter Jentsch, Hudson Valley Research Laboratory; and Steve Young and the staff at the Northeastern IPM Center, especially to former center director Carrie Koplinka-Loehr, for helping me understand and appreciate the many wonders of integrated pest management.

Erik Nicholson and colleagues at United Farm Workers introduced me to Jose Onate, Rosa Torres, and Angelica Ruiz-Rodriguez; I am deeply grateful for your trust, grace, and humor.

To all the farmers and farm advocates who help me understand and appreciate what it takes to grow food, especially my Iowa circle: Denise O'Brien, Ann Franzenberg, Mary Swalla Holmes, Jan Libbey, Laura Krouse, and Susan Jutz.

My thanks to librarians Mary Bennett, State Historical Society of Iowa, and Marty Schlabaugh, Cornell University Albert R. Mann Library, and all the libraries and cafés that lent me a quiet, cool place to work when I needed it, especially the State Historical Society of Iowa; Iowa City Public Library; Patten Free Library, Bath, Maine; Curtis Memorial Library, Brunswick, Maine; and the Albert R. Mann Library at Cornell University. Support your local libraries and public archives; they are invaluable, and they need us.

I'm thankful for wise and kind teachers Laverna Larson and Patricia Foster for their friendship and encouragement, and for Mary Swander, generous mentor and steadfast friend, for her presence and advice and for offering me a quiet place to write.

Thanks to Catherine Cocks, editor, and everyone at the University of Iowa Press for their support and dedication to producing excellent books, and to Faith Marcovecchio, copy editor, for astutely and kindly making this a better one.

I am grateful for the support, advice, and wisdom of many writing colleagues over the years, too many to name without missing someone, and I'm richly blessed to be part of a community of writers who love to read each other's work. Hope Burwell is a steadfast and fierce editor; she, Jo Futrell, Michael Rozyne, and Dan Cooley each read the entire manuscript at crucial stages and gave me honest, astute suggestions that make this a far better book than it would have been without their wisdom. Any flaws that remain are all mine.

Sharon Lake, Jackie Loesche, Jesse Singerman, Jane Tenenbaum, Lalli Drobny, Glenda Yoder, and my many kind and wonderful friends too many to name, thank you for the friendship and counsel that keeps me whole.

Frances Tenenbaum was a dear friend and my home away from home for the first few years of my time working in Boston. The last time I saw her she whispered, "I am so excited about your book," before even I knew there was going to be one.

A lifetime of thanks to my mom, Lucy Futrell, my sister, Jo Futrell, my family, Steve, Alice, Harrison, and Lydia Futrell, Bill Futrell, Mary Volkman, and my entire Jennings family for their support, patience, and encouragement; and in honor and memory of my dad, Gene Futrell, who is with me in spirit.

Gibson, thanks for hanging in there with me the whole way: cats don't need to read because they already know.

Will Jennings, who is my home; who is always willing to go the distance with me, apple orchard included; who knows when I need to sit down and get to work and when to take the hike; who believes in me, and more than that, helps me believe in myself: thank you for sharing this writing life.

GOOD APPLES

Soul of an Orchard

"DO YOU WANT TO *run* the orchard?" my husband, Will, asked carefully. I'd just told him that our local bank had given me a letter of credit, based on only my own savings and income, promising to loan me more money than our own house was worth to buy an orchard I'd never seen. "No," I said firmly. "And I don't want to move there, either." Still, I raced to the copy shop to fax the bank letter to Sullivan Auctions somewhere in Illinois in time to be registered as an authorized bidder for the 6:00 p.m. auction.

It was February, and raining. I had planned to drive the hour and a half south from our home in Iowa City to attend in person so I could see what was happening and gauge my steps accordingly. I stuck stubbornly to that plan until midafternoon, when the rain turned to ice and the reasonableness of the drive (never mind the reason for it) became a serious question. I made nervous calls to the auction house, drove across town to fax them my registration to join the auction online, and raced back home in the growing dark. Not quite able to look Will in the eye, I made a cup of tea to calm myself down.

In my upstairs office, lit only by the computer screen, I scrolled back and forth between plat maps and photographs, trying to picture a place I had never seen and get a feel for what was about to happen. Sleet lashed at the window. My slightly crazed reflection looked back at me from the dark glass. The other parties—the family selling the orchard to resolve a dispute between two brothers, neighbors, developers, and who knows who else—were gathered in a motel banquet room a hundred miles away on the outskirts of Fort Madison, Iowa. For all they knew, the lone bidder on the phone was a serious fruit producer looking for another farm, or a rich college-town food enthusiast looking for a hobby, or a developer looking for a piece of flat ground with good drainage. I was Paddle No. 3000. Beyond that, I was having trouble figuring out for myself who I was in this situation.

I'm a fifth-generation Iowan. Like the brothers selling the orchard, my family came west to the prairie in the 1800s. My ancestors were sometimes tenants, moving from farm to farm, so my roots in Iowa are not as deeply planted in one piece of ground. I grew up in Ames, a college town. Still, those nostalgic associations with apple pie at Grandma's are actually true for me, as are memories of big pots of applesauce bubbling in my mother's kitchen and hours spent sitting in the fruit tree at the edge of our backyard.

The neighborhood where I grew up, like so many others, was once woods, then farmland, then subdivision. A few blocks away, surrounded on three sides by sidewalks and ranch houses, the remnants of an apple orchard filled a pocket of land along the main road. The Jensens, the old German couple who owned it, were as gnarled and odd to my child's eyes as the old apple trees they tended, and the baskets of apples they sold at their fruit stand every autumn were equally lumpy and imperfect. But each fall we made regular stops to buy their fruit, my dad always taking time to talk about the weather, the season, and his favorite apple, Grimes Golden.

The little old farmhouse was dark and set back from the road. It was sometimes hard to understand the tiny stooped woman because of her heavy accent. On Halloween, kids were always afraid to knock on the Jensens' door for trick or treat. The year I was old enough and brave enough to go up their dark gravel driveway and ring the bell, I came away with the best Halloween score ever: a whole bag of splotchy apples. Never mind how heavy they were, I proudly lugged my bulging treat sack the rest of the way around the neighborhood. I was never afraid of the old couple after that, sometimes stopping to buy apples and venturing my own conversations about how the apples looked, finding my own favorite: dark-red, tart, crisp Jonathan.

My father was an agricultural economist at Iowa State University. He grew up on a farm, the youngest of seven and the only one to go to a four-year college and on to graduate school. He spent his career working for the extension service at Iowa State, helping hog and cattle farmers survive in the changing marketplace. My mom grew up on a farm, paid her own way to college, then left school to raise four kids. She cooked our meals from scratch, grew a big garden, and made jelly every summer from the grapes in our backyard. Our parents made sure we did well in school, went to church, and saw much of the country on summer trips to wherever the American Agricultural Economics Association was holding its meetings that year. My sister, brothers, cousins, and I spent many weekends on both grandparents' farms, straddling fences, hiding in the root cellar among the blue jars of canned goods, and daring each other to go into the henhouse among the chickens. Big Sunday dinners with lots of relatives crowded around the table filling plates with vegetables from the garden and homegrown chicken gave me an early understanding of where food comes from. I took for granted that farms were part of the landscape and of life.

As it turned out, the last-minute effort to set up proxy bidding so I could see and hear the auction on my computer failed. There was some fumbling around, then the auction assistant suggested that since I was the only online bidder, he would just hold his phone up so I could hear and give him my bid. Clutching my phone as the auctioneer started his reeling, rhythmic patter, I tried hard to imagine the faces in the room. Were the family members all there? Were they lined up on opposite sides of the room? Were there bankers, speculators, curious neighbors? Was it tense, sad, exciting, or just another land auction in a county that has seen more than its share?

The orchard being sold was the oldest commercial apple orchard in Iowa, in the same family for five generations. I'd first learned of it a year before while helping the Leopold Center for Sustainable Agriculture establish an heirloom apple competition at the Iowa State Fair. The family took home the blue ribbon for heirloom apples and several other categories. At the time, the orchard seemed like a proud survivor.

But when the father died, his sons couldn't agree about the future of the farm. As happens fairly often in farm country, those differences were being settled on the auction block. Someone had posted the sale announcement on the Practical Farmers of Iowa listserv, where it sat thrumming in my inbox for several days while I waited for someone to respond and say they were rallying to save the orchard. No one did. I began to imagine the old trees being ripped out by bulldozer, their rich leaf mulch pressed into the mud, the slopes cleared for a parking lot, a factory, a housing development named Orchard Lane.

The more I let myself imagine, the more worked up I got. Finally I sent the rallying email to a few people around the state I knew cared about Iowa's farm heritage. Did they know anything about the orchard? Was someone going to keep it in operation? Anyone looking for a farm in southeast Iowa? Anyone interested in putting together a joint bid? With only the barest information gleaned from the bill of sale and an article in the local newspaper, we commiserated from a distance about the tragedy of it all. In the end, it was clear there was no time, not enough money, and no one to take it on. Which was equally true of my own situation, but at some point I stopped letting that matter. I didn't want to run the orchard, I didn't want to move to southeast Iowa, and I didn't want to drain my life savings. But neither did I want the orchard—or the idea I had of it—to disappear.

I WAS A SHY, bookish town kid, but I spent a lot of time outdoors, playing in nearby woods and pastures, going on family camping trips and Camp Fire Girls nature hikes. When I was twelve, I helped start the Welch Jr. High Environmental Action Club and campaigned to Save the Ledges, a nearby state park about to be flooded by a proposed dam. I wrote leaflets and letters to the editor, sat at card tables with petitions, and knocked on neighbors' doors. Ultimately we failed to stop the construction of the dam, but it was my first taste of the satisfaction of getting involved with other people to advocate for something we cared about.

The environmental action club advisor was our seventh-grade biology teacher, Laverna Larson. It was 1967, and one of the books she suggested to her earnest crew of budding activists was *Silent Spring*, by Rachel Carson. I read it avidly, then ordered a set of Carson's other books—*The Sea Around Us*, *Under the Sea Wind*, and *The Edge of the Sea*—from the Scholastic Book Club, and devoured those too. *Silent Spring* rocked my world as it did for so many. I became passionate about environmental issues and a bit insufferable, as only teenagers can be, uncompromising and certain about my beliefs. Carson's work is still my touchstone for understanding the intersection between nature and humans. It's taken me many years to realize that intersection is far more complicated than I understood then.

My love of farms and concern for the environment converged when I encountered the natural food and organic farming movement as a college student. Food became a lens, a lever of change, and a means of connection to everything I wanted the world to be. I spent the next twenty-five years of my working life doing marketing and sales for Blooming Prairie Warehouse, a cooperatively owned natural foods distributor that reached tens of thousands of eaters all over the upper Midwest.

One of the most meaningful things I had the opportunity to do at Blooming Prairie was connect our work with that of other people and organizations that cared about food and farming. At the beginnings of the farm crisis of the 1980s, as part of an initiative called Peoples' Commission on Food, Land, and Justice, I helped draft and co-signed a national call to action to support family farmers and environmental justice. In 1985, I camped overnight near Champaign, Illinois, with my sister and two friends to get a good seat at the first Farm Aid concert to benefit family farmers. A few years later, Blooming Prairie shipped a truckload of food to the Farm Aid concert in Chicago. With others in the industry, I advocated and helped draft guidelines for what became the Organic Foods Production Act of 1990. We were part of many exciting changes in the food supply and culture.

In those early years of the natural and organic food industry, I discovered I love business when it's done right. I've spent my career since trying to figure out how to do business right in the food industry. But when I left my job as director of marketing at Blooming Prairie after more than two decades, I was worn out by the intense competition and steady consolidation of the industry, even in our still-small corner of it. I wanted to reconnect more directly with farms and the environment.

So it probably made sense for Will to worry when I told him I might buy an orchard.

ADRENALINE PUMPING, I waited for the auction to start. I knew my limit after talking with the bank. I was barely going to be at market value. But I reasoned, if the place went for nothing, at least a developer wouldn't get it easily.

At 6:01 the auctioneer called the auction open, describing the property, giving a nod to its history and an indirect acknowledgment that not every family member was happy to see it sectioned off into seven bite-sized plots. He opened the bidding at $50,000. I listened for someone to bid. The auctioneer dropped to $25,000. *My g-d*, I thought, forgetting how auctions usually go, *I could afford that!* Then bang, I heard the first bid of $175,000, and then another, come through the phone. Before I could react, much less squeeze in a too-low attempt, it raced past me. Lively bidding from at least two parties quickly overtook my paltry limit. $200,000, then $210,000, the auctioneer cajoling, wheedling for $225,000. At 6:24 his rolling, tinny voice through the phone asked, "All in? All done? SOLD, $215,000." And just like that, it was over.

Breathless, I told the nice fellow holding the phone, "That went past me pretty fast. I'll follow the other sections online. I'm glad for the family, and appreciate being able to call in." I hung up the phone and sat in the dark, shaking. My eyes burned, and I wasn't sure if the tears were tension, or sadness, or some murkier kind of grief. Mostly, I was relieved. With the wind and sleet snarling outside, I knew I had just been given a reprieve from what could have been the first of many anxious drives south.

I had a candle on the desk next to me, some kind of gesture to the universe to help "the right thing," whatever it was, happen, except it wouldn't stay lit. The online auction still glowed from my small computer screen, and I watched the numbers being entered as the rest of the farm was sold off tract by tract. At 7:05, the auctioneer gaveled the last forty acres of Tract #7 sold.

It took long breaths and a good ten minutes for the adrenaline to dissolve enough for me to go downstairs. Will, carefully quiet but tensely ready for relief or for our life to upend, let me describe the auction and talk myself down before letting out his own breath. Bless him for never telling me I was foolish and impractical to have even entertained such an idea, because I'd have had to agree.

The next day, weather clear, I drove to Fort Madison for the auctioning of the tools, household goods, and miscellanea of the century farm. The parking lot was filled with trucks and cars from all over Iowa and nearby states, a few painted with names of other orchards. It was a cold, blustery day, but there was a good crowd, a bittersweet blessing for people holding an auction that's not entirely welcome. Before the bidding got started, we all clustered around a flatbed truck piled with boxes of hand tools, carpentry chests, and machinery. The auctioneer gestured toward a young couple standing at one end of the flatbed. They were the new owners of the orchard, he announced, there to purchase what they needed to take over the operation. He congratulated them and reminded people to be respectful but not to hold back from bidding on whatever they wanted. Relief, deference, and curiosity rippled through me and the rest of the crowd.

The young couple followed closely as the auction moved around the farmyard, carefully bidding on orchard equipment and other things, and usually winning the items. By the end of a long day everything was gone except a few piles and pieces of equipment left to be collected later. I came home with a few wooden crates, some hand-painted signs, and a scuffed-up, gracefully tapered wooden orchard ladder, reminiscent of but much more manageable than the orchard itself.

EVEN YEARS LATER, I can't easily explain why I clutched the phone so tightly that night of the auction. It was illogical and impractical and undeniable. Why would something as everyday, common, enduring, and iconic as an apple orchard engender such intense feelings of nostalgia and loss? It's not as if we are in danger of never seeing or tasting apples again, or even in danger of never seeing an apple tree or orchard. But something about the loss felt irreplaceable.

My grandfather died when I was in college. He had stopped farming years before, and his house and belongings were sold off in an auction to resolve a dispute among his sons and daughters, too. Maybe that's partly why I needed to bear some kind of witness to the orchard passing. But there was something else about that venerable orchard sliding off the auction block into the icy telephone lines and away. It had something to do with farms, a connection to history, caretaking the land, and apples. I've known all my life that those things matter, but I've never felt it so deeply in my bones as I did that night.

The sense of loss that I felt so viscerally continues to be very real in farm communities. Across the countryside, very large farms are increasing in number and size. Very small farms are also increasing in some areas, although many are too small to support their owners without outside jobs. Medium-sized family farms, still the majority of farms in the United States, are having a tough time staying in business. Secretary of Agriculture Tom Vilsack spoke at a joint USDA/Department of Justice public workshop on competition in agriculture in 2010, stating that over eighty thousand midsized U.S. farms disappeared in the five years between 2002 and 2007 alone.[1] When these farms go out of business, the farmland is lost to development or industry, and farming knowledge disappears rather than being passed along to a new generation. Rural communities collapse, losing businesses, churches, and schools. Those losses affect urban residents' access to locally grown food as well as rural beauty. They represent not just land changing hands but degradation of the ecosystems that feed soil, air, and water for surrounding communities. At some point, we lose the capacity to rebuild a locally based food supply.

Losing local apple orchards is particularly wrenching. Apples are familiar to almost everyone from childhood, whether picked from a backyard tree or a grocery store shelf. Trees can produce fruit for generations. Mention apples to almost anyone, and you'll prompt a story, the name of a favorite variety, a recommendation about where to pick them, or a promise to introduce a friend who has worked in or owns an orchard.

On the night of the auction I felt like I was trying to hold on to all of that. There was more at stake than a small orchard in an out-of-the-way part of a flyover state. It was about the soul of something—me, the land, the country. It was about how we feed ourselves, not just our bodies but our sense of connection to each other, to our history, the land, and our responsibility for all of it.

Years ago, reading Michael Pollan's *The Botany of Desire*, I noticed a reference to an essay by Henry Ward Beecher, a prolific writer and orator in the mid-1800s (and brother of writer Harriet Beecher Stowe) in which he called the apple "the true democratic fruit."[2] The phrase stuck in my mind, but for a long time I focused on the eaters' view of what I thought he meant: apples are common and affordable, they're diverse and everyone can choose a favorite, they're grown and sold and available everywhere. Then I began to work with farmers who grow apples for a living. I began to learn about varieties and biology, pests and disease, packaging and market pressures and crop loss. I began to realize that a wider meaning of *democratic* would take these into account too, that a democratic apple isn't just about who is eating apples but about who is growing, picking, packing, studying, buying, and selling them.

Pondering my own response to everything that phrase means has led me deeper into the world of apples and apple growing in the United States. I've barely scratched the surface of all there is to know about this humble, delightful fruit. But it turns out that understanding the geographic, ecological, and economic forces shaping the choices of those who make a living growing apples and, at the other end of the supply chain, of the people who buy their fruit, is a powerful way to understand what's at stake for all of us as we shape the farm and food system.

LOCAL
Liberty Apples
Wilson's Orchard

CHAPTER ONE

At the Intersection of Apples and Local

ON A SATURDAY MORNING in autumn, the Iowa City Farmers Market is bustling. Baked goods, meats, cheeses, sauces, and jams along with handmade tamales and egg rolls crowd tables loaded with a colorful array of fresh fruits and vegetables. Several apple vendors with beautiful fruit offer new varieties to choose from every week as the season goes on. Duchess is the earliest to ripen, followed by a dazzling parade that includes new offerings like Zestar!® and oldsters like my longtime favorite, Jonathan. Iowa has among the highest number of farmers markets per capita in the United States,[1] which might surprise those who think of it as corn, soybean, and confinement hog land. Farms here once produced a much wider range of crops, including fresh fruits and vegetables, than they do today, supplying markets across the country. Iowa State University's Leopold Center for Sustainable Agriculture reports that in 1920, thirty-four different crops, including apples, were grown commercially

ABOVE: Local apples at New Pioneer Food Co-op, Iowa City.
Photo by Susan Futrell.

by at least 1 percent of farms in the state. By 1997, the number had nar-
rowed to just ten, and apples were not among them.[2] The center estimates close to 85 percent of food consumed in the state now comes from
elsewhere.[3]

Farmers markets have grown profusely all over the country. There
were 8,268 and counting in 2014, up 180 percent just since 2006.[4] Still,
direct-to-consumer outlets such as farmers markets and farm stands
account for less than 3 percent of U.S. farm sales according to the 2012
USDA Census of Agriculture.[5] Most people still buy their produce at
the grocery store, where the percentage of produce marketed as locally
grown, although not widely tracked, is loosely estimated to be under
2 percent, staggeringly below what demand could support.

In part, this is because the infrastructure and systems for growing,
distributing, processing, and selling food from regional farmers to local,
regional, and national grocers have been reshaped and reengineered
over the past fifty years to provide a year-round supply of cheap commodities with no connection to place or season, shipped anonymously
worldwide in high volume. Consumer buying patterns have helped drive
this shift, even though many say they would choose fresh, local, seasonal
products if they had easier access to them.

As I make my way around the Iowa City market, it's obvious we still
have the soil, climate, and skilled farmers to produce the diverse bounty
that once grew here. The same is true in most regions of the country.
Still, in the middle of September, when apple harvest is in full swing, it
is rare to find a local or even a midwestern apple in the grocery store. My
local co-op, which makes a point of supporting Iowa growers, has a few
local varieties on offer next to many more from elsewhere. The gigantic
Iowa-owned Hy-Vee grocery stores on the outskirts of town carry local
apples for a few weeks in autumn, but even then their displays are dominated by piles of shiny fruit from far away. Almost everywhere in the
country, local apples are a novelty nestled in among apples from Washington State and New Zealand that will be as abundant in January and
June as they are in September.

WHEN I LEFT my longtime natural foods job, I found a new sense of home in the local food movement. In the past decade, support for local food has blossomed for all kinds of good reasons: buying local supports farmers, keeps money in the community, provides fresher produce, and promotes stewardship of the land. The turn toward local food is a logical extension of many of the values that motivated the natural food, organic farming, and cooperative movements.

For me, the most exciting thing about local food isn't counting miles, it's connecting with farms. At the time of the orchard auction, I was living in Iowa but had just started working for a small nonprofit near Boston. Red Tomato was started in 1996 by Michael Rozyne, a friend I have known since college days. Michael helped found Equal Exchange, the first fair-trade coffee company in the United States, and has spent the past twenty years finding ways to bring those fair-trade values to his work with local fruit and vegetable farms. At Red Tomato, I found a satisfying opportunity to apply my experience in food distribution to a small organization that worked directly with local farms. Within a couple years I was working there full time, dividing my time between home in Iowa City and the office in Plainville, Massachusetts. Working with fruit and vegetable growers to market their crops to local eaters was exactly what I wanted to do (never mind the irony of traveling halfway across the country in order to do it).

Buying local produce is indeed a powerful way to support local farms, but growing local food presents challenges that aren't obvious at first. Rebuilding a locally based food supply intersects with a whole range of big questions, about pest management, regional differences, climate change, farm labor shortages, economics, and the role of public support for farming as a livelihood.

Getting local produce from farm to table isn't as simple as it sounds, either. Just because the farms and customers are close together doesn't make the logistics between them easier; it actually makes them more complicated. Red Tomato doesn't sell directly to consumers, but rather to retail grocery stores, cafeterias, and wholesale distributors, the invis-

ible part of the food supply chain that handles most of the food sold in
the United States, in the places where most people shop most of the time.

When the phone rings at Red Tomato, Laura Edwards-Orr, the exec-
utive director, or Michael, or one of several young, savvy account managers might take a call from a grocery store or cafeteria interested in
buying fresh produce from farms in the region, or from one of the several hundred stores already set up to place an order, or from one of the
forty-some fruit and vegetable farms across the region whose produce
they coordinate, market, and sell. Thanks to years of nurturing relationships with trucking companies and buyers throughout the region, Angel
Mendez, director of operations and logistics maestro, can line up a
trucker ready to pick up fresh produce at a farm or an on-farm packinghouse and deliver it to the customer's dock, sometimes the same day
it's picked. The logistics and timing of getting orders from farm to store
are complicated: growers from several orchards might bring fruit to one
farm where it is loaded together onto that farmer's truck or picked up by
a third-party trucking company and taken to a distribution center to be
divided up again for delivery to individual stores. It works most of the
time. When it doesn't, someone from Red Tomato answers phone calls
in the middle of the night.

Marketing and explaining "local" to shoppers and produce buyers
also turns out to be more challenging than I expected. Depending on
when, where, and how it is grown, local produce doesn't easily fit into
the kinds of either/or definitions—large or small, organic or not, from
ten miles away, a hundred miles, or the next state over—that seem to
make sense from a distance when you are writing promotions and advertising claims.

My first hard lesson in how complicated local can be came from a network of Northeast apple orchards, part of a program developed by Red
Tomato called Eco Apple. After decades of thinking of farms as either
organic or conventional, I quickly learned that conventional didn't come
close to describing these orchards, or the orchardists who ran them.
Certified organic apples sold in U.S. grocery stores are rarely local—
93 percent are from Washington, most of the rest from New Zealand or
Chile, where a dry climate makes organic practices especially effective.

The orchards certified as Eco Apple grow fruit using ecological production methods that suit the Northeast with its wetter climate and considerable range of pest and disease pressures. Without understanding the complex challenges and choices involved in producing a commercial apple crop, the decisions made by these growers don't always make sense to shoppers, or at least not in a way that can be conveyed on a tiny label or shelf sign.

Despite tough odds, these growers are managing to keep a foot in the wholesale fresh apple business. Their orchards are in a region ideal for producing crisp, flavorful fruit. Their oldest trees harken back to the earliest days of fruit production in the American colonies. People in New England love their apples, yet here too, local apples in the grocery stores are dwarfed by the mounds of apples from out West, even at the peak of harvest.

THE HIGHWAY BETWEEN my home in Iowa City and the orchard that was sold at auction passes through a corner of the state that was once a major fruit and vegetable growing region. Tomatoes were processed at a big Heinz canning factory outside of Muscatine. A bend in the Mississippi River creates a microclimate and good sandy soil that makes the flat fields of Fruitland famous for their Muscatine melons. The drive today passes through a landscape defined by what Iowa musician Dave Moore sings about as "Pork, Poker, and Prisons." Corn destined for livestock feed and ethanol, riverboat casinos, and the state penitentiary in Fort Madison are big economic drivers here now.

Our dominant food and farming system in the United States has gone off the rails in too many ways. Some 40 percent of the entire U.S. land base is devoted to agricultural production, much of it in the vast Mississippi watershed. Potentially a tremendous natural resource for future generations, instead, soil, fertilizer, and pesticides from the region wash down the river into a massive dead zone in the Gulf of Mexico. The City of Des Moines waterworks department has the most sophisticated nitrate management equipment in the world and cannot keep up with what it takes to purify the surface runoff in the three rivers that converge at their doorstep. Fields grown using organic agriculture and conservation practices have been shown to practically eliminate erosion and nitrogen leaching, and significantly reduce pesticide use. Yet nearly thirty years after the passage of the Organic Foods Production Act in 1990, less than 1 percent of U.S. farmland is certified organic.[6] Practices on the other 99 percent vary widely, some damaging, some highly restorative.

Most of the food that feeds small towns, rural areas, and big cities alike is imported from far away. All of it, even if it's organic, is grown using equipment and materials that depend on petroleum. Millions of families living in poverty, including many of those who harvest and prepare our food, don't have access to and can't afford fresh, sustainably grown local food. Record-breaking harvests force prices down for apple growers all over the country, while more orchards every year join a long and proliferating line of towns, housing developments, and shopping malls to be named after the orchards and trees they've erased.

The public discourse about these issues is noisy and polarized. Proponents of industrial-scale agriculture loudly proclaim everything is fine, no harm is being done, just leave us in charge, while consumer advocates and activists sound loud alarms about poisons in our food, dead bees, and evil corporations. At the same time, more eaters want wholesome, ecological, ethical food grown by real people they can trust. As more social and environmental costs are linked to the current industrial food system—epidemic rates of obesity and diabetes, food safety scares, illnesses linked to toxins in water and air, labor abuses—it seems clear that this desire for good food is not just a fad but a deeply felt call for something better.

In the midst of that clamor, the voices of farmers on small and midsized family farms are mostly quiet. Their stories are not quick sound bites, are not always what consumers want to hear, and are not the same for every farm.

The longer I worked with apple growers in the Northeast, the more I wanted to know about apple growing in general. For the past ten years I've had the opportunity to meet and learn from apple growers in many parts of the country who follow a variety of growing and marketing practices on farms that range from tiny to thousands of acres.

Working with, learning from, and getting to know these growers has tested a lot of what I thought I knew about where farming and food need to go. After my years in the organic movement, excitement about Slow Food and local food, and years of living in the middle of so much industrial agriculture, I thought organic, heirloom, direct marketing, family farm, small scale, and local seemed like the right stuff. Apple growers are doing all of that, but a lot of them are also trying new high-density planting of the latest new varieties, using ecologically responsible growing methods other than organic, and trying hard to hold on to their wholesale markets. They've complicated my picture of what "right" in farming looks like.

It turns out apple growers are doing a lot of things right. Apple orchards in the United States are still mostly family owned, and their farms are of all sizes, tiny to very large. The infrastructure—packing, shipping, marketing—is also mostly grower-owned, a lot of it by co-ops. Production practices are becoming more ecologically responsible, not less, on a large scale as well as small. Apple researchers at public institutions work with diverse genetic material and use traditional breeding methods to advance new varieties. Orchards and heritage collections are preserving the old varieties too, and heirloom apples have growing numbers of fans. There are lots of really good-quality apples in stores all over the country, all year long, at prices that make them affordable for most households, schools, and restaurants. Apples are good for you—healthy, mostly eaten fresh, real food for real people. Apples are also deeply full of story and culture and history—quintessential American food.

I've learned that growing apples for a year-round wholesale marketplace in ecologically sustainable ways and making a living at it is one of the most complex and challenging things a farmer, or anyone, could decide to do. The growers, scientists, and other apple caretakers described in this book represent some of the most creative, dedicated, smart, and skillful fruit producers in the country, and there are thousands more like them.

John Lyman of Lyman Orchards in Connecticut is the eighth generation to farm his family's land. He is a leader in helping to develop innovative marketing and growing practices for ecological fruit in the

Northeast. Lyman Orchards sells its fruit directly to consumers at its retail store, café, and pick-your-own, and also wholesale to grocery stores
and institutions. John is a co-founder of the Eco Apple program. After
275 years on the same piece of land, it is still a constant challenge to keep
the orchard viable and around for the next generation. Aaron, Dana, and
Brian Clark and their families, of Clark Brothers Orchards in western
Massachusetts, who sell most of their fruit through wholesale channels,
are also part of the Eco Apple program. It's one of the ways they have
held on to wholesale customers they have had for decades, in a market
where price is way more powerful than loyalty. Peter Ten Eyck is another
longtime leader in ecological fruit production. His family's Indian Ladder Farms in the upper Hudson Valley is a phenomenally popular pick-
your-own orchard, market, and café. These orchards all sell their fruit
almost entirely within the Northeast.

Across the country in Washington, the heart of the nation's dominant
apple region, Wynne Weinreb and Scott Beaton have nurtured five acres
of rich organic ground high above the Columbia River in Chelan, producing dozens of varieties of apples for loyal farmers market and mail-
order customers. A few miles up the shore of Lake Chelan, Mark Gores,
a second-generation grower, has met the challenge of staying afloat by
remaking the orchard planted by his parents as he adopts the latest varieties and growing techniques. A bit farther to the northwest, the Stennes
family operates a multi-generation orchard that is fully integrated into
the large, complex, and mostly grower-owned packing and marketing
infrastructure that supplies Washington apples to the rest of the world.
All of these growers produce fruit that is sold to customers across the
country, and in some cases around the world. Yet they too struggle each
year to keep up with changes and make the complex decisions that will
keep their orchards thriving.

And in the middle of the Mississippi River valley, surrounded by corn,
is a small orchard of found and grafted and tested varieties lovingly
tended and nursed from cuttings for over seven decades by orchardist
and experimenter Harold Linder.

Thumbtacked to the bulletin board above my desk is a quote from
the photographer Lewis Hine: "There are two things I wanted to do. I

wanted to show the things that needed to be corrected. And I wanted to show the things that needed to be appreciated."[7] This book offers some of both. All of these growers and many others like them have found their own ways to make a living growing apples, and they have helped me realize some of what it will take from the rest of us to make their choice of livelihood sustainable for the future. To understand how much there is to appreciate, I started with some history.

CHAPTER TWO

Immigrant Apples

APPLES ARE SO well adapted to North America, it seems as if they've always been here. They're grown in every state in the United States: in Alaska, old Yellow Transparent trees have stood for over a century; in Hawai'i, apples have grown high up on the mountainside of sacred Mauna Kea since 1890. They thrive in backyards, farmyards, urban orchards, commercial orchards, nurseries, parks. Whether abandoned, haphazard, or well tended, all of them are immigrants.[1]

The ancestors of the modern apple first grew in the Tien Shan mountains of Central Asia, in what is now Kazakhstan. This pocket of land at the juncture of modern China, Pakistan, and Afghanistan seems remote and harsh to most Americans, but it sits at the hub of some of the oldest civilizations and trade routes on Earth, midway along the Silk Road that has connected India and China to Europe and Africa for centuries.

The modern-day city of Almaty (formerly Alma-Ata) in Kazakhstan, sometimes translated as "full of apples" or "father of the apple," sits amid

ABOVE: Harvest on display, 1800s, Lyman Orchards, Middlefield, Connecticut. Photo by Lyman Orchards.

remnants of fruit forests that once stretched hundreds of miles. Nikolay Vavilov, the Russian agricultural scientist credited with collecting over 250,000 seeds, fruits, and tubers, first explored the region in 1929. Observing a forest of apple trees unlike any he had ever seen, he concluded this must be their place of origin.

Vavilov, who did perhaps more than any other person to preserve and catalog the biodiversity of plant life on Earth, starved to death in a Soviet gulag in 1943. His colleagues guarded his seed collection, many starving themselves rather than eat the genetic storehouse that might someday feed the world. Stalin's suppression of Vavilov's science kept his work from being recognized for many years, but he left a legacy in the apple forests of Almaty.

A million apple trees disappeared there during WWII alone, burned as firewood. Writer Gary Nabhan[2] estimates that 70 to 80 percent of the remaining wild apple forests surrounding Almaty have been lost since 1960, mostly to urban development. But local guardians such as Dr. Aimak Dzangaliev, once a student of Vavilov, and scientists and apple breeders around the world have continued to collect and preserve these ancestors.

The original Alma-Ata apples were a mix of sweet, sour, and bitter, of many shapes and colors. Their seeds journeyed along wildlife trails and trade routes, tossed into the bushes by passing caravans, mixing with crab apples and related species and sprouting new versions along the way. The domestication of wild horses, around 3000 BC, carried them farther faster, accelerating their movement beyond Central Asia. By the 1400s, *Malus sieversii* had become *Malus domestica*, well established in the orchards and gardens of Europe.[3] From there it crossed the seas to another continent.

The ancient mountain-born apple had its heyday when it reached North America, planted where it had never grown before. John Bunker, founder of the Maine Heritage Orchard, who has explored and tracked down more apple varieties in Maine alone than most people will ever taste in a lifetime, has found evidence that Scandinavian fishermen planted seedling orchards on islands off the coast of what is now Maine as early as 1550.[4] Portuguese fishermen, explorers, and settlers brought apples to what is now Nova Scotia well before the Pilgrims set foot on

Plymouth Rock. Small wooden boats that carried settlers to Phippsburg in Maine and Jamestown in Virginia in 1607 brought apple seeds saved from favorite trees or gathered quickly from cider pressings in preparation for the long, uncertain journey. By 1634, Lord Baltimore was instructing settlers in the Maryland and Virginia colonies to carry and plant apple and other fruit "kernalls."[5]

Fruit trees were an anchor to the new land—a way of claiming it, taming it, and investing in it for the long haul. Planting an apple seed was an act of faith, a declaration that the future would extend beyond the next harvest or the coming winter. It made the choice of place intentional and the act of planting more than casual; a seedling apple tree needed tending, patience, and many years to bear fruit.

Most apple historians consider the first American orchard that endured to be the one planted by William Blaxton on Boston's Beacon Hill around 1625. The first named apple in the United States, Roxbury Russet, grew a few miles away in the village of Roxbury at around the same time. It is a delightful apple, crisp and delicious eaten fresh, a good keeper that tastes even better in January than it does when first picked, and it makes a nice pie. I've walked by the dozen or so trees that still grow on top of the hill in the Roxbury neighborhood in Boston, overlooking the traffic below. Friends tell me the old apple trees at the top of Mission Hill a few blocks away were once so prolific that in autumn apples rolled down the streets to the houses below.

Nearly everyone in the colonies grew their own food; a few apple trees along with plums, grapes, and other fruit graced the backyards and fields of every farm and settlement. Large landholders, including George Washington and Thomas Jefferson, had orchards that were a point of pride. While they exchanged advice and varieties with their neighbors, slaves and tenants cleared, planted, and tended their land, a common way to expand and improve landholdings.

Like the western land speculators to come, wealthy eastern landowners often made planting of fruit trees a requirement of tenancy. George Washington required a tenant to plant two hundred trees on a parcel of his land in Virginia in 1774.[6] He wanted them planted forty feet apart, fenced, and well pruned, an undertaking neither for the faint of heart nor the transient.

Native peoples adopted the imported apple too, selecting favorites and propagating the best among them.[7] There were well-established Iroquois and Seneca orchards in upstate New York in Revolutionary War times that were methodically destroyed by the U.S. Army around 1799 in order to uproot the settlements.[8] Apple trees were first planted in Iowa just a few miles from the orchard I tried to buy, near what is now the tiny town of Montrose. They are usually credited to Louis Honore Tesson, a French trapper, but a more plausible story based on firsthand accounts suggests that a Sac and Fox native known as Red-Bird brought young trees across the river from Saint Louis around 1795, planted them amid the forest near his home, and tended them so well they were still bearing fruit a century later.[9]

Agricultural tribes of the Southeast also planted fruit trees as part of permanent settlements and in clearings across the region. Apple historian Creighton Lee Calhoun notes in *Old Southern Apples* that President Jefferson directed government Indian agents in 1801 to distribute fruit-tree seeds to the southern tribes to encourage them to become "more agricultural and less warlike." After the Choctaw, Chickasaw, Creek, Seminole, and Cherokee tribes were expelled from their homelands in the 1830s, settlers taking over their lands "found seedling apple trees by the thousands, particularly in North Carolina, Georgia, Alabama, and Tennessee."[10] For decades after, nurserymen and pomologists found some of their best varieties of southern apples in old Cherokee seedling orchards.

LIKE THE HUMANS who planted them, each apple seed is one of a kind. If you fall in love with an apple you've eaten and save its seeds to grow more of the same kind of apples, you will be disappointed. No seedling tree produces the same fruit as its parent. They are an unruly rabble, a little bit of everything, and they make for a grand experiment.

The proliferation of apple varieties and characteristics is a result of genetics: apples are heterozygous. Heterozygous organisms, called heterozygotes, do not "breed true." It helps to know that humans too are heterozygous—all of us resemble parts of our parents, and for the most part have basic human components like skeletal structure and organs, but no two humans, unless they are identical twins, are exactly alike.

Heterozygosity is not a trait of a species per se, but rather of individual characteristics. Characteristics such as color, amount of sugar, acidity, or shape are controlled by genes. Two alleles combine to form each gene, and that fact accounts for much of the variation in apples. Some pairs of alleles match, and thus are homozygous. Other genes have two different versions of the allele, unmatched, making the outcome of their pairing heterozygous, and therefore less standard and less predictable.

Apple cells have a nucleus that contains all the genes for that apple, organized into distinct packets called chromosomes. Apples have seventeen chromosomes, and each chromosome contains many genes.[11] Apples are estimated to have an astounding 57,386 genes, one of the larger genomes that have been identified. Humans, by comparison, are estimated to have 22,333 genes.

Add to this the profligate pollination habits of the apple. They are hermaphrodites, carrying both sexes within each flower, but are mostly what's called self-incompatible, meaning they can't pollinate themselves but just about any other apple can. Grains of pollen from a crab apple, apple seedling, or a carefully selected variety, new or old, can be carried to thousands of blossoms by thousands of bees and other pollinators, matching up millions of heterozygous bits of genetic material. One apple tree, if it produces one hundred pieces of fruit, each typically containing ten seeds, drops over a thousand unique genetic packages into the world every season. Think of a classroom full of kindergartners in all their wildly energetic individuality—the quiet ones, the ornery, the ones who can carry a tune, the ones fascinated by ants, the fast, the slow, the witty and serious; not to mention the physical array—dark hair, hazel eyes, tall, short, gangly, freckled, dark or light skin, long fingers, big feet, small ears, and on and on and on. It starts to make sense that every apple seed grows into a different batch of apples.

The only reliable way to grow fruit of the same variety is to graft: a cutting (called a scion) or bud from the tree being propagated is spliced onto already established rootstock. Every Roxbury Russet tree ever planted and growing today was grafted from that original tree on Beacon Hill.

Grafting techniques had been known since at least Roman times, but grafting wasn't a common skill among the early colonists. There were many reasons, many of them economic, to choose seedlings instead. Hard cider was a common use for apples; most everyone drank alcohol, and any apple would do for making it. Some cider was turned into vinegar, a staple of colonial and frontier kitchens. Fruit and mash left over from cider-making were both used as animal feed. None of this required particularly good fruit flavor or keeping quality.

In colonial times, the choice of seedlings over grafted trees was sometimes a matter of logistics. As settlements moved inland, transport of grafted stock was difficult. Seeds were easy to carry. Grafted trees were expensive; first, rootstock had to be grown from seed, then grafts had to be tended until they were established, or shipped from across the ocean on a voyage that took months. European varieties didn't always survive their new surroundings. Those who could afford it—owners of large orchards and big estates—planted grafted trees; everyone else planted seeds. Millions of apple seeds were planted all over the South and East in seventeenth- and eighteenth-century North America, in possibly the greatest burst of genetic diffusion and apple evolution ever seen.

Given the wildly variable offspring of every bag of seeds, those early settlers likely figured that if they planted two hundred seeds and even half of them survived weather and wildlife for a few years, odds were good that at least one or two would produce edible fruit. Maybe not the predictable favorite of a grafted Roxbury Russet or Newtown Pippin, but if you were strapped for money, traveling by horse or wagon, and concerned with immediate needs for food and shelter, tasting a few sour fruits on their way to the cider press was a decent alternative to paying for, carrying, and tending grafted trees. Settlers who found an apple worth keeping among their seedlings might find someone with the skill to graft it, or if the tree produced sprouts around the trunk, they could replant those for additional trees or trade with other orchard owners for additional varieties.

While apple trees transformed forests into settled farmland, apples were transformed in the process. New varieties suited to new conditions began to replace the old European cultivars. By 1800, over seven thousand named varieties of apples were grown in the United States. Some may have been the same fruit named more than once, or the apple may have changed names, like a game of telephone, as fruit and trees were passed along. But most of them were indeed unique, and the more seeds that were planted, carried farther west, or left behind to drop apples full of seeds of their own, the more varieties came to be. The sowing of all those individual seeds in anticipation of random and unpredictable results suited the pioneer spirit: democratic but also expansive, adaptable, and independent.

TO PROMOTE THE expansion of white settlement after the Revolutionary War into what was called the Ohio Territory (the region west of the Appalachian Mountains, later expanded to the Mississippi River and renamed the Northwest Territory), Congress claimed vast expanses of land as an ever-expanding buffer against the native residents. They sold it cheaply to land companies that in turn sold it parcel by parcel to settlers. A condition of every sale was the planting of apple and other fruit trees. The Ohio Land Company (based in Massachusetts) called for fifty trees per claim; others required two hundred apple trees and a hundred pear trees to be planted and maintained, and payment made yearly to secure the claim. Failure to plant the trees or pay the yearly installment meant the claim reverted to the land company. Thousands of settlers pushing west from what was already being called the "crowded and farmed-out" East created a steady market for seedling trees. Whether the trees themselves survived long enough to produce fruit mattered less than that they were planted, like flags, to signify ownership.

The most famous agent of that seedling migration was John Chapman, the mythic Johnny Appleseed. Theories about why he planted apples abound,[12] but it's generally agreed he brought more apples to the western frontier than any other single person. Born in Leominster, Massachusetts, in 1774, near the same time and place as the new nation, he headed into the new territory on foot at age eighteen and became an itinerant preacher, wanderer, and nature lover.

Chapman found a trade carrying bags of apple seeds to tracts of newly "available" land across the Ohio Territory. He cleared a plot, planted seeds, put up branch fences to keep away deer, stayed awhile to get the trees established, then moved on. He spent winters warm and dry with his sister in Pennsylvania, where he could replenish his supply of apple seeds from nearby cider mills. Eventually, he trod a yearlong circuit by foot and canoe to visit and tend his seedling nurseries until settlers in the market for fruit trees arrived to stake their claims.

Chapman seems to have been a restless soul, eccentric as well as a proselytizer. It's not entirely clear that apples were as central a purpose for his life as legend would have it. Seeds fit his belief in kindness to other living beings, less cruel than cutting and grafting. Planting them allowed him to stay on the move, to live mostly outdoors and on his own. A devout follower of the theology of Emanuel Swedenborg, winters in Pennsylvania gave him access to the latest writings and teaching as well as the company of brethren followers. Preaching Swedenborg's doctrine provided access to a meal and a pallet on the kitchen floor or in the barn at many a frontier household. Walking and paddling the circuit between his sister's home and his network of seedling orchards lent a suitable rhythm to his life. The sale of seedlings and the occasional profit from a land claim kept him mostly solvent and moving west.

The river bottoms where Chapman often started his orchards had plenty of water during the months he was away and were easy to reach by boat when he was ready to sell to the next wave of settlers. But they were low, damp, and prone to flooding: not ideal land for producing good fruit, which suggests the trees were at least as much about land claims as about apples. Land companies benefited from his renown, and settlers likely recommended him to new arrivals. It's not hard to see how his reputation grew and spread. When he died in 1845, near Fort Wayne, Indiana, he held title to 1,200 acres of land claims scattered across what is now Indiana, Ohio, and Pennsylvania: not worth much, but evidence of how far he had roamed. Trees claimed to have descended from his seedlings are still scattered around the countryside.

Chapman's seedling orchards were considered by some to represent a coarse lower class, an unruly democratic version of life, in contrast to the orderly grafted commercial production of fruit seen as emblematic of prosperity and industry.[13] His seedling nurseries were by no means the only supply of fruit trees in the new territories. Prince's nursery on Long Island, founded in 1730, is reputed to be the first commercial nursery in the colonies. By the time Chapman set foot in Ohio, a number of established nurseries there offered both seedling and grafted trees. Many nurseries employed their own versions of Johnny Appleseed, sales agents who traveled on horseback to remote farms and villages with trees, seeds, and catalogs, carrying news of the latest variety, advice on cultivation, and no doubt the latest gossip. Nurseries enabled not just seeds but whole trees, roots already reaching for new ground, to be moved from place to place, and the best varieties to be established and spread.

The early settlers carried apple trees farther and farther into the western forests and the far western plains. A few seedlings produced fruit of note—good tasting, good for keeping, talked about, shared, and traded. If the fruit was especially good, maybe it was given a name. As settlements and farms began to fill in an area, nurseries followed, perhaps acquiring a supply of cuttings from the lucky neighbor with a tasty named fruit, grafting a few to list in their catalog. New trees joined the catalogs of other local nurseries, which served as proving ground to select the best varieties, pushing out older varieties that were no longer so popular. Bigger nurseries picked up new varieties, selling trees farther north, south, and west. The best varieties (or those chosen by shrewd marketers) were planted in greater quantities. Settlers pushed west, plopping seedlings into new ground, and the process continued, a pre–gold rush path to fortune on the frontier.

AS THE EASTERN SEABOARD grew more settled and populous and the first homesteads became towns and cities, a transformation not just of apples but of farming itself was under way. Once, every farm was self-sufficient by necessity, growing a cornucopia of fruits, vegetables, grains, and animals so each family could feed itself, make it through the winter, and have a little left over for trade. By the early 1800s, there were more jobs in town, more people to feed, and farming became a more commercial enterprise. That meant growing crops for market, which meant choosing crops that would store, transport, and sell best. As backyard fruit gave way to commercial production for city markets, profitable qualities such as being durable, keepable, and pretty were favored, sometimes displacing flavor.

Around the same time, the temperance movement began to take hold, driving the ubiquitous makers and drinkers of hard cider into back rooms and subterfuge. Farmers with seedling orchards where a mix of trees could provide plenty of fruit for cider and vinegar but not much else did one of two things: cut down or burned their trees, clearing land for grain and vegetables or for grazing dairy cows and sheep, or topworked their seedling orchards to more popular commercial varieties.

Because orchardists can't plow up rows of trees every year to plant a new crop like corn or tomato farmers do, topworking remains one of the main ways to respond to changing tastes and markets. It involves cutting off the tree just where the branches begin and grafting a new variety onto the established trunk and roots. In the early nineteenth century, thousands of seedling orchards were, in a short span of time, topped off and converted to a few popular named varieties that could be shipped to town, taken by boat to cities such as Boston, New York, Charleston, and New Orleans, and even exported back to England and the port cities of Europe. A few old trees still marked farmsteads and fencerows, but by the mid-1850s, as people moved and the meaning of *West* shifted, most of the seedling orchards in the East had been grafted over.

First Pennsylvania, then Ohio, then Illinois, then the Mississippi River marked the threshold of the frontier. Fruit trees in the new territories anchored the kind of homestead-based agriculture already waning in the East. Early settlers were eager for fruit, as well as trees for windbreaks and woodlots. They brought familiar apple varieties from back home and hoped they would thrive in the open windswept plains.

The first nursery stock crossed the Mississippi to Iowa on riverboats from Ohio and Indiana. A nursery in Burlington advertised eastern fruit trees in 1839, and by 1857 there were two or three nurseries in every one of the state's ninety-nine counties. Iowa apples, grapes, melons, and other fruit and vegetable crops flourished in the freshly plowed fertile prairie soil and became a source of food not only for nearby settlements but for cities back East.

A few miles from the Mississippi River just north of the Missouri border is the tiny town of Salem, Iowa, a short drive from the orchard auction I attended. The Quakers who first settled Salem in the 1800s had split off in a branch called the Anti-Slavery Quakers and made their community one of the first stops on the Underground Railroad in the years leading up to the Civil War. The head of the Anti-Slavery Quaker congregation in Salem was a man named Henderson Luelling.[14]

Son of a nursery owner who had settled in Indiana, Luelling headed to Iowa Territory in 1837, bringing cuttings and seeds to start a nursery of his own. For ten years, he and his wife Elizabeth tended trees, a large family, and many freed and escaping slaves coming up from Kansas and Missouri headed for the free North. Luelling and his brother John built up a successful fruit tree nursery that supplied farms and orchards across Iowa. But after ten years of settled life, Luelling felt the pull of the western frontier again. His next migration was as epic as John Chapman's, although nowhere near as well known.

Sometime in 1846, Luelling began preparing to take his family, and his nursery, west to the fertile river valleys of the Oregon territory. He'd spent two years carefully selecting and grafting the hardiest trees in his nursery. With the help of a neighbor, he obtained a strong wagon and built two large wooden boxes, each twelve inches deep, to fit into the wagon bed. He filled the boxes with a mixture of soil, manure, and charcoal, and packed them with some seven hundred bushes and small trees—apple, pear, cherry, peach, quince, plum, grape, and more—some as large as four feet tall, protected by strips of hickory stapled on posts along the wagon box. It looked like a rolling thicket of improbable folly.

In late spring, the Luellings—Henderson, his wife, Elizabeth, and eight children—left Salem with two other families in a seven-wagon train. The wagons were heavy, loaded with household belongings, food for the journey, and water for the trees as well as the animals and people who trudged alongside on foot. They likely relied on a popular do-it-yourself booklet, Joel Palmer's "Guide to Crossing the Plains," for advice. There's no record of what Elizabeth had to say about the plans, but everyone else predicted Luelling and his trees would never survive.

A few days after setting out, they encountered another caravan led by Lot Whitcomb, a seasoned traveler who had assembled 154 wagons, the largest wagon train ever to attempt the crossing. The huge encampment looked like a small city gathered on the plains. Whitcomb was headed for land he owned along the Willamette River, in Oregon, and they agreed that it would be safest for the small party to join them.

The trip got harder instead of easier from there. One of Luelling's partners and two of the oxen perished along the way. The other travelers became increasingly aggravated with Luelling and his trees, certain that the weight would kill the rest of the oxen, slow the caravan down, and get them stuck in the mountains. Luelling's vision of a nursery in the new territories, or his attachment to his fruit trees, or perhaps just the stubbornness of a strong-minded Quaker caused him to rebuff every entreaty to abandon the rolling nursery. He reportedly watered each tree and cutting daily, thundering "No!" to his detractors.

Eventually they parted ways and the Luelling family continued on alone, the trees bobbing and waving above them. Midway across the plains a party of much-feared native riders came upon the wagons. As was recounted many times afterward, "The Indians believed that the Great Spirit lived in trees; they thought that [Luelling] must be under the special care of the Great Spirit, and so they did not harm him."[15]

Wagon trains traveled about fifteen miles a day, moving between water sources when possible, traveling in groups for protection and help with hunting and chores. Today the trip from Salem, Iowa, to Salem, Oregon, takes twenty-nine hours by car, driving the speed limit on interstate highways along a mostly direct route of 1,969 miles. By wagon, the trip took more than half a year, winding up, down, and around river valleys, mountains, and rock formations. The trail stayed close to the Platte River until midway across the high, arid plains of what is now Wyoming, then turned north into the Rocky Mountains. Even crossing in summer, those weeks and months must have been brutal.

The shallow ruts were etched so repeatedly into the dirt and grass of the dry, high plains by the hard wooden wheels of hundreds of wagons that a century and a half later they are still visible in places. I've seen them in western Nebraska, from a little roadside pullout where I stopped to read a sign identifying the faint traces I would otherwise have missed. Even now, the rolling, unbroken grassland stretches out in all directions. The faint impression in the thick grass isn't dramatic, but it stays with you. It makes it easier to picture the Luelling wagon lumbering off with its load of rocking twigs, barely visible above the waving prairie grasses on that ridge, the relentless wind and the Platte River never too far away, and the great unknown stretching ahead of them.

One mishap after another slowed the arduous trip across the plains. Oxen drowned, the wagons overturned more than once, the trees and dirt having to be scooped up and repositioned in their boxes. River crossings were especially perilous, and the Snake River was almost the undoing of the whole venture. There, Luelling reportedly told his son, "We may as well go back to Iowa. We're ruined. Everything has gone against us."[16]

Instead, they persevered, crossing the dry plateau of eastern Oregon and reaching the Columbia River around the first of October. They unloaded the wagons and built two wooden boats to make their way down the Columbia River to the Willamette. The trees were taken out of their wooden boxes and carefully wrapped in cloth to protect them from the coming winter. Another month of travel landed the party across the river from Portland, where they purchased land just north of that owned by Whitcomb, their erstwhile wagon train leader. The next spring, nearly a year after being nestled into their boxes of dirt, the trees were unwrapped and finally planted. Some had grown as much as three feet on their journey west.

Luelling established one of the first nurseries of grafted trees in the West. Soon joined by his brother Seth from Indiana, his brother John from Iowa, and his future son-in-law William Meek, who arrived with a bag of seeds, the family prospered. Meek's seedlings provided rootstock for Luelling's cuttings, other settlers followed, and soon they were holding what might have been the first scion exchange in the Northwest.

Seth Luelling stayed in Oregon, expanding the nursery and breeding new fruit, especially cherries. Working with the varieties that had come across the prairie, he and his longtime orchard employee, a Chinese man named Ah Bing, developed a variety of cherry named after the employee that now represents a third of the fresh cherry crop grown in the region.

Henderson Luelling, meanwhile, still felt the pull of new horizons. In the gold rush fever of 1853, he picked up again and left for California. Once again, he established a nursery, in an area now part of East Oakland called Fruitvale. Eventually he took his dream of a free society to found a utopian settlement in Honduras, where he perished. New waves of immigrants came to Fruitvale to work in the orchards. Many stayed to put down roots in what is now a mostly Latino neighborhood with its own long history of farmwork and farm labor organizing.

Apples also migrated to California from the south. As early as the 1500s, Spanish explorers brought apples to Mexico and South America, and by 1659, missionaries and traders had introduced them in the Southwest, still part of Mexico at the time. Orchards planted by settlers still exist in the high, dry mountains of New Mexico and Arizona. Mission gardens in Southern California were outposts for apples and other fruit; when the gold rush brought new waves of settlers, commercial orchards expanded rapidly as the gold rush ended and railroads opened up eastern markets for western fruit. By the late 1800s, there was a thriving fruit industry in California. The immigrant apple had taken root across an entire continent.

WHEN LUELLING HEADED west with his wagonload of apple trees, the United States was a profoundly rural nation. The U.S. Bureau of Census reported 80 percent of the population lived in the countryside and 59 percent of the total labor force was engaged in agriculture. Of the 4,009,000 farms established before the Homestead Act of 1862 that pushed new settlement farther west, 97 percent were smaller than 260 acres. Only twenty-nine farms in the entire country had one thousand acres or more.[17]

But agriculture, especially in the eastern states, was becoming more specialized, more commercialized, and more complex. A shift away from subsistence farming in the early 1800s was accompanied by a fervor to bring "book learning" and more scientific approaches to the production of crops for market. Farm publications such as Hovey's *Magazine of Horticulture*, *The Western Farmer and Gardener*, *American Agriculturist*, and *The Ploughman* flourished. They were promoted and supported by growers associations and co-ops, as were research farms, breeding programs, and exhibitions devoted to fruit growing.

Grower-led associations promoting cooperation among apple and other fruit growers, active since colonial days, proliferated around the same time. The New York State Horticultural Society began in 1855, Iowa's and Minnesota's in 1866, and every other state's within a few decades. They supported research, publications, and fairs, and provided a means of support and sharing of information among growers that still exists today.

Dozens of smaller regional societies for fruit, vegetables, flower gardens, and beekeeping were affiliated with the state organizations, and they often held meetings and reported their proceedings jointly. The yearly record of observations and advice was published in hardbound volumes that must have been pored over avidly by those who could not spend the several days it took to travel by horseback to attend the meetings. In the flowery, expressive prose of the day, they provided advice directly from peers—with no intermediary from academia, journalism, or commerce. Ideas and wisdom were contributed by and available to anyone who aspired to practice pomology—the science of growing tree fruit—or dabbled in backyard trees, or engaged in their own experiments with variety and flavor.

State horticultural associations helped the apple industry through Reconstruction, the prosperous twenties, and the Depression years, providing a place for growers to exchange ideas, collaborate, and promote their fruit and fruit-growing practices. Their members paid annual dues to support research, publications, exhibitions, and gatherings, as well as representatives advocating on behalf of their members before state legislators and Congress.

The growers associations were a strong civic force in those days. Their members represented over half the population. When they took that strength to Congress, they helped bring about far-reaching policies that have had as great an impact on apples and farming as any other act of government since. As the cities grew and the portion of the population engaged in farming grew steadily smaller, people close to agriculture recognized how dependent the rest of the country was on sustaining farms. In 1862, with the country deeply embroiled in the Civil War— losing many of its farmers to bloody battles and its southern farms and orchards to devastation—a group of visionaries set out to create public institutions that would educate the farming and working classes and support the development of agriculture as a public good. Vermont senator Justin Morrill, son of a blacksmith, authored and shepherded passage of the Morrill Act. The federal law granted land to each state, in proportion to their representation in Congress, to be sold and the proceeds applied:

> To the endowment, support, and maintenance of at least one college where the leading object shall be . . . to teach such branches of learning as are related to agriculture and the mechanic arts . . . in order to promote the liberal and practical education of the industrial classes in the several pursuits and professions in life.[18]

That same year, President Abraham Lincoln established the United States Department of Agriculture (USDA) and Congress passed the Homestead Act, opening millions more acres of western land to new settlement. Iowa was the first state to accept the terms of the Morrill Act, on September 11, 1862, establishing Iowa State Agricultural College (now Iowa State University) in my hometown of Ames. Other states followed, either purchasing land for new colleges or designating existing institutions, both public and private, to fulfill the land grant mission. These colleges came to be known as land grant institutions.

Twenty-five years later, in 1887, the Hatch Act was passed, creating state agricultural experiment stations whose purpose was, in part, to promote "a sound and prosperous agriculture and rural life as indispensable to the maintenance of maximum employment and national prosperity and security" and "to assure agriculture a position in research equal to that of industry, which will aid in maintaining an equitable balance between agriculture and other segments of the economy."[19]

Morrill intended the 1862 land grant institutions to admit freed and former slaves, but most former Confederate states were unwilling to do so. A second Morrill Act was passed in 1890, requiring states to either remove race as an admissions criteria or to establish separate land grant institutions for people of color. Seventeen states established separate schools, and along with Tuskegee University and Central State University (Ohio), these historically black universities, still called "1890 institutions," are now part of the land grant system. Not until 1994 was the land grant system expanded to include thirty-one tribal colleges, most of them in the West and upper Midwest.

In 1914, recognizing that the research and knowledge of the land grant schools needed to be shared as widely as possible with the farming public, the Smith-Lever Act created the Cooperative Extension Service "in order to aid in diffusing among the people . . . useful and practical information on subjects relating to agriculture and home economics, and to encourage the application of the same."[20]

These systems of public support continue to be critical resources for U.S. farmers with farms of all sizes and crops. For generations of apple growers, the research, education, and independent support of growers associations and land-grant scientists has helped firmly root the apple not just in the landscape of its adopted country but in our economy and culture as well.

CHAPTER THREE

The People Who Grow
the Apples We Eat

IN THE MID-1970S, when I was first getting involved with the natural and organic food movement and learning to shop and cook for myself, natural food stores carried mostly bulk grains, flours, and the basics of a simple whole-food diet. There were few processed products and almost no fresh produce in the tiny stores that served the hard-core faithful. If there was produce, it was usually limited to oranges, yellow onions, carrots, and Pippin apples, all labeled organic, all a bit scruffy and road weary, in big twenty-five- or fifty-pound bags, mostly from California. The Pippins were greenish-yellow, thick-skinned, squat little things, russeted around the stem, a bit grainy but sweet and zesty tasting. They had the waxy feel of having been around a while, and indeed, you could keep them in the refrigerator for weeks before they'd start to soften.

They weren't the best apples I'd ever tasted. But for years, these were the apples I ate most of the time. They were organic—before that term

ABOVE: Harvesttime at Blue Hills Orchard,
Wallingford, Connecticut. Photo by Diane Rast.

always meant the same thing. Determined to do my part to support a food supply that was good for farmers and good for the environment, eating those apples felt virtuous and hopeful. I took great pleasure in them, sliced and eaten with good sharp, undyed cheddar cheese or spread with fabulous natural peanut butter that came in unwieldy white plastic thirty-five-pound buckets and had to be stirred with the biceps of a baseball slugger to mix the oil back in. We baked them into muffins and pies, diligently made with 100 percent whole wheat flour, sweetened with honey: no lard, no white flour, no cornstarch for us!

It sounds dour, but it was mostly a lot of fun, and fostered lifelong friendships with big bountiful potlucks, recipe sharing, and regular gatherings on the front porch of one or another group household to "break down" the bulk orders from our food co-op buying club. We scooped the dripping peanut butter into our reused glass jars, dug into boxes of raisins and bags of rolled oats to weigh out portions, found big flat knives long enough to cut into five-pound blocks of cheese. Everybody joined in, talking, laughing, helping out, figuring and refiguring to get the tally of what each person owed to come out right, and then we trooped home with our bags and boxes to fill the jars and bins in our own kitchens. I learned to cook all kinds of things I'd never tasted before. Nutritious and wholesome, it was adventurous in its own way and never felt limiting. The food was hearty and delicious, and a lot of it I still cook today; well, maybe not the heavy carob and whole wheat sweets, but brown rice and vegetables, thick lentil soup, beans and tortillas, giant salads.

Those round yellow-green Pippins, though, have disappeared, at least from stores in the East and Midwest. Natural food stores and mainstream supermarkets alike now carry an array of red, green, and yellow organic apples, all the main varieties, all year round, mostly from Washington, where 65 percent of all apples and over 90 percent of organic apples in the United States are grown.[1] Apples still populate the entire country, but the way they are grown, the size of orchards and trees, the varieties, and the ways apple growers have found to make a livelihood would be unrecognizable to the Chapmans and Luellings of earlier centuries.

A FIRST STEP in understanding the orchards of today is to meet some of the people who own and operate them. The center of U.S. apple growing has shifted west again and again, but its roots are in the East. John Lyman is the eighth generation to farm his family's land in central Connecticut. His ancestors arrived in Boston in 1631. Some moved west and south to Connecticut, some to New York, spreading out as so many families still do. The Lymans began farming their current land in Middlefield, Connecticut, in 1741, more than a century after the first European settlers carried apple seeds to Maine and Virginia, but still twenty-five years before the start of the American Revolution. John's forebearer made a three-mile trek across swampland to start a self-sufficient farm "like they all were back then," John tells me, clearly having recounted the story many times.

Like most farmers, the Lyman family had apple trees from the beginning, but they didn't start serious commercial fruit-growing until the 1890s. By then they'd established themselves as vocal opponents of slavery, the farm a stop on the Underground Railroad, and the family had been farming the same land for over 150 years. John's great-grandfather first planted peaches. Connecticut was well situated between New York City and Boston, and peaches were a high-value crop, so investing in them made sense to the Lymans and many other farmers in the area. But the winter of 1917–18 was so brutal it killed peach trees across the region, some dying outright, some slowly over the next couple of years. The Lymans were in dire straits through the 1920s. As the Depression approached, John's grandfather, just becoming involved in the farm, decided apples would be hardier than peaches, and he planted 150 to 200 acres of apple trees.

The standard trees John's grandfather planted took ten years or so to bear fruit. By the early 1930s, farms across the region had lots of apples coming in. Newfangled ammonia cooling systems went into low brick storage buildings on many farms, allowing growers to sell the crop over a longer period of time; the Lymans built theirs in 1931 and still use it for packing. When the Depression hit, times were hard but they kept the farm.

John and his brothers and sisters grew up on the family farm, just as seven generations before them had. John went off to school, and after graduation he took off for the Netherlands. He told his parents he didn't know when he was coming home, and meant it. "That year, 1979, was a pretty rotten time in the U.S.," he recalls. "I expected to stay away three, four, five years before I would be ready to come back." To immerse himself in another culture he found a job in an orchard. At the time, he wasn't thinking of it as preparation for anything, just a good experience.

The Netherlands wasn't what he expected. He found the Dutch interested in and appreciative of America and curious to hear about his home. Instead of being critical of the politics and economic issues he had left back home, people kept asking, "Why aren't you back there?" The more he talked about home and the more he got that reaction, the more he started to think, *Well, why aren't I back there?* "I became a really strong, patriotic American in that year away," he recalls with firm pride, sounding ready to defend his change of heart to his listener and perhaps to his twenty-something self. He came home after one year, and stayed. "I came back with a full commitment," he says.

John is a quiet person, deliberate and thoughtful in the way he speaks. He's a tireless innovator, putting a combination of generations of experience and the latest research from the region's land grant scientists to work in his orchard. Using integrated pest management (IPM),[2] John relies on monitoring and biological controls like mating disruption and natural predators to minimize the use of sprays and manage his orchard in a way that is healthy and harmonious for his workers, his customers, his family, and the farm's ecosystem of bees, pollinators, and wildlife. For over two decades, he has been a pioneer and leading practitioner of IPM in the Northeast because he believes it's the right thing to do.

In order to differentiate his fruit from all the other apples in the grocery store, John Lyman has been part of several efforts over the years to educate consumers about this ecological approach to fruit growing and to build a market for himself and other ecological growers in the region. In 2004, along with Red Tomato, five other New England orchards, and a group of scientists from the IPM Institute of North America, the University of Massachusetts, and Cornell University, he helped found the Eco Apple program, which combines a progressive ecological growing protocol with Eco certification, marketing, and sales coordination. There are over a dozen orchards now participating in the program from throughout the Northeast.

To sustain their farm for nine generations and keep a place for their apples in the supermarkets where their family and neighbors shop, the Lymans employ strategies as sophisticated as the largest food marketers around. They operate a business so diverse and complex it would challenge the sharpest biologists, chemists, engineers, and MBA graduates. They overcome daily obstacles as mundane as lack of shipping options for orders not big enough to fill a truck. Their employees pack apples in bags labeled Lyman Orchards as well as Big Y, Red Tomato, and whoever else's brand is ordering their apples this season.

Lyman Orchards operates a scratch bakery and a large, popular farm market, the Apple Barrel, where they sell their own fruit along with an assortment of products both local, like Farmer's Cow milk, and global, like bananas and Pepsi. Their apple-cider doughnuts are a big attraction, their pies renowned. A few years ago, the Lymans saw an opportunity to add value to more of their crop by expanding their pie-making capacity. Their fruit pies, sold frozen, are a regional favorite, baked off and sold at supermarkets from Connecticut and Massachusetts to Pennsylvania, Maryland, and New York City.

During apple harvest, from August through late October, Lyman Orchards is also a pick-your-own (PYO) destination. Thousands of families from nearby Hartford, New Haven, and even New York City drive out to spend a few hours doing their own version of farming—roaming over designated sections of the rolling orchard to select and pick their own fruit. They pay a premium for the experience. It's entertainment, educational for the kids, time outdoors, and a little exercise. For many, it's a surprisingly powerful way to connect to something they don't often touch in daily life: a nostalgic past, close to the source of food and rooted in something even more fundamental: the land.

Because the orchard is close to large urban centers, taxes are high and the pressure to sell the land off for development is intense. Every inch of the ground at Lyman Orchards needs to help pay for itself as well as support multiple generations of Lymans. The old, graceful homestead at one end of the orchard with its sweeping porch and lovely gardens is rented out for weddings and other events. And, the family operates two championship eighteen-hole golf courses and a nine-hole short course on the property, which are also busy on a sunny day. It's a full-service farm.

Still, Lyman Orchards has had to reinvent itself many times over to stay afloat as a family farm. Although the one-hundred-acre orchard is considered big by comparison to some eastern farms, it has much in common with other orchards in the region and with orchards in the upper Midwest.

IN 1903, THE USDA reported that the biggest fruit-growing region in the country was the Mississippi River valley. The East had urbanized and begun to shift to other crops. Fruit production in the West was barely a factor. Today, Michigan vies with New York for the second and third largest apple crops in the country.[3] Fruit growing in the two states is similar in many ways: both have northern climates buffered by the Great Lakes; produce top-quality apples for a mix of fresh, processing, and export markets; and have enough wholesale orchards left to support the infrastructure and research needed to keep a foothold. The Fruit Ridge region in northwest Michigan is known for its apples, cherries, and other tree fruit. Michigan growers provide leadership in national organizations and are innovators in the adoption of varieties and technology. For the most part, though, except for Michigan and a few big orchards in Wisconsin and Minnesota, the legacy of apples across most of the Midwest persists on small-scale pick-your-own and backyard orchards. A rich heritage is kept alive on those farms and in places such as Seed Savers Exchange orchard in northeast Iowa, but very little of that heritage reaches the wholesale market. Fifty years after its mid-continent heyday, the center of gravity has moved northwest.

THERE IS NO WAY to fully understand the apple industry in the United States without knowing what it is like in Washington. Even the production of all the other states combined doesn't come close to what is grown east of the Cascade Range, along the Yakima, Columbia, and Wenatchee River valleys. When Henderson Luelling and his family arrived at the western edge of the continent, they found few other farms. Until the great waterworks projects damming the Columbia and other rivers in the 1950s made it possible to irrigate with the surge of glacial melt and surface water that pours down out of the mountains every spring, much of the region east of the Cascades and Sierras was too dry to farm. Those public water projects made the water supply seem as vast and unending as the land in those days. Now, climate change and receding snowpack raise questions about whether farming here will be sustainable in a few more decades.

For now, the Pacific Northwest is one of the largest apple-producing regions in the world, representing a collage of the entire spectrum of fruit growing in the twenty-first century: everything from a tiny few acres to tens of thousands, some 100 percent organic from their first planting, some shifting to organic on a large scale, most growing apples in what are generally called conventional ways. Trees, planting systems, and apple varieties are as diverse as the orchards. Large packing and marketing companies such as Stemilt Growers and Starr Ranch own thousands of acres, but even those companies are still family-owned, like much of the rest of U.S. farmland. If they are growing and selling for the wholesale market, most orchards belong to one or more packing and marketing co-ops that combine their fruit with that of hundreds of other orchards, consolidating the packing, selling, and storage on their behalf. Many small orchards sell directly to consumers, with owners or their employees sometimes driving many hours each week to get to farmers markets in the bigger cities along the coast.

Western fruit-growing is a young industry, not so steeped in old traditions. Uniform fruit is the industry hallmark, and vertical integration is the driver—the same companies own and control the orchards, the pack lines, and the brands and manage shipping, sales, and marketing. Big packing co-ops grow as much as 80 percent of their own fruit, as well as what they pack and sell for their co-op members. The large grower-packer-shippers continue buying up land, and the size of the remaining family orchards is increasing too, sometimes providing a refuge when other family orchards are ready to sell out.

It doesn't take long, though, just a few conversations with growers at various points on the spectrum, to understand that whether the orchard is a few acres or a few thousand, selling direct or wholesale, organic or not, making a living growing apples is a year-by-year, high-stakes, headache-inducing challenge for these families. Here at the epicenter of the industry, the pressures, competition, and pitfalls are especially intense. Apple prices everywhere rise and fall on the fate of the Washington orchards; the biggest packers are here, supplying the highest-volume exports via shipping ports that are the gateways to China and the Asian market. There is a lot of innovation here, a lot of infrastructure, and a lot of fruit.

Driving up the Columbia River valley between the Tri-Cities (Richland, Kennewick, and Pasco) and Wenatchee is a good way to take in the scale of the Washington State apple industry. Interspersed with views of the arid, brown river valley laid out wide and flat against the foothills of the Cascades, rows of candelabra-pruned semidwarf trees[4] stretch beyond sight along both sides of the road. I've made my first visit in December after the harvest so I can attend the big annual statewide tree fruit conference, and because that's when more people have time to talk. Even in winter, the trees are recognizable as fruit trees—long straight rows, ten to fifteen feet high (just reachable with a tapered orchard ladder), thick at the trunk with carefully shaped branches reaching up in rounded canopies or stretched sideways along wires, staked every few trees. In some orchards, brown leaves and wrinkled translucent apples, evidence of an early freeze, hang thick on the branches, unharvested and unusable. In others, the limbs are mostly bare: graceful gnarly fingers tracing against a steely gray sky, row after row, orange-brown leaves carpeting the ground beneath.

It's the scale that lets you know where you are. Signs at every cross-roads mark grower-packer operations whose names are common in the storerooms of supermarkets across the country: Starr Ranch, Stemilt, Columbia. From late July through November they bustle with trucks, ladders, people picking and moving fruit. By Thanksgiving, large concrete cold-storage buildings, several stories high with no windows and just a few doors visible along one side, are packed to the ceiling with bins of apples for the winter market.

A big neon apple at the entrance into Wenatchee proclaims it The Apple Capital of the World. These days, the center of high-volume apple production and most of the biggest companies that combine growing, packing, and shipping have moved south toward Yakima and the Columbia Basin, but the roots of Washington's apple industry are here. Nestled between the Columbia River and the Cascades in the center of the state, orchards and vineyards radiate in all directions from Wenatchee. The Washington Apple Commission's office on the outskirts of town has a small, cheery visitor center filled with brochures and apple T-shirts, apple pins, apple cookbooks, and apple bumper stickers. Flyers advertise farmers markets and fruit stands. The annual calendar of events includes the Washington State Apple Blossom Festival, the bicycle Tour de Bloom, the Sunrise Rotary Apple Century Bike Ride, and the Chelan County Fair. The local baseball team is the Apple Sox, and the Apple Capital Loop Trail winds through town along both banks of the Columbia River. One brochure brags the region is "ripe with bumper crops of seasonal bounty that nourish our children, our souls, our economy, and our world."

A map on the wall shows seven apple-growing regions in the state, five major regions filling the center of the state and two smaller ones to the east and west. One hundred acres is the average orchard size, with some as large as five thousand acres. The rich lava-ash soil, dry climate, and three hundred days of sunshine a year made fruit growing attractive to the earliest settlers. Over 3,500 apple growers now farm more than 172,000 acres. However, the number of orchards in Washington has been decreasing steadily for decades. The USDA Census of Agriculture showed a drop of 11.4 percent between 2007 and 2012.[5] Orchard acreage increased by 5.4 percent in that same period. The big are getting bigger. The small are hanging on. The midsized folks are making tough choices about the future.

Just outside of Wenatchee, U.S. 97 Alternate runs north along the river to the small town of Chelan, passing some of the largest apple-processing facilities in the world. The road winds around the edge of steep hills to a breathtaking view at the end of long, narrow Lake Chelan. The Cascades tower above. Tucked against them a few miles from the south end of the lake is the improbably named Jerzy Boyz Farm.

Wynne Weinreb and Scott Beaton are first-generation organic fruit growers in a county with an economy that depends more on a single crop than any other county in the country. Expressive, generous, and wise, Wynne is a fount of information on everyone and everything in the valley related to apples. When I arrive for a visit on a blustery morning in early December, she rattles off a list of people I should meet and makes phone calls, arranging introductions and lunch. Fiercely committed to the choices she and Scott have made for their own orchard, she is equally insistent that I understand and respect other growers in the area who've made other choices.

When I ask how she ended up on an organic apple orchard on a hillside overlooking the Columbia River valley in tiny Chelan, Wynne looks amused. "Well, the motorcycle broke down." In her loose, colorful clothing and sturdy boots, striding through the orchard, she looks more like an artisan potter than a motorcycle babe. But she and I are about the same age, and I can absolutely picture her at twenty, long hair, lean limbs, bold and free spirited, astride a road bike on the open highway. It wasn't such a strange thing forty years ago to travel without knowing where you were headed or how long you'd stay, nor for happenstance and impulse to set the course for the rest of your life.

Wynne grew up in New York City; Scott's from north Jersey. On their first date as college students in Boston in the early '70s, Wynne nixed the Greek restaurant Scott had in mind and instead took him to buy apples at Erewhon, one of the first natural food stores in the country. She figured if it was going to work between them, he was going to have to find out what mattered to her sooner rather than later. After college, they headed west. When the bike broke down, they made their way to Chelan for an apple-picking job. By the time the bike was fixed, they'd met other kindred spirits, decided they liked it there, and settled in. They worked for a few years for one of the prominent local orchard families, raised two kids, and eventually bought land and planted their own orchard.

My old favorite Pippins might have come from an orchard like this, the kind of place where I've sometimes imagined I could make a life. Set high up on the hillside, rocky ground overlooking the broad valley, a winding road leads to the house. The farm equipment is old but well maintained. The work is hard, but manageable on five acres. There is a deep, saturated stillness and dignity, an almost holy feeling in the orchard as we walk among the trees, birds chirping and a happy dog bouncing around Wynne's ankles. Mountains slice the horizon in three directions, and a steep slope stretches above the orchard that hugs its side. Small things rustle in the brush along the path. The trees are bare, dark, thick, and sturdy with decades of growth. The place, and the people who tend it, have become so interwoven over the years it's impossible to separate them—Wynne from the orchard, the orchard from the strength, dignity, stubbornness, and wisdom of the orchardists.

Wynne and Scott started out farming with another couple, selling mostly to the wholesale market. The partnership, the fruit business, and the orchard have been through many changes in the twenty-seven years since. Now, they own their land outright, something not many first-generation farmers manage these days. Now it's just the two of them. They do most of the work themselves, each tree pruned by Scott, who has a full-time job off the farm as well. They follow organic growing practices and market all their fruit directly to consumers by mail order and at weekly farmers markets. Most of their crop goes to Seattle—not the big Pike Place Market where tourists go, but the University District Market. It's a three-hour drive over the mountains before dawn to set up and sell out every week.

Wynne stands at the edge of her orchard, looking out over the Columbia River valley at acres of spindly, regimented orchards planted below. A trill of birdsong makes me look back at the rows of sturdy, slightly wild-looking trees lining a narrow dirt roadway leading to the house and pack shed. There is a palpable presence in the orchard here. The trees are not tall, they're well-tended and carefully pruned, but they look old and wizened, vigorous and rooted, and the orchard alleys are beckoning and enveloping even on a gray, coldish day. There is a raw, simple beauty in this place.

"What a beautiful setting!" I exclaim. She nods. "Aren't they gorgeous? Isn't this amazing? I get to come to work here every day!" She sweeps a hand to take in the orchard and view together. "I can look people in the eye and tell them I grow the best fruit in America. I have no problem telling you that, and I'll hand you the fruit to back it up. But you can't do that alone. It takes lots of help, from my husband, friends, neighbors, fairies . . . " She smiles with satisfaction.

Wynne has a sturdy, determined gait, always a few steps ahead as we move through the orchard, pointing out this tree or that. In the jumble of the packing barn I admire the bold design of their Jerzy Boyz box, a nod to Scott's boyhood home. She says, resigned, that they don't use them anymore, can't afford it, so they pack in generic boxes, but she gives me one of the colorful Jerzy Boyz postcards that goes into each one. As I look around, she clicks the answering machine on the cluttered shelf that passes for a desk, and I hear the recorded voice say, "You have nineteen messages . . . " Wynne buzzes through them, looking for a call from the grower she's arranged to meet us for lunch, at the same time putting down a bowl of water for the dogs and clearing a space on the counter so I can take a photo.

I follow her dusty green Toyota pickup back into town and park in front of a small, colorful door tucked below an appliance shop, marked only by a small sign in the shape of a fish. It's the kind of place you have to know about to find, and it's clear when we walk in that she and Scott are family here. Scott, taking a lunch break from his full-time job managing a regional recycling program, and Mark, another local grower who has driven in to town to meet us, are already waiting. The lunchtime conversation is part neighborly catching up and telling stories of the old days and part commiseration about the challenges of the apple business. They've clearly been around the block with each other on some issues, but there's deep respect evident, and a persistent desire to be understood.

Mark Gores is a midsized conventional grower, his operation similar in scale to the Lymans', Clarks', and thousands of other family orchards and farms in the United States. Mark earnestly and generously tells me the winding story of his own path to growing specialty varieties, which he markets through one of the local grower-owned co-ops. With short dark hair, a big firm handshake, and the rolling walk of someone who spends his days climbing in and out of pickups and tractors, he's full of enthusiastic energy, so eager to say all that's bottled up in him that he doesn't always finish his sentences before rushing on to the next thought. A self-effacing guy, bursting with pride in his orchard and livelihood, he's quick to compliment Scott and Wynne and other growers he's worked with, and just as quick to point out his own mistakes and missteps along the way. He has a dry humor about the way his wife puts up with him and earnest gratitude that his father let him take over the orchard and make his own decisions. He has bucked conventional wisdom in his own way, and has held on to his orchard through a combination of stubbornness, paying close attention to what other successful growers were doing, and making some hardheaded, smart decisions.

Mark's father grew up on a North Dakota wheat farm. After serving in the U.S. Navy during World War II, he earned an engineering degree and had a successful career with Boeing in Seattle. But he missed farming and used to drive across the Cascades on weekends to help his brother and uncles work their apple orchards in the valley. Eventually he bought an orchard of his own, and when Mark was four, they moved to Chelan. His dad worked nights in a lumber mill, and his mom worked days in the fruit warehouses until they were able to farm full time. "It was just me and my three sisters and Mom and Dad, we did everything but pick it," remembers Mark.

Mark graduated high school just before the end of the Vietnam War. He had a draft number. Scared about his future, he was getting ready to join up when his dad suggested he stay around for the summer before committing to such a big decision. It was the only time his dad ever made a suggestion about what he should do, and it was a turning point.

Mark spent the next few years hanging out with his buddies, hunting, skiing on the lake, getting into some trouble, and working in the orchard he knew so well. Eventually, he says, he "met the right people," including his wife, Marcia, and Tom Auvil, nephew of a prominent local orchardist and a horticulturist at one of the local warehouses who became a life-long friend.

Mark has known Wynne and Scott since they first came to Chelan. He alternates between sheepishness at not having the dedication to organic principles that Jerzy Boyz has and head-shaking skepticism that either of them could farm the way the other does. Scott, wiry and energetic, agrees they've each made different choices but face the same competitive pressures.

Wynne and Scott chose to farm organically, plant lots of different varieties, and stay small. "We learned within a couple years that to stay in business we had to market and pack our own fruit," Scott recounts. "The recession hit about the time some of the big orchards started getting into organic. You know, it's a nice thing that more acres are going organic, but . . . pretty much all of a sudden, you've got ten thousand new acres going onto the organic market." The flood of organic fruit brought prices down just as demand was increasing.

Mark wasn't among those looking to shift to organic, but as the owner of a midsized orchard without a lot of clout, he didn't think he could make it against the competition unless he came up with his own strategy to stand out. He took a hard look at the varieties he and his dad had planted and began to think about how he could restructure his orchard to offer newer varieties to the changing market.

"I didn't think of it at the time, but looking back, I had my own fundamentals. I just think there's certain things you like to hang your hat on, and hopefully they don't move too much, you know?"

"Like trees!" Wynne wisecracks. "That's one of the good things about trees: you can hang your hat on them."

We all chuckle, but Mark turns serious again. "You get lucky."

"Or have good instincts," inserts Wynne, encouraging him to take some credit. Mark persists. "Well, that's nice, but we didn't have a hailstorm at the wrong time, or . . . " His voice trails off, knowing they've all had some good and bad years.

THE CHELAN FRESH OFFICE is only a few blocks off the main street where Wynne, Scott, Mark, and I had lunch. From the outside, the long, low brick building of shared offices looks like an elementary school, not the headquarters of one of the largest fruit marketing companies in the world. Wynne has put me in touch with the Stennes family, growers for Chelan Fresh and longtime growers in the area. Like nearly everyone I meet in the apple world, my interest in apples is all Kevin Stennes needs to hear to say, "Sure, come by the office, I'd be glad to talk." When I mention that I heard someone with the same last name speak at the Washington State Horticultural Association meeting earlier in the week, he grins. "Yeah, that was my twin brother, Mark."

In a conference room with a window looking into the sales office— two rows of low cubicles bustling with phones and activity—are two large photographs of beautiful orchards, one taken from above so you can see the sweep of the river and the mountains behind. Kevin points out the big yellow house where his grandparents and now his parents live and two smaller homes nearby, one his, one belonging to his brother. His pride and enthusiasm are contagious.

Kevin's father, Keith, is the fourth generation of a family that settled their land in the Methow Valley north of Lake Chelan in 1894. They have a 550-acre orchard, midsized for here, with hills and valleys that allow them to grow twenty-five varieties of apples, pears, pluots, and cherries. Keith took over the orchard after his father died in 1966. Of the fifty-some families that were growing fruit commercially in their community then, only three are still farming. The Stenneses have persevered, adding acres, finding export markets for their cherries, and certifying part of the orchard as organic (they market the fruit under the name Cascade Crest Organics). Keith provides a lifetime of knowledge and experience. His sons, Kevin and Mark, in their thirties, started managing the orchard in 2003. They hope to nearly double their acreage in the next five years.

Like John Lyman in Connecticut, the Stennes's Cascade Crest orchard mostly grows fruit using integrated pest management (IPM) and what some would call conventional practices. Kevin manages the organic program for his family and about ten other growers. "I have the easy job;

I get to sell the organic fruit. My brother's got the challenging part of making everything line up in the fields," he laughs. Organic fruit sales are growing, but it's a big challenge to get more growers to convert. "Once they make that decision, you know, the challenges have just started," Kevin points out.

The Stenneses are members of Chelan Fruit Cooperative, which markets fruit from about three hundred family orchards. A decade ago there were close to a dozen packing co-ops in this part of the state. Of forty-some fruit cooperatives in the state in 1950, only six or seven are left after years of mergers and consolidation. A number of them joined to become Chelan Fruit, and in 2004 the co-op and Gebbers Farms, one of the state's and the world's largest family-owned orchards, joined forces to form Chelan Fresh, the marketing company where Kevin works. The co-op has six packing plants and six hundred employees year-round, double that number during the peak season. Their packing facility on the outskirts of Chelan is one of the largest in the world.

Kevin is proud that all of the co-op member orchards, as well as Gebbers, are family owned, as are most of the other large orchards in the state. "Even though it's a huge organization, it's comprised of over three hundred pretty small family farms, some literally as small as two or three acres, up to thousands of acres." Large by eastern standards, at 550 acres his family's orchard feels small to Kevin. He compares it to the region just south of Wenatchee. "I mean, it's just thousands of acres of orchard, flat. In Quincy, you can go like eight miles for one orchard, because of the way the land lies. That's mass production down there, for sure."

Most of the state's apple volume is sold through companies like Chelan Fresh. The biggest orchards, like those he's just described, might bring their fruit to four or five major companies to pack and market, but the Stenneses sell nearly all their fruit through the co-op. "It's rare for somebody that's decent-sized to have all their fruit in one packing and shipping company like my family does. We used to have our fruit in nine different companies, but as we got bigger we felt a need to be a bigger part of a single group. I've got a friend that's one of the bigger growers in the state that takes fruit to almost twenty-five different packers. So there's no one grower alike."

When I ask what made him decide to stay in the family business, he doesn't hesitate. "I love it. As far as the fruit industry as a whole, I've always wanted to be part of it. I never had aspirations to do anything else. My brother never did either; he always wanted to be the farmer. We're neighbors, and we're having fun."

Chelan Fresh is big, forward looking, diversified in terms of both organic and more conventional production methods, and vertically integrated with its own packing and marketing. As with many parts of U.S. agriculture, what looks like industrial mass production from the vantage point of the anonymous supermarket smorgasbord is mostly made up of midsized family farms with generations of experience, land, and relationships. Yet even with that scale, resourcefulness, and stability there are no guarantees.

At the end of our conversation, Kevin mentions that his family is featured in the latest issue of *Seattle Metropolitan* magazine. Almost as an aside, he says the article is about the huge 2014 Carlton Complex fire, then the largest in the state's history, which tore through this area. As we stand up to leave, Kevin turns around and points again to the beautiful photo of his family homestead to show me how close the fire came to the houses. The flames devoured stacks of wooden bins, equipment, and six miles of deer fencing, and the fire was hot enough to melt aluminum ladders. The Stenneses were lucky; they lost some rows along the perimeter, but most of their orchard, and their homes, were spared. Other growers in the region lost tens of thousands of acres and millions of dollars in fruit. It will take six to seven years for some of the trees to get back into production.

Kevin and his counterparts—whether Scott and Wynne's five organic acres, Mark Gores's midsized orchards, or John Lyman's diverse operation a continent away—take tremendous risks and pour so much of themselves into growing tasty apples. I'm awed by their dedication. The more I learn about what it takes to grow apples in the United States today, the harder it is to take even one bite for granted.

CHAPTER FOUR

Making Apples

TREE FRUIT GROWERS live in an altered time frame, even compared to other farmers. When gardening and farming magazines and catalogs lush with colorful photos arrive in midwinter, home gardeners and vegetable farmers order seed for the coming season; barring too much rain, drought, hail, or early frost, most of their crops grow from seedling to table in a matter of months. It's different if you're planting trees. "Time to Plan for 2017 and 2018 Rootstocks" announces an advertisement in the January 2015 issue of *Good Fruit Grower*. "Reservations Highly Recommended." Another ad blares "For this year, next year, and EVEN THE YEAR AFTER THAT, demand for trees is very strong and quantities are limited."

Growing good apples takes a combination of horticulture, biology, botany, plant pathology, entomology, weed science, chemistry, physics, soil science, meteorology, math, engineering, mechanics, and management, mixed with equal measures of creativity, philosophy, and stub-

ABOVE: Apple seeds, Pete Ten Eyck, Indian Ladder Farms, Altamont, New York. Photo by Susan Futrell.

bornness. It also takes patience, attention to detail, hard physical labor, long hours, love of the outdoors, and some unknown amount of pure wizardry. Marketing your own apples takes all of that plus a strong suit in human relations and psychology, more patience, and a thick skin. Political savvy doesn't hurt. Faith and a prayer now and then also help. Every season there's a chance that something significant will go wrong. Despite planning one, two, even ten years ahead, things change every day, sometimes every hour.

Old books on fruit growing devote entire chapters to each element of orchard success, and some basics haven't changed since the days of Jefferson. Good pomology starts with selecting the right location and orienting the trees just so. John Chapman and his river-bottom nurseries notwithstanding, the best places to plant apple trees are on hillsides sloping gently enough that cold air moves to the bottom, protecting the trees from frost while providing good drainage and exposure to sunlight. In the dry Pacific Northwest, access to irrigation is key. In northern regions, planting near a large body of water reduces risk of cold and frost damage. Proper drainage and controlling erosion are crucial to avoid root rot or nutrients leaching away.

The foundation of the orchard lives in the soil that holds and nurtures the trees. Soil is a community of living organisms. It takes constant care—testing, adding amendments, planting cover crops—to keep it free of pathogens, parasites, and disease, and to maintain organic matter and good tilth with the proper balance of pH, nutrients, and fertility. Healthy soil also plays an important role in sequestering carbon, meaning orchards have an increasingly important contribution to make in mediating climate disruption.

Once the orchard is sited and the ground prepared, the choice of rootstock is the next long game. Rootstock provides not only roots but also the tree trunk that holds all the growth above. Rootstock determines size, resistance to some diseases, how long the trees live, and how much work is needed to tend them. Some growers and nurseries prefer rootstock grown from seedlings, but most rely on carefully selected, well-tested cloned or grafted lines like M-7, M-9 from the Malling-Merton research centers in England and G-11, G-16 from the Cornell apple rootstock breeding program in Geneva, New York. Others come from Sweden, Poland, and elsewhere, each with unique characteristics suited to different needs and climates. Rootstocks require a few years to establish, even longer than the varieties grafted onto them. Desirable lines are in short supply, hence the years-long wait for orders.

Old-fashioned trees on standard rootstock generally have more vigor and live longest. Gnarly and full of character, these full-size trees still grace old farmsteads, fencerows, and a few subdivision backyards. They grow thirty or forty feet high and take as long as ten years to bear fruit. Almost every commercial orchard I've visited has a stand of old trees like these somewhere on the farm, kept for beauty or sentiment—Lyman Orchards has kept a block of Baldwin trees planted the year John's father was born—but almost no one plants them nowadays. They must be spaced at least thirty feet apart; require more mowing, pruning, and maintenance; are harder to pick; and too often shade their own apples with too many branches.

Semidwarf trees, common since the 1960s, are shorter, can be grown much closer together, and produce fruit within seven years. They still look like trees but are more compact and easier to prune, dotting the hillsides like a Grant Wood painting. They are popular rootstocks for backyard orchards, and their fruit is easier to reach for pick-your-own and professional pickers alike.

Dwarf trees are the trees of today. The trend toward high-density planting of dwarf trees began in the 1990s and is now the norm. Planted as many as several hundred to several thousand trees per acre, they're ten to twelve feet at their tallest and start producing small amounts of fruit in the first or second year after planting. Fewer, sparser branches mean more efficient pruning, making it easier to grow apples with good color because they get more sun. They are easier to mow around; keeping grass cut short is a good nontoxic way to control mice and weeds. But dwarf trees have wrist-thin trunks that can't withstand wind and snow, so they must be supported on stakes or wire and don't live as long as larger trees. There are many designs for support structures in high-density plantings: individual stakes, overhead wires, V-trellis. All of them cost thousands of dollars per acre to put in place, holding row after row of trees planted as close as two feet apart in rows just wide enough for a ten-foot piece of equipment to pass. Even at full growth, dwarf trees look like saplings, orderly and prim.

Choosing apple varieties (also called cultivars, for cultivated varieties) brings into play an even more complex mix of factors: reliable stock, suitability for geographic region and site, climate tolerance, disease resistance, personal affection, and market appeal. To acquire a lot of identical and predictable fruit, a chosen variety is grafted onto the chosen rootstock. At its most basic, grafting involves splicing the thin cambium layer just below the bark of a piece of rootstock to the cambium layer of a cutting, or scion, of the cultivar, or variety being propagated. The two are held in place with tape or wax until they grow together. There are many grafting techniques, but they all have one purpose: to attach a cultivar that will produce fruit to a rootstock that will support it.

Then there are sports, or mutations. Even grafted trees of known varieties sometimes produce shoots with slightly different characteristics than the parent tree had. As Henry Ward Beecher quaintly explained, "A sober apple-tree will sometimes let down its dignity, in what gardeners call a 'sport,' *e.g.*, a sweet apple may grow on a sour tree and vice versa."[1] Sports are not generally a result of pollination but of a single cell that mutates for any number of reasons and forms a bud that grows into a shoot or branch. That variant itself can then be grafted, making its own contribution to diversity. Red Delicious trees, for example, widely propagated from a single persistent tree that originally grew in an Iowa field, sometimes send out branches with fruit that is even redder, thicker-skinned, or more handsomely shaped than the original. Dozens of those sports have been further selected and propagated, some with new versions of the name, such as Double Red. Over time, the selection and promotion of these redder, harder, or more dramatically shaped sports are part of the reason that the Red Delicious you buy in the grocery store are sadly more red, but less delicious, than their name implies.

With good rootstock in place, you're a step ahead when it's time to regraft or topwork the next variety. In an older orchard, you weigh the costs and risks of pulling up and starting over. These days, new is usually the way to go, but even then there are risks.

When planting new trees into old orchard ground, some trees are victims of a not yet understood disease called apple replant. A mixture of microbes and microscopic worms called nematodes feed on the roots of old established trees. Larger rootstocks withstand this, but when new dwarf rootstocks go into the same soil, they may not fare as well. Growers who've had soil tested and found replant disease use treatments such as adding organic matter or new soil or using highly toxic fumigation chemicals to ensure new trees won't have their roots destroyed.

THE RISKY, LONG-TERM decisions don't stop with the selection of rootstock and variety. Once trees are in the ground, they are assaulted daily by pests, diseases, and competitors. A chart of major apple pests in New York produced by scientists at Cornell University shows twenty-nine insects, fifteen diseases, and six classes of weeds representing dozens of weed species east of the Mississippi River. Only a handful of those pests are a serious problem in the arid climates west of the Rockies, which is one reason most of the organic fruit in the United States is grown in that region. But growers everywhere need to be constantly vigilant to manage insects, mites, fungi, and animals, balancing economics and ecologically sound practices. No matter what their growing philosophy, they must follow a dizzying regimen informed by chemistry, botany, biology, and both EPA and state-level pesticide regulations to manage a voracious parade of insects and diseases that can leave their beautiful apples spotted, speckled, brown, soft, or lumpy.

Many growers throughout the United States rely on integrated pest management (IPM), an approach that uses ecological methods as the basis for pest control. (The word *pest* is used in IPM to mean diseases, weeds, microbes, animals, and all things that eat or damage apples, not just insect pests.) IPM practices can dramatically reduce the need for and costs of spraying insecticides or fungicides, but they often require considerable investment of knowledge and attention. For example, John Lyman in Connecticut hangs red sticky balls treated with aromatic chemicals in his trees to trap apple maggot flies. Using this method to catch and count the flies has become standard practice in most apple orchards to monitor when and where flies emerge. That helps reduce frequency of spraying and allows growers to target only infested parts of an orchard. But John goes further, using the pheromone balls to "trap-out" enough of the pests to avoid spraying altogether. Spraying for apple maggot or any pest can also kill off the beneficials that would otherwise eat apple pests, and that means having to spray for other pests as well. Entirely eliminating that one spray application helps foster more beneficial insects that in turn keep other pests under control. Using pheromone balls to trap-out helps create a more diverse orchard ecology that manages all pests more effectively.[2]

Most of the pests and diseases that plagued apples a century ago—rot, rust, scab, and a multitude of borers, moths, worms, aphids, and beetles —still bedevil apple growers today. In addition, some pests are moving into new regions as climates change and others are arriving from outside the United States as global trade expands. Some pests have become resistant to specific pesticides. Along with constantly evolving pest ecology, there are constantly changing regulatory restrictions as well as new research on health and environmental effects. "There is always risk," says John Lyman. "Every farm has microclimates, so it's an ongoing experiment."

Apple growers in the United States first began to use chemicals to manage diseases and insects about 120 years ago, and the practice has generally intensified ever since. Knowledge about the biology of pest species, the roles of other insects and soil microbes as effective controls, and sophisticated chemistry that allows more targeted treatments have all evolved significantly over time, leading to better precautions for workers and surrounding environments. Arsenic and lead, for example, once considered major advances, have not been used for decades because of their severe toxicity. But previous decades of lead arsenate spraying left soil in many old orchards saturated with high levels of lead and arsenic. As orchards are plowed under to make way for housing developments, playgrounds, and even other farms, soil testing and remediation are major undertakings. That progression of newly discovered solution becoming long-term problem has been repeated many times over in the constant search for new pesticides that do the job but do no harm.

When I listen to discussions about pest management among growers and scientists, I don't always understand the details and chemistry. But I'm fascinated by the language. A decidedly practical and down-to-earth group of farmers and scientists becomes unabashedly poetic talking about stages of growth in an orchard: Dormant. Silver Tip. Green Tip. Half-Inch Green. Tight Cluster. Pink. Popcorn Bloom. Bloom. Petal Fall. As in, "it's best to treat between green tip and pink, and definitely not after petal fall."[3]

Pesticide product names are something else altogether. They could just as likely be cosmetics, cars, cleaning products, or pharmaceuticals (they're often produced by the same companies), and it's hard to distinguish the highly toxic from the eco-friendly or the chemistry from the spin. The "softer," reputedly greener versions have names such as Vanguard, Reliant, Assail, Agree, Deliver, Avant, Disrupt, Esteem, Entrust, and Apogee. (The cowboy-sounding weed killer Roundup was once considered to be in this category, but new research indicates it may need to move to more restricted use.) The harsher "use-only-if-you-have-to" options have equally inventive names: Captan, Disperss, Nova, Procure, Firewall, Flint, Rely, Scythe, Lorsban, Clutch, Proclaim, Secure, Zeal, Intrepid. And the really bad actors sound just as bold: Pristine, Prism, Apollo, Asana, Warrior, Pounce, Calypso, Pyramite, Goal, Prowl, Kerb.

The word *label* comes up frequently in pesticide discussions, sometimes as a noun, sometimes a verb. The verb *to label* means it's legally allowed for a location, crop, pest, or all three. As in, "X is labeled for apples in New York, but not for aphids, and not after petal fall." The noun *label* is where you find the fine print: application rate, precautions, target pests, more precautions, risks. The two meanings of *label* don't always align. A product label, for example, might indicate the pesticide is effective against a common apple pest. But that same product might not be labeled for use on apples, or it might be labeled in Massachusetts but not in New York, or it might be labeled for use as a growth regulator, but not as an insecticide. To stay legal, you have to know both kinds of label.

Add to that an array of certifications, standards, retail rating systems, and constantly evolving advice from researchers in multiple states, and growers have at least a half dozen different prohibitions and recommendations to consult before deciding whether to apply a given product to their crop. That's all before reaching an actual decision for their specific situation: Is the pest threat above a threshold that makes it worth treating? Is it too hot or cold or dry or humid for the treatment to work properly? Is it windy, and from what direction? Is it going to rain before, during, or within a few days after spraying? How long will it take to spray the orchard? How long an interval between spraying and harvest does the label require? Is fruit already forming, and exactly when will it be ready to pick? These questions all matter, whether for greener, organic-approved sprays or any other category. It's mind boggling. And there's more.

The behaviors, life cycles, and sheer number of pests and diseases an orchardist must understand are also mind boggling. Arthur Agnello, tree fruit entomologist at Cornell University's New York State Agricultural Experiment Station in Geneva, New York, produces *Scaffolds*, a weekly report on pests during the apple-growing season. The May 4, 2015, issue is nine pages long just for New York State and includes these upcoming events: redbanded leafroller peak catch; spotted tentiform leafminer first flight peak and first oviposition; European red mite egg hatch. That's not all, and each week there's a new list. Another page tallies the weekly trap catches of things such as apple maggot flies, peachtree borer, and obliquebanded leafroller. A lead article covers management for San Jose scale, rosy apple aphid, tarnished plant bug, European apple sawfly, and plum curculio, all at pink. This is followed by four pages of advice on the best way to deal with the disease fire blight.[4] Next week, and the next, there will be more lists and articles.

Although they are sometimes named for specific crops, the insects themselves are actually much more profligate. To many of them, apple wood tastes just as good as peach wood and green leaves of all varieties make a good lunch. Ironically, when it comes to pesticides, insects are more particular; some substances affect one species and not another, or are effective at one point in the life cycle but no other, or work better only at certain temperatures. Many of them wash away when it rains. It's complicated, for sure. But simple isn't always better. The only approach recommended for black stem borer, for example, is all too simple: "Infested trees should be removed and burned."

Diseases require another set of considerations about timing, treatment, labels, weather, and local/regional outbreaks. The biggest issues in the East are plant diseases that prosper in humid climates. Agnello's counterparts in plant pathology generate regular advice on disease management. Land grant scientists and private crop consultants around the country keep growers updated on assaults and options. Like almost everything else in farming, dealing with disease means balancing trade-offs. To ward off fire blight without antibiotics, the recommendation is to keep trees at low to moderate vigor (growth rate and size); to fend off borers, high vigor is the best strategy. For scab, planting resistant varieties eliminates the need for scab fungicides. But the apple varieties customers want are generally not scab resistant, and in fact may be quite susceptible; to give customers the pretty Honeycrisp and Gala they want is hard to do without spraying. For cedar rust, the most important preventive measure is to get rid of any nearby cedar trees, but that may not be possible if your suburban neighbors have just planted a nice cedar hedge along the edge of their newly landscaped yard.

Weeds not only compete with trees for nutrients and water, they provide cover and habitat for insects, voles, and other pests. Keeping weeds at bay is another balancing act, usually involving mowing or shallow cultivation with special equipment to avoid root damage—or a preventive spray of an herbicide such as glyphosate (Roundup).[5] And even eliminating weeds requires delicate timing to preserve pollinator habitats and avoid treatments when pollinators are feeding on weeds that bloom before or after the apple trees.

In addition to deciding which substances to use for which problem at what point in the tree or pest life cycles, there are application methods to consider. To get the stuff to go where you want it, dispense proper amounts, and eliminate or minimize drift to the woods or a neighbor's backyard, sprayers need calibration. Calibration is as much art as science, a balance of nozzle selection, pressure in the system, driving speed, and other variables. It's crucial to effective and economic pesticide application. And adjustments need to be made for individual blocks of trees in most orchards. When an application is done, the sprayer has to be safely cleaned and checked before it's put away for the next time.

Growers who use IPM, whether they are spraying organic-approved substances such as kaolin clay and sulfur, or synthetic chemicals, scout and monitor for levels of pest infestation, which allows them to spray only when and where needed. The alternative, without scouting or where orchard size makes covering a large block in a short time frame difficult, is to spray everything on a regular schedule, called calendar spraying.

Employees must be trained and certified to apply pesticides and must wear personal protective equipment (PPE). They must avoid spraying when the wind is too high, or so low that it makes air movement unpredictable. They must avoid high temperatures, low temperatures, and too much or too little humidity, protect bees, and place warning signs on sprayed blocks or sections of the orchard. They must keep application records, including date, time, weather, operator, sprayer, field ID/location, targeted pest, pesticide name and EPA number, formulation, rate applied, and acres treated, and post those records where all employees can see them. Pesticides must be stored separately from PPE in a frost-free, secure, ventilated building, in original containers, powder above liquids, abiding by correct rinsing and disposal methods, with an inventory list of products and emergency plan plainly posted. Apple growers need to be very smart about all of it, and most of them will tell you it's their least favorite part of growing apples.

AT INDIAN LADDER FARMS, an Eco Apple certified orchard in upstate New York, I got my first look at an especially vicious orchard threat, a disease called fire blight. The telltale signs are brownish-red leaves, completely dried up and stiff, a branch here and there in the midst of otherwise lush green foliage like they've been selectively torched.[6] Certain tree varieties have been especially hard hit this season. In an orchard that's not restricted by eco or organic certification, this never would have happened—the trees would have been treated, usually with a targeted antibiotic. Eco Apple protocol does allow some targeted use of antibiotics, but owner Pete Ten Eyck tries to avoid using them because he knows some customers are concerned. Now that the trees are infected, the only thing to do is cut out the diseased wood.

I ask if the trees will make it, and Pete says probably. But fire blight makes apples vulnerable to another disease, a fungus called black rot. That's now flourishing, especially on his Honeycrisp, which are particularly susceptible and also particularly valuable. So the decision not to treat for fire blight will have consequences far beyond the loss of fruit and branches on the infected trees we're looking at. It all looms: extra pruning, disposal of the infected wood, the loss of more fruit and tree limbs to black rot, plus uncertainty next year about whether the fire blight has wintered over or diseased branches have been missed in the pruning and how that will affect next year's crop. A proactive, targeted antibiotic could have kept the bacteria from getting a foothold to begin with. Pete shrugs it off; he's committed to ecological production methods, and these are the kinds of risks he juggles constantly in this business.

When a few customers complained about apples showing a bit of scab, another disease causing mainly cosmetic damage, Pete started carrying around a clipboard. He told customers he was keeping a list of anyone who wanted perfect apples without spots. He would grow a special block for them next year with just a few more sprays, and when the apples were ready he'd let them know. Funny thing, no one wanted to be on his list. Pete loves to tell this story. His dry wit is the perfect way to explain what customers don't want to hear: there are trade-offs in all of this.

ANOTHER BALANCING ACT that plays out for much of the growing season is the effort to maximize fruit set, which happens when there is good pollination, and the counteraction of thinning back the fruit if there is too much of it. Experts call this crop management, but to the uninitiated it amounts to wizardry.

Apple blossoms need pollen from another apple or crab apple tree to successfully produce fruit. Some cultivars are better pollen sources than others. Some produce sterile pollen, some are "self-fruitful" when pollinated by another tree of the same variety, and some require cross-pollination from other varieties. Bees, butterflies, and other pollinators carry pollen from tree to tree, and the timing of bloom, weather, hour of day, pollinator species, and the presence of competing blooming plants nearby all affect pollination rates. Some orchards keep their own bees year-round, harvesting honey as an added bonus. Others bring in bees for hire every spring. One hive of fifteen thousand to twenty thousand bees can pollinate an acre of semidwarf trees. Higher density dwarf plantings need two or more hives per acre to do the job during the small window when they are in bloom.

Commercial beekeepers with healthy hives are in high demand for a wide range of crops. Booked far in advance, they travel cross-country with stacks of hives, moving from crop to crop over the course of many months. Devastating bee-colony losses have been a persistent and serious threat in recent years. The parasitic varroa mite, a diet of sugary feed, stress of travel, and a complex array of chemicals including a class of pesticides called neonicotinoids have all been implicated. Loss of commercial bee colonies puts the apple crop at risk in orchards without native pollinators.

Wild pollinators are a significant asset in orchards that foster their habitat. Clark Brothers Orchards, an Eco Apple–certified farm in western Massachusetts, has a healthy population of wild pollinators, as many as sixty or more species including bumblebees and blue orchard bees. The Clarks know pollination will be good when they look out on a nice day and see a column of bees rising up over the trees.

After spending the early spring carefully tending to the bees and trees so they produce bountiful, beautiful fruit, it's time to knock back the amount of fruit that will be allowed to remain and ripen for harvest. Thinning in a small orchard can be done by hand-cutting fingertip-sized fruits off each tree and leaving one apple every six to ten inches to grow to full size. In a commercial orchard, thinning usually involves chemistry.

"Thinning is the hardest thing we do in the orchard," explains Dana Clark with a frown. "It has the biggest impact on the current crop and on next year's crop of anything we do, especially for varieties like Honeycrisp." If the trees are allowed to bear too heavily one year, they will produce a very light crop the next year. A very heavy crop can send the tree into a biennial cycle, producing fruit only every other year. In addition, if there is too much fruit on the tree, the apples will be smaller. "The end result is too much small fruit that doesn't bring a premium price, plus a heavy crop that brings prices down, followed by not enough fruit to sell next year." Dana shakes his head and runs a hand through his short-cropped, just-graying hair. "I lose more sleep over thinning than anything else we do. It's so hard to get it right."

While it's possible to thin fruit by hand, labor shortages and costs have led growers to depend on chemical thinners. The impact of a given thinner varies with weather, apple variety, and the amount used. One of the most common substances used for thinning, because it is less sensitive to these variables and works so reliably, is carbaryl. Part of a family of substances called carbamates, it is under increasing scrutiny because of health concerns, and one large retail chain now prohibits its use by their apple suppliers. There is a lot of research under way and interest in finding effective alternatives. But alternative thinning agents are more weather-sensitive. Some don't work well in the cool, damp weather that can last for weeks in late spring in the Northeast. Some work best during bloom, before you really know how much pollination and fruit set you will get. Other treatments go on after the fruit is set and still small, but those tend to be stronger and more likely to negatively impact tree growth and the next year's fruit set. Some take multiple applications. Some have multiple benefits—reducing russet and sunburn, for example. None of them is inexpensive.

Even when all the conditions and the guesses and the leaps of faith are aligned, thinning sometimes works and sometimes doesn't. Some varieties thin more reliably than others. Some thin well one season and not so well the next. Land grant and grower-funded research on thinning methods continues, invaluable to growers trying to navigate this annual dance.[7]

Just to complicate things a bit further, some apple varieties need another treatment after thinning, to help them retain the fruit that's left. Growers don't want fruit to drop and rot on the ground before it's fully ripe instead of sizing up, coloring well, and staying on the tree to be picked. Red color is more prized than any other quality—including flavor—in commercial fruit marketing. Apparently we humans just can't help but be attracted to shiny red fruit. Redness develops with exposure to sunlight, so the planting, pruning, spacing, and staking of trees are all geared toward exposing ripening fruit to just the right amount of light. Too much results in sunburn; not enough keeps them too green. Shade from a leaf or branch can produce exquisite leaf prints and pale patches on an otherwise red piece of fruit—a bit of found art that will cause the apple to be rejected on most pack lines. Color and ripeness do not always correlate; some varieties continue to sweeten and improve in flavor for weeks or even months after being picked. None, however, turn redder once they are off the tree.

While it's a cliché that farmers start every conversation with talk about the weather, it's a preoccupation for good reason. Rain at the right time, not too much, not too little, is the orchardist's dream. A hard winter can wipe out entire swaths of orchards. Extremes of heat and cold are becoming more frequent. Good weather out of season can force blooms too early. Frost a few weeks later can turn those blooms brown. The risk of codling moth infestation goes up when the weather in spring is warm and wet, but a warm, wet spring is better for treating fire blight with biological methods. Hail in midsummer, when apples are big enough to make good targets but still too soft and thin-skinned to withstand fast-falling balls of ice, is devastating. The anguish of seeing a good crop develop on the trees, ripen well, and color up in the summer sun only to wake up one day to fruit pulverized and nicked by pellets of ice is especially cruel. The less predictable weather patterns become, the more vulnerable the fruit.

Weather that's too cold kills fruit buds and even whole trees, but winters that are too warm can be just as bad, preventing apple bloom and fruiting. Meanwhile, in Alaska, warming climate trends are making it possible to grow apple varieties that couldn't survive there in the past. In another century, those same warming trends may mean it is no longer possible to grow apples in all fifty states.

The most hopeful thing about weather is that farming may have a significant role to play in sequestering carbon. Expanding the number of ecologically managed orchards with rich soil and healthy trees may be one way to contribute to long-term climate stability.

HAVING FOUGHT THE PESTS, encouraged the pollinators, thinned for maximum value, and survived summer storms, when it is finally time to harvest, orchards fill up with people. From July into November, depending on the region and apple varieties, harvest crews move through the rows, spot picking to get the best fruit for fresh sales, going back to each tree as fruit is ready. For processing, the crews strip trees all at once. We'll learn more about the people who do this orchard work in chapter 9, but for now we'll focus on the fruit.

Apples are transferred from the pickers' bags into large wooden or plastic bins in the orchard. A person driving a trailer or forklift brings the bins to the packing barn. Bins are moved from orchard to packing shed to cooler as they're filled. In the packing shed, equipment needs maintenance and operators need training. The bins, boxes, and packing areas must be kept scrupulously clean; bits of decayed fruit removed; bins, floors, everything cleaned and sanitized. Sanitation with water, heat, ozone, or chemicals such as bleach kills bacteria, yeast, and fungal spores that can spoil fruit after it is moved into storage.

Midsized orchards in the West often send their fruit to a large packer-shipper once it is harvested. The Lymans, Clarks, and many orchards in the East and Midwest pack, store, and ship their fruit on their own farms. The process can be done by hand or with sturdy generations-old machines that are tended and kept in motion the way old tractors are. Increasingly, though, even on midsized farms, the old pack lines are giving way to sophisticated machinery costing hundreds of thousands of dollars and powered by banks of computers linked to monitors and service techs on the other side of the globe. The new machines work basically the same way the old ones do, but with head-spinning speed and accuracy.

A full bin is lifted onto the packing machine at one end and lowered down into a tank until it is submerged in water, so the apples float rather than tumble out, keeping bruising to a minimum. The apples bob and float cheerily along toward a conveyor that brings them, gently dripping, up onto a smaller belt to be individually weighed and, in the newest pack lines, photographed by hundreds of tiny cameras to sort for color and blemishes. Small apples fall through the sorter and are swooshed along in water to a separate chute that dumps them unceremoniously into another bin to be sold for cider-making. Right-size apples are carried along into a covered section where blowing air dries them.

If the customer the orchard is packing for requires it, the machine applies a thin coating of paraffin or naturally derived shellac that makes apples shiny. Many supermarkets require waxing, and even organic apples are sometimes waxed with an organic-approved version. It's another step many growers would rather do without. Apples develop their own waxy coating over time, and a good polish on a shirtsleeve is all it takes to brighten them up naturally. If the customer the orchard is packing for requires it, a tiny sticker with a price look-up (PLU) code and, if there's room, the apple variety and name of the orchard is applied. Stickers stick to machines, fingers, and floor, not just apples, and they add a small cost to every piece of fruit.

Dry, glistening, sorted by weight and color, buffed and stickered, the apples rumble along the conveyor belt to a series of pack stations. Ideally, those of the same size and quality end up together. Actually, density and therefore size varies, so a human packer sometimes sorts them further before packing them into bags or boxes. Bruised or misshapen fruit that has made it past the sorter gets tossed into the cider bin as the packers move quickly to keep up with the conveyor. Some varieties like McIntosh and Macoun are more delicate, and it can take as long as forty-eight hours for bruises to show up. During harvest, the Clarks' packing machine in western Massachusetts runs twelve hours a day, six days a week. In Washington, large packer-shippers like Chelan Fruit run dozens of machines for months to pack the 240 million bushels grown in the state in an average year. Once packed, some fruit is shipped immediately; the rest goes back into cold storage along with full bins yet to be packed, for shipment throughout the winter.

Difficulties don't end with harvest. Even sitting quietly in the cooler, apples need protection from injury and damage. Growers need to know just the right length of time to hold each variety to maintain—and for some varieties, to develop—peak flavor and texture, with no mold, no rot, no infestation, no stem punctures, no bruising. The biggest factor in maintaining quality is cooling the apples as quickly as possible after picking and then keeping them cool. For most apples, thirty-two degrees Fahrenheit is best. Colder, they freeze; warmer, they're susceptible to all manner of problems. But McIntosh like to be kept at thirty-eight degrees Fahrenheit; otherwise, they can develop internal browning, which, as the name suggests, you won't see until you bite into the apple.

Along with improved cooling technology, the greatest boon for apple quality was the advent of controlled-atmosphere (CA) storage in the 1940s. CA storage rooms are sealed once they are filled with fruit, and most of their oxygen is replaced with carbon dioxide, which dramatically slows ethylene absorption, ripening, and respiration. CA storage can keep apples crisp and firm for many months after harvest.

If you've noticed the apples you buy seem crisper than ever, it may also be due to post-harvest treatments such as SmartFresh, a proprietary form of hydrocarbon molecule dispersed in storage units that temporarily blocks ethylene receptors then biodegrades naturally when apples are brought out of storage. These storage technologies have helped reduce waste and bring firm, crisp apples to shoppers year-round.

Properly stored apples are still vulnerable to a host of postharvest disorders and diseases such as scald (skin blemishes), carbon dioxide injury (which causes internal browning), moldy core, bitter pit, and fungal rots. Treatments with calcium, fungicides, and the antioxidant diphenylamine (DPA) are used to manage these injuries, which affect some varieties more than others. Fogging applications now allow much lower application rates than drenching entire bins as was once more common. Less susceptible varieties can be managed with good bin sanitation or calcium treatments on trees. Storage treatments must be used according to label, just like treatments in the orchard.

THE WORK AND DECISIONS don't stop when the leaves fall. Pruning is done in the winter, after most of the orchard workers have gone and snow blankets the rows. It's the end of the year, but also the start of the next one, with the preparation for new growth and a new season. In a big orchard a crew does the job, but in smaller orchards it is a solitary task, something growers do themselves, relearning the trees at their essence. It can be meditative for someone who knows what they're doing, but takes attention and skill; it's not repetitive in the way of mowing, hedge trimming, or other tasks that involve a sharp blade and a straight line. Pruning is about learning to see what you can't see: sap moving, buds still dormant, leaves yet to appear, sunlight moving in a shifting arc, branches and shadows that don't exist until sometime next spring. Invisible apples.

On a piercing blue-sky day in late winter, I follow Zeke Goodband as he points out different varieties among the trees arching over the rolling hills of the Scott Farm orchard in Dummerston, Vermont. Each variety has a unique shape and distinctions of bark color, size, and line that are at first inscrutable: essential bones, bare branches, an alphabet waiting to be translated.

"Here you go." Zeke holds out the pruner, a long pole with a cutter at one end controlled by a stiff handle at the other. I am not quite ready to have that kind of power over the shape of future branches and the color of future fruit, but I try to grasp it with confidence. I'm pretty sure someone who knows as little as I do about apple trees shouldn't be taking a sharp implement to their tender branches.

My first lesson: pruning isn't about aesthetics, although the bare, gnarled branches of the trees against a painfully bright sky are exquisite: quiet, stark, and open. The ideal shape for an apple tree is about strength and light and where the energy of the tree will go—fruit, leaves, or branches. A properly placed cut allows sun to reach and ripen fruit that would otherwise be shaded and slow to develop its lovely blush and color. Trimming out branches that cross and crowd each other lets the main structure grow stronger and bear more fruit. "They used to say you should be able to throw a cat through that tree in July," Zeke says helpfully.

Zeke walks his entire orchard each winter, pruning every tree himself. "When I first came here, I couldn't discern the pattern, couldn't figure out where to make that first cut. It's the first cut that helps everything fall into place. Walking around and around, I realized there was no pattern, just chaos from years of contract cutting. Eventually I cut through the chaos of those years and found a pattern of caretaking from earlier years. Fred, the original owner, spread the branches really well. Contract pruners tend not to make heavy cuts—takes too much time. The way the trees are shaped is a historical record."

Zeke knows the particular characteristics of each of the more than seventy-five varieties in his orchard. Blue Pearmain is a very spare tree. Cox's Orange Pippin is feathery. Gradually, looking up into the branches as he talks, I begin to see choices, like a fuzzy picture coming into focus—the direction of a bud, where two branches might crowd one another, the shadow that leaves will make when the sun's angle is higher. "A certain number of typos are allowed," Zeke offers by way of encouragement.

I fumble with the handle of the pruner, take a deep breath, and make my first cut. The branch—okay, it's barely a twig—drops to the ground. I slowly circle the tree, staring hard at the scribble of branches until I can see lines and space. I won't say I become confident, but I make some bolder cuts here and there, and Zeke is tolerant.

Light moves. Empty space is useful. Each cut changes the future shape of the tree. Timid pruning isn't very efficient. Wise cuts are a kindness. It's a lesson not to be attached to the individual branch, to your idea of beauty, to the power of the sharp implement. Look at stark, bare branches against cold blue sky, and see next season's perfect apple.

Zeke likes apple trees. You can see it in the way he moves among them, and hear it in his voice. When I remark on this he admits he's partial. "What kind of relationship can you have with a vegetable?" he asks, trying not to smile.

CHAPTER FIVE

Grafting Remnants

IT'S MARCH, cold and windy, with clouds scudding through late-winter slants of sun. I'm clutching a pencil and a large, crookedly folded sheet of graph paper marshaled onto a clipboard, trying to walk and write fast enough to keep up. Both the writing and the walking are wobbly. The dry grass in the orchard tangles around my ankles, and the short, young trees intermingled with sprawling old veterans mean I have to look both up and down to avoid stumbling into a trunk or branch. Wind whips at the paper and blows hair in my eyes as I try to keep up.

The speedy pace is a surprise. My guide is ninety-one years old; one might expect a certain slowness of step and movement. But this is Harold Linder's orchard. He knows every footstep and branch. He eats apples all day, every day, and it seems to be keeping him very spry. He never stops. He's full of stories, full of information, full of ideas, and full of plans. Harold has spent a lifetime working with trees and plants. He doesn't waste time when there is something to be done.

ABOVE: Drawing of a Newport apple from Denmark, Iowa, by William Henry Prestele, 1890. Courtesy of the USDA.

Harold keeps a few steps ahead of me. He knows the name of every tree, where it came from, when it was planted, what kind of apples it produces, when they ripen, how they taste, how long they'll keep, and which ones make the best sauce. For the next couple of hours I trail him between the rows, Harold giving a steady commentary, me writing as fast as possible and asking questions in between scribbles. I stop every so often to steady my pencil, but Harold keeps moving.

The small orchard, stretching in orderly rows along a sunny hillside just to the north of his house, has trees in every stage of growth, from new starts planted last year to gnarly old trees that he's tended for decades. There's a graft from the original Hawkeye Delicious, the Iowa parent of the now-ubiquitous Red Delicious. Liberty, Duchess, Wolf River, Chenango Strawberry—each tree has a story. Two young seedlings he's named Schoolkid because they were found along the roadside and brought to him by local schoolchildren. There are familiar standards too: Macoun, Jonathan, Gala. At this time of year, their twisty branches are beautiful, and I can recognize the older trees as apples by their shape. But without leaves or fruit, his ability to know them each so intimately seems magical.

The scratches I'm making on the graph paper I plan to turn into a map of the orchard marking the name and location of each of his one hundred or so trees. We're making a map because even apples won't keep Harold here forever, and when he is gone the few trees that have tags will eventually lose their labels and then no one will know which tree is which. Knowing the name of an apple tree will at least recall its story. Without a name, they're wild and mysterious.

The white house sits near the road, a mile or so of gravel off the main highway. A white picket fence surrounds a yard full of flowers. Cracked corn and birdseed line the sidewalk leading up to the house. Outbuildings full of aging machinery ring the farmyard. There's a well-stocked fishing pond just beyond the garden. Many years of hard work and attention have kept this place going. When I pulled into his driveway this morning, Harold met me at his back door with a clipboard, a sharpened pencil, and a no-nonsense greeting: "Hello! Let's get started!" Thin, wiry, and energetic, with thick glasses and a thick head of hair, he reminds me of my grandfather.

Harold's sitting room is stacked with books and papers. His reading is eclectic; *Fast Food Nation* sits next to books about farming, health, and history. A map of the world hangs on his living room wall. In one corner is an upright piano, in another a computer keeps him in touch with friends and fellow orchardists. A prolific writer despite having no schooling beyond the eighth grade, he's authored several books on local history and has just self-published a compilation of everything he knows about apples.

The only spot in the room that seems quiet is the empty chair where his wife Mildred always sat. She passed away only a month before, after a long illness. He had spent the last several years taking care of her, and they would have celebrated sixty-eight years of marriage this month. Harold insists I sit in Mildred's chair while we talk. Its worn cushion is used to another body, and I have to lean forward to keep from sinking in too deeply. I'm eerily aware of the hole she has left in his days, until we step outside to meet his other true love.

Harold Linder loves apple trees. He's not stuffy about their pedigree. He's more interested in studying their properties. Are they disease and insect resistant, will they thrive in Iowa's weather, do they produce early or late, are the apples tasty? He doesn't produce fruit for commercial sale anymore. He takes bushel baskets to town for the women at church to cook into pies and sauce, and his neighbors come by to pick in the fall, but he's long since stopped farming for a living. He's part of a long tradition of devoted enthusiasts and pomologists whose love of apples is as much about the trees themselves as about enjoying the fruit. Any tree is worth investigating and nurturing along if it promises to add to the body of knowledge acquired over his seven decades as an orchardist.

On the way to the orchard, we detour through an outbuilding with a dirt floor, his greenhouse and makeshift breeding lab. Wooden shelves and benches line the sides, and a row of neat black plastic pots stretches down the middle, each holding a young twig-sized tree with a carefully written label.

Harold started work as a farmhand at age fifteen and began pruning apple trees soon after. His stepfather was a tenant farmer and hired hand, and the family moved often as farms were sold out from under them. "Raising a family and trying to survive on a small farm, it's a problem," he asserts, remembering the ups and downs. "It's still hard to be a small farmer these days—either you inherit a farm or a lot of money."

He remembers many orchards and nurseries that used to dot this part of the state when he came to this farm in 1943. He can name half a dozen within thirty miles that have gone out of business, only one that is still in operation. A cider mill a few miles down the road is also long gone. "People practically lived on apples and vinegar then," he muses. "We live so differently today."

Among the trees in his orchard is one he calls Burlington Leopold. Aldo Leopold, beloved conservationist and author of *A Sand County Almanac*, grew up in nearby Burlington, Iowa, in a big house on the bluffs above the Mississippi River. Harold was friends with Aldo's youngest brother, Frederic, and on a visit to the old Leopold orchard in 1974 he noticed a particular tree with an unusual shape—a long horizontal limb just a few feet off the ground that made it a favorite for kids to climb. Frederic didn't know where the tree had come from, only that it was over one hundred years old. Intrigued by its age and shape, Harold went back later for a cutting to graft and plant in his own orchard. It produces over two bushels of good fall apples each year, mild flavored, similar to McIntosh, good for both cooking and eating. Harold has found records of a Burlington apple that fits this description and believes the one he grafted is the original. The tree in his orchard has a long horizontal limb in perfect sitting position, uncannily like its parent.

Once the tree was well established in his own orchard, Harold sent a scion to the heritage orchard at Seed Savers Exchange in Decorah, Iowa. A sturdy tree labeled Leopold Apple now stands among the more than six hundred varieties of apple trees there. This is the way apple history is written: twigs marked with paper tags and attached to stories, passed from one apple collector to another.

Harold tends his trees himself, with help from a friend who's interested in learning the craft and a neighbor who helps with pruning and harvesting in exchange for apples. He tells me he's trying to use as few sprays and chemicals as possible, learning from other growers what works. There is always plenty to do; maybe it's easier while he's among his trees to imagine that Mildred is busy in the kitchen or resting in her well-worn chair.

At the end of my visit, the ground outside still frosty and the trees not yet budded, Harold fetches a sack of apples from his cool room. "Those are the Johnny Appleseed apples; I still have a lot of them left," he offers. He's named them for a tree he grafted from one reputedly planted by its namesake. On the hour-long drive home the car is fragrant with apples, still crisp after a winter in storage. Back home, I spread the wrinkled graph paper on our dining room table. Over the next few days I carefully recopy it onto a fresh sheet, in pencil in case I've made a mistake that only Harold would catch. I drive back down to show it to him, and after he's looked it over approvingly, recopy it in pen so the record of his labor of love will last longer. I roll the inked version into a cardboard tube and mail it to him with a thank you note. I keep the pencil copy, although at the time I'm not sure why.

OLD APPLE VARIETIES have been disappearing as long as there have been apples, and what gets saved has long been a matter of debate. In 1926 Liberty Hyde Bailey, a prolific horticulturist and author of dozens of books for fruit growers, bemoaned that eaters had lost the appreciation for true flavor, deprived by the presence of tasteless fruits in the commercial market:

> Most fruit-eaters have never eaten a first-class apple or pear or peach, and do not know what such fruits are; and the names of the choice varieties have mostly dropped from the lists of nurserymen. All this is as much to be deplored as a loss of standards of excellence in literature and music, for it is an expression of a lack of resources and a failure of sensitiveness.[1]

The Slow Food project Renewing America's Food Tradition estimates that around fifteen thousand to sixteen thousand varieties of apples have been grown in the United States over the past centuries.[2] Eighty percent have disappeared. Of those that remain, 94 percent are considered commercially endangered, meaning not only the apples but grafting stock and the knowledge of their unique characteristics are disappearing from nursery catalogs, markets, and tables. It might seem unimportant when there are thousands of new apple seeds ready to add their genes to the mix every season, but the old varieties represent knowledge and diversity that isn't easily replaced.

The steady narrowing of varieties and the loss of diversity has consequences for apple growers and breeders as well as eaters. Apples suited to different climates and resistant to different insects and diseases become harder to find as nurseries and commercial breeders focus on a few high-volume varieties grown in a few major apple-producing states. Apples that thrive elsewhere don't get saved, researched, or planted as often. For southerners who want to buy local apples, for example, this isn't just a sentimental issue; the ability to find suitable southern varieties is disappearing along with the apples. Climate change is making heirloom orchards even more crucial as breeders look for apples that can withstand warmer summers and colder winters. Pest and disease issues also shift with the climate, making resistant varieties ever more valuable.

The apple varieties grown and proliferated in the 1800s were extensively documented. One of the earliest chronicles of apple cultivars, *The Fruits and Fruit Trees of America*, was compiled by brothers Charles and Andrew Downing in 1845.[3] After Andrew's death, Charles continued to add new material and reissued several editions until it had grown to twice the size of the first edition. *Nomenclature of the Apple*, compiled by W. H. Ragan and published by the USDA in 1905, is an exhaustive catalog of "The Known Varieties Referred to in American Publications from 1805 to 1905."[4] Detailed descriptions of growing habits, flavor, keeping qualities, disease resistance, and more, acquired over decades and even centuries, fill volumes. Those thousands of well-documented varieties were already carefully selected and maintained out of the millions of other apples that have been grown and tasted. Why toss that all aside and reinvent it, even if we could?

Old apple books are remnants of another kind, many of them traces of publicly supported investigation, knowledge, and thought. I've acquired my collection at library book sales, secondhand bookstores, and online auctions; it includes several of Lippincott's Farm Manuals, many books by Liberty Hyde Bailey, an 1878 edition of Downing's *The Fruits and Fruit Trees of America*, and my most-prized, *Apples of New York*.[5] My first look at this classic was in Harold Linder's living room. On the way outside to his orchard, talking about his work on breeding and collecting apple trees, he stopped to point out the two-volume set on a small table near the door. The books were in beautiful condition, loaned by a fellow member of an Iowa fruit growers association. He smoothed them reverently, opening to one of the exquisite color plates to show me the outside and inside views of a long-gone variety.

Every serious apple obsessive covets these volumes. Published in 1905 by the State of New York Department of Agriculture (as part two of the Annual Report of the New York Experiment Station for 1903), the books are officially authored by Spencer A. Beach, who credits a long list of other contributors. Volume one covers winter apples, and volume two the early and fall varieties. Beach made a point of including not only varieties recommended for growing in New York but also varieties *not* recommended, reasoning it was just as important to know what not to plant. He cataloged the most popular varieties then being grown, new varieties still unfamiliar to many, and some old historical varieties that were falling out of use but which he felt deserved notice. After forty pages of introductory material on the origins of apples, the apple industry in New York State, and the system used to classify varieties, he devotes the rest of volume one and all of volume two to alphabetical listings of each named variety in astounding detail, interspersed with finely illustrated plates, most in color. A ninety-page index chronicles the listings.

Sixty-seven years earlier, in 1838, John James Audubon had completed publication of the first edition of *Birds of America*, his life's work represented by 435 large, carefully executed lithographs, hand-pulled and hand-colored, accompanied by two volumes of detailed text about the species portrayed. The books were issued in sets of five over more than ten years to subscribers who paid—or at least promised to pay—in installments to fund the long and arduous process of bringing them to print, a low-tech precursor of a Kickstarter project.

Apples of New York is almost certainly a direct descendant of Audubon's work, the coffee-table books of the time. It was followed over the next few years by *Plums*, *Peaches*, *Cherries* and other fruits of New York, all in the same careful mode: beautiful color prints, exhaustive descriptions, history, and cultivation tips. Rather than being the province of the wealthy, these beautiful and useful references and works of art were for the public, available on request for farmers, schoolteachers, small-town libraries, and citizens. *Apples of New York* is a massive opus—a labor of love and a testament to a time when the New York legislature's idea of "the public good" included the conviction that the public was owed not just access to information collected under its auspices, but information in a beautiful and useful form. Something is lost without this window into the culture as well as the agriculture of fruit growing; it's worth stopping to appreciate what it represents, and what has changed in the ensuing century.

Old apple varieties—Wealthy, Grimes Golden, Wolf River, Yellow Transparent, Stayman Winesap, and hundreds more—can still be found at farmers markets, pick-your-own orchards, and backyards. Libraries of apple trees, lovingly tended repositories devoted to nurturing and sustaining this riotous diversity, are tucked away on the slopes of orchards like Harold's, Seed Savers Exchange, Maine Heritage Orchard, and Jefferson's Monticello. The heirloom "librarians" who tend them, such as Zeke Goodband in Vermont, John Bunker in Maine, and Lee Calhoun in Virginia, are devotedly keeping old varieties alive. They're quintessential apple growers, encyclopedic, a bit obsessive, intelligent, generous with knowledge and cuttings. Zeke Goodband is the kind of person who can walk through an orchard of hundreds of trees during harvesttime telling the story behind each apple, why he likes it or doesn't, where it comes from, what it's known for, and a dozen other details. Pocketknife in hand, he pulls an apple gently, cuts a slice for tasting, then before he's reached the next tree, tosses the partially eaten fruit and turns to select another from another tree and recite another story. Zeke told National Public Radio in 2014 that eating and growing heirloom apples is "sort of like a chain letter through history."[6]

HAROLD LINDER showed me how to graft while standing at his kitchen counter, confidently making and wrapping the cuts, his movements so practiced and quick I could barely see how carefully he positioned the wounded slices together. His hands steady and sure, he pulled a well-worn knife from his pocket and deftly cut a thin incision into the top of the scion and another into the top of the rootstock, each no bigger around than his finger. He fit the twigs together and wrapped them with a supply of tape and rubber bands he kept handy. The graft is only the start of nursing the young tree along, making sure the graft takes and the roots take hold when it's planted, and keeping track of what you've done.

For a longer lesson, my friend Maggie and I drive a couple of hours to Seed Savers Exchange to take a grafting class from master orchardist Dan Bussey. In a room off the back of the century-old barn, a dozen of us sit in a semicircle around makeshift plywood-on-sawhorse tables, bundled in flannel, wool sweaters, and sweatshirts, mud stuck to boots and shoes. Hands and a few sun-darkened faces, even though it's winter, distinguish those who work outside from the hobbyists. Along one wall, white plastic five-gallon buckets hold bundles of sticks about two feet long. A paper label on each bucket tells the name and growing characteristics of each twig: Golden Russet, Wealthy, Black Oxford, all heirlooms from the Seed Savers orchard.

Bussey is an heirloom guardian. His tally of named apples historically grown in the United States since 1769 is seventeen thousand, the highest I've heard. He may be the definitive source: for decades, he's been diligently cataloging every apple he can track down and has spent years preparing a multivolume opus in the tradition of Downing and Beach for eventual publication. Lately, the numbers are gaining again.[7]

"Grafting is like living carpentry," Bussey instructs. There are many types of grafts, all with specific uses and advantages. We've each been given three stalks of M-7 semidwarf rootstock with a few wispy roots. Dan tells us it is sturdy, won't need to be staked, and is susceptible to only a few pests. We shuffle around the buckets, deliberating and sorting through the twigs until we've each settled on three varieties to practice on and take home after class. We pull out our tools: a good sharp knife and a rubber band. I've brought my own well-used Swiss Army knife, but I'm eyeing Dan's sleek grafting knife with its special easy-to-maneuver blade.

The goal of a successful graft is to combine a thin layer of cambium on the scion with a matching layer on the rootstock. Always cut the scion wood first, then cut into the rootstock, Dan instructs. Finding a spot on each stick that is about the same width around, he makes a shallow cut to expose a wider surface of the cambium layer, at a slant and about three times as long as the diameter of the stalk. He slides the two smoothly together. Next, he cuts the scion down to about five inches and wraps a rubber band around the two to hold them together, tucking the last bit of bark under to cover the graft. We gingerly make cuts in our own branches while he circles around giving advice. Old-timers used wax to seal the graft union and keep it from drying out. We cover ours with a stretchy material called Parafilm that will degrade once the graft has taken and the tree is planted outside.

Once we've started to get the hang of it and some are already on their second graft, Dan becomes rhapsodic about his deep love of old apples. Older trees on standard rootstock can live one hundred years or more. There are lots of trees scattered around the country nearing the end of their life. He encourages us to get out there, find them, and graft them before they are gone. He rattles off lists of old reference books and tips on where to find both old books and old trees.

Dan sends us off with our delicate new creations, telling us to wrap them in a plastic bag and place them in the fridge for three or four weeks to harden off and heal. "Plant them for the first year in a 'nursery' spot in your garden, sheltered and with good soil and sun, where you can keep an eye on them and protect them from rabbits and mice," he cautions. "In the second year, move them to a permanent spot, and you'll have apples in six to seven years."

Maggie and I trudge back to the car, carefully holding our plastic bags, the fragile-seeming grafts still intact each time we peek at them. After they've spent a few weeks in the refrigerator, we plant all six of them in her yard, tiny leafless twigs about ten inches high. They leaf out, but after a year all but one have succumbed to rabbits, a couple of the grafts failing to take, the small twigs leafed out from the rootstock instead. I have a new appreciation for the difference between gardening and growing fruit trees.

GRAFTING REMNANTS of the past on to rootstock for the future can take many forms. For an ephemera-lover like me, a box of papers from the archives at the Cornell University Albert R. Mann Library makes for a fun afternoon. I pull out a few folders labeled "Geneva, NY Experiment Station, 1951" and flip over the sheets of paper one by one, reading letters requesting grant funds, research reports, and minutes of meetings written in extensive, earnest detail. The papers were all hand-typed, many on onionskin, copies made with black carbon paper and sometimes the faded purple-blue of mimeograph, an occasional note penciled in the margins or an inked signature. A powerful wave of recognition makes me suddenly and intensely miss my father.

My dad was an agricultural economist who worked for the extension service at Iowa State University. I remember many nights growing up, listening to the sound of him typing away, index fingers only, fast and firm on the black Royal manual typewriter in his office across the hall from the bedroom my sister and I shared. We'd hear the ripple of paper being pulled from the roller and dropped to the floor, the soft clatter of a new sheet being rolled into place, and the high, clear *ding* of the carriage return as he finished a line. The papers in my hands felt and smelled the same as the ones scattered over Dad's desk and in neat piles on the floor, the rejects saved for us to use for drawing.

This is how information got recorded, communicated, and kept not that long ago. Creating copies meant typing the document with thin sheets of carbon paper between the white paper, or typing a stencil for the Ditto machine that printed out fuzzy purple-blue copies, or making a mimeograph transfer and cranking out one page at a time.

The lump in my throat and the intensity of missing Dad caught me by surprise. The papers I was holding were from the same years he would have been in graduate school, the reports and letters much like his own. The blue copies reminded me of all the files I had helped Mom move out of the university office where he had worked until the day before he died in 1991, at age sixty-two. Even though his closest coworkers knew he had ALS (Lou Gehrig's disease, amyotrophic lateral sclerosis), no one expected that he would be gone so quickly. His office—desk, papers, books, drawers—looked just the way he had left it, intending to come back. It's been more than twenty years since he stopped reading and writing his own reports and left the earth. I miss him especially when I am around extension service and land grant folks at conferences, and I often wish I could talk with him about the changes in agriculture, his research, and my own work. I hadn't expected the reminders here to be so tangible, and so potent. "Your dad would be proud of you," my mom says when I tell her later about my trip. Kindly and without irony, she adds, "The apple doesn't fall far from the tree."

The detailed proceedings of horticultural associations are no longer chronicled in hardbound volumes, and hand-painted drawings of apple varieties are no longer considered a good use of public funds; today's versions are found on the Internet and in emailed newsletters. The USDA *Yearbooks of Agriculture* that lined the bookshelf in my dad's office no longer pass through the hands of hundreds of congressional and extension offices. Every year I waited for him to bring home the new one, with its special title and topic: *Grasses* or *Soil* or *Marketing*. Every few years the yearbook would feature a fruit and apple report with a page or two of colored plates. The yearbooks too ceased publication in 1992, another casualty of funding cuts.

Apple trees leave a particular kind of imprint on the landscape: part familiar, gentle, and immediately recognizable; part mysterious, unpredictable, and completely wild. When you pass an old field or homestead once planted with apple trees, their gnarled trunks and a few fruits hanging from the high branches can still be seen along old fencerows and overgrown farmyards. The shape of the tree and the fruit, the bark, the flavor and color, all give clues that are distinctly apple. They're like the traces of wagon wheels in the Nebraska plains, or Downing's notebooks[8] with their ink tracings crusted with old apple juice. Remnants, but a stubborn imprint, enough to suggest there's something there to reconstruct.

A few years after we'd plotted the map of his orchard, I received a letter from Harold Linder, the return address a nursing home an hour away from his farm. In his neat cursive script, shaky but clear, he wrote,

"There have been many changes in the orchard since you did the map of it. I had some of it taken out due to the extra work." He had arthritis in his knees and could no longer take care of the trees that were left. "I miss working with the orchard. I had hoped that someone would take over, but . . . " His children have busy lives elsewhere, and it's not clear what will happen to the orchard now that he can no longer keep it up.

When I first visited Harold, I'd thought of his endeavor as an effort to preserve heirloom and old varieties, maybe find a seedling that would produce tasty fruit. When I unroll the yellowing map that has been sitting on my shelf for nearly ten years, I can see his vision was far bigger. Choice old varieties such as Duchess and Winesap are planted next to new Cameo, Gala, Granny Smith, and Jonagold. Schoolkid, the roadside seedling, is there along with the Burlington Leopold and a tree Harold and I labeled "darn if I know."

Thinking back to our first conversation, I remembered how curious he was to learn whatever he could from other growers with different approaches than his. On the bulky desktop computer in his front room, he stayed in touch with other members of various growers associations, with the extension horticulturist who had helped me find him in the first place, and with apple growers all over the country. He invited friends out to pick his fruit in the fall and delivered apples to churches and friends in town.

There is plenty of romance in Harold Linder's stories and the apple names that float up from the pencil marks on his map. But he was in pursuit of something that is not the least bit sentimental. Collecting old books is a way of saving knowledge. Grafting and saving old trees and old orchards is about saving knowledge, too. A desire to help preserve some of that knowledge is part of why I had drawn the map of Harold Linder's orchard, why I've kept my copy of it, and part of what led me to visit him in the first place. In a democracy of apples, diversity and knowledge are virtues.

CHAPTER SIX

Give the People What They Want

IT MAY SOUND LIKE sacrilege to call Red Delicious an heirloom, but it has an impeccable pedigree. Harold Linder has an original Hawkeye Delicious tree in his orchard a few rows away from a more common Red Delicious. A chance seedling in an Iowa orchard, a stubborn sprout and a stubborn farmer boosted by fairs, nurserymen, and fellow growers turned what would otherwise have been a humble footnote into the world's most iconic apple. It's been fueling the hopes of chance seedling growers everywhere ever since.

Jesse Hiatt was a good Quaker, the youngest of twelve children and father of ten, who farmed in Madison County, Iowa. Tending his orchard one day in 1870, he cut down a disorderly seedling that had grown up between the rows. The next year it grew back. He cut it twice more, then reportedly acquiesced with the words, "If you must live, you may." After ten years, the seedling produced just one apple. Ever patient, Hiatt

ABOVE: Baldwin apples, Alyson's Orchard, Walpole, New Hampshire.
Photo by Diane Rast, courtesy of Red Tomato.

waited until it ripened to full strawberry-red, cut a slice on the edge of his pocketknife, and proclaimed it the best he had ever tasted.[1]

Over the next few years, the tree produced more fruit, and he named it Hawkeye, his state's nickname. None of his nursery and orchard buddies were convinced of its superiority, but Hiatt believed. After twenty-three diligent years, in 1893 he sent four specimens off to a fruit show in Louisiana, Missouri, where nurseryman C. M. Stark was making the rounds with a little red notebook and a list of possible names, looking for apples to acquire for his nursery. He'd reserved his best name for perfection, and when he tasted the Hawkeye he knew he'd found it. But the tag on the plate had gone missing, and Stark couldn't trace the apple. At the following year's show, he gleefully recognized its strawberry shape and color, this time properly tagged, and sent an entreaty off to Hiatt, who replied: "I am nearly seventy years old and have raised apples all my life . . . if it is not a better apple than any in your large list, it will cost you nothing."[2]

Stark paid for the rights anyway and renamed the apple Delicious. His nursery spent three quarters of a million dollars to introduce and promote its new favorite. The nursery sold eight million of the trees over the next twenty-five years. The original striped fruit was eventually supplanted by solid red versions as sports emerged. By 1966 there were more than eighty different versions of Delicious on record, and Iowa State University fruit specialist Paul Domoto estimates there are now more than two hundred variations developed from the original.[3]

Red Delicious's makeover became its undoing. Red started out as a tasty, distinctively shaped apple with a bit of yellow and green blush and a crisp, juicy gold-tinged flesh. Over time, sports were selected and selected again to favor redder, firmer, less juicy versions. The apples looked beautiful with their deep red skin flecked with small white dots, prominent bottom lobes, and oblong shape. They were also increasingly hard, thick skinned, and green tasting. But what mattered most was that they withstood shipping and still looked great in the grocery store, gas station, or decorative bowl of room-temperature fruit in a hotel lobby. The move toward redder, harder, shapelier versions was relentless. Flavor, because it was invisible, lost out.

The apple industry owes Red a lot. In the 1980s, Red Delicious represented 75 percent of Washington State's apple harvest. By 2000, it had
dropped to less than half, and by 2003, even though still number one, it
had dropped to under 37 percent of the harvest.[4] It's the top U.S. export
apple; its unmistakable shape and color signify American fruit around
the world. And it can still be a tasty apple. Apples grafted from the original tree, which still grows in a field in Iowa, are reported to taste as good
as the name. John Lyman in Connecticut grows a variety that, when
picked at peak flavor, rivals the best in his orchard. But today the once-
celebrated Delicious is considered a workhorse apple, not a prized specialty fruit. A parade of newer varieties is lined up to jostle for its place.

THE PERIOD AFTER the Civil War began a new era of scientific plant-
breeding in the United States, with much attention and ambition devoted to finding commercial varieties that could please the changing
tastes of consumers and meet the growing need for efficient, predicable
fruit volume. Farmers, businesspeople, and politicians began to see that
science and research could improve prospects for agriculture in general.
The establishment of land grant institutions further encouraged the development of plant breeding as a professional science.

In 1874, the year Jesse Hiatt decided to let his errant apple tree grow,
J. L. Budd joined the Horticulture Department at brand-new Iowa State
College. The aptly named Budd was an avid collector of trees and scions
and a popular speaker, and apples were his greatest enthusiasm. Born in
the Hudson Valley, Budd taught in New York and Illinois before buying
a farm in Iowa, where he established a nursery and began testing and
breeding fruit trees.

Finding apple varieties that could thrive in harsh midwestern and
northern winters was a priority for apple breeders at the time. Pomologists had a theory that Russian cultivars, being closer to the origins of
the first apples and growing in a climate with harsh winters, could be
the key to hardier fruit. The Massachusetts Horticultural Society had
brought four varieties of Russian trees from England in 1835. Breeders
across the country began testing them, and they were promising enough

that Budd and a colleague embarked on a collecting spree. They made
several trips to Europe, Russia, and England, returning from Moscow
with two hundred varieties in 1878, and four years later with one hundred more, along with a large collection of other fruits. Budd began to
distribute the Russian trees from his nursery and became a leading promoter of the theory of Russian varieties.

His enthusiasm was not shared by all of his fellow nurserymen and
orchardists. Great debates ensued in horticultural societies around the
country. Some disagreed with bringing in Russian trees to compete with
established varieties; others felt the trees would taint efforts to develop
vigorous native sources. After many years of testing, the Russian trees,
aside from a few that are still grown, such as Red Astrakan, Duchess of
Oldenburg, and Yellow Transparent, proved mostly to be a failure. They
ripened too early in the hot midwestern summers and produced small,
bitter fruit. They did, however, turn out to be important breeding stock.
One Russian offspring, the Wealthy, stood up well to the harsh winters
and became a popular apple throughout the Midwest.[5]

At the time of the Russian experiments, the Red Delicious was still
undiscovered, and the most popular American apples were the Baldwin
in the northeast and the Ben Davis grown farther south. Baldwin, discovered in 1740 on a farm in Massachusetts and favored in both home
and commercial orchards for its flavor and versatility, was shipped to
markets around the world. Ben Davis, first grown in Kentucky around
1799, was better known for its keeping quality and durability than for its
flavor. The long popularity of both encouraged growers and marketers
to focus on narrowing the varieties they grew and promoted in hopes
of finding the next big apple success. In 1928, the extension services of
the six New England states, with support from the Massachusetts Fruit
Growers Association, issued a booklet titled "The New England Seven"
in which they argued:

> In this section of the United States no less than fifty varieties can be
> found in the commercial orchards of today. Growers have become
> convinced . . . that market needs will be better served and produc-
> tion and marketing simplified, if the number of commercial vari-

eties is reduced to a minimum.... No longer can the commercial grower with a few bushels each of thirty varieties compete on the wholesale market with the grower who has specialized in the growing of three varieties. This point is well illustrated in the business world where the factory focuses its attention on mass production of a few popular and recognized brands.[6]

The authors selected McIntosh, Baldwin, Rhode Island Greening, Delicious, Gravenstein, Northern Spy, and Wealthy. They acknowledged that their advice was geared toward big city markets such as Boston and New York and that other varieties might still have a place in local farm stands. They advised growers to stick to these varieties but to test a few new grafts each year and stay alert for other promising varieties, especially red sports of "The Seven" that might replace the originals over time. Fruit growers all over New England topworked acres of trees in response.

Planting only a few varieties did make things simpler, more standard, more predictable, and more efficient, but as with monocrops of all kinds, it also made growers more vulnerable. In 1934, a few years after anointment to the New England Seven, thousands of Baldwin trees across New England were split and killed by a great freeze. Growers who had invested in the popular variety suffered huge losses, and the Baldwin never regained its place as a top apple.

Rather than spur a return to more diversity, the Baldwin's loss sent apple growers and marketers off in search of the next big winner. There's no end in sight to that pursuit, and it remains as risky as ever. New dwarf-trellised plantings can produce fruit within two or three years instead of the eight to ten it used to take for larger trees, making the turnaround time to replace one variety with another shorter and shorter. Still, these are trees, not cornstalks, and change is a major investment.

WITH MORE THAN 2,500 varieties available and new seedlings sprouting every year, apples provide endless combinations of taste, color, shape, and texture to please any palate, eye, and preference, from the mundane to the adventurous. Yet just eleven varieties make up approximately 90 percent of apples sold in American grocery stores.[7]

The reason lies in part with the fickle fads and tastes of eaters and persistent attempts by marketers and public servants to shape a market that meets those tastes and still allows growers to make a living. In part, it's a result of the steady march toward consolidation and efficiency that is the modern-day grocery industry.

In the past, apples were named for people, places, their looks, and an occasional sweet something. Today's new apples are made-up words with a trademark symbol after them, meant to conjure up taste and looks and excitement but rarely a place or a story. Even in colonial days, nurseries and marketers were paying for rights to varieties and growers were watching their seedlings for the next big find. Even then, apple experts were bemoaning the loss of variety and the fickle tastes of eaters. But while the pressures of commerce were once diffused among thousands of nurseries, tens of thousands of orchards, and many more local markets, today extreme concentration of both production and markets dominates the process and makes the stakes exceptionally high.

The difference between a commercial success and a variety relegated to backyard orchards is sometimes flavor, sometimes beauty, but more often it's about being versatile, reliable, and a good "keeper" that's easy to grow and transport. Innovations in refrigeration and transport have made greater varieties of fruit available year-round. Self-serve supermarkets, replacing the fruit stand and corner grocer, have encouraged choosing fruit by eye rather than by taste, favoring redder and redder fruit.

Supermarkets and growers both followed the red beacons right to the brink of troubles for the whole industry. By the late 1990s, apple consumption in the United States was dropping—today it averages nineteen pounds of fresh apples per capita per year. Apple prices declined steadily and were pushed even lower by apple concentrate imported from vast new apple plantings in China. In 2001, according to the US Apple Association, the national apple industry lost $700 million.[8] Finding ways to make people want to eat more apples is serious business, and finding the latest new varieties to tempt them is an irresistible strategy.

THERE WERE ONCE thousands of associations, nurseries, and public breeding programs testing, cataloging, and trading new varieties, and both costs and rewards were widely shared. Over the past few decades, however, concentration, high-stakes competition, and cuts in funding for public breeding programs have prompted ever more creative and entrepreneurial strategies to find and market the next big apple. Some cultivars are still released for general use by public breeding programs and private enthusiasts, but more and more new varieties reach the marketplace today via a tangle of licensing agreements that govern who grows them, where they are grown, where they are sold and under what name, and who gets paid for every aspect, from breeding to propagating nursery stock, growing, packing, and marketing the fruit.

Restricted varieties, with trademarked brands and marketing, are often called "club" apples because in order to have access to them, orchards must join a marketing association, buy a license, and adhere to production and quality standards. Those who don't follow the agreements can be kicked out of the club. The rationale is the ability to control quality, and just as important, quantity and availability, in hopes of building strong retail and consumer demand that will lead to higher prices and profits.

Licensing agreements can vary for different parts of the process, such as purchasing trees and growing, packing, marketing, and selling fruit. Trademarks and licenses differ from country to country, covering varying time periods. Tree licenses and brand trademarks are sometimes managed separately, sometimes together. Access to and flow of product is complicated by relationships among regional and global players, public and private breeding programs, big packer-shipper-marketers that can manage at a national scale, small and large wholesale growers, and large retailers that want exclusive offerings. Because the success of a variety depends on things such as consistency, reliable supply, and brand marketing power, club licenses tend to favor a small number of large orchards, packers, and marketing organizations in each country.

Even so, new varieties, including club brands, have been a lifeline for
midsized farmers like Mark Gores in Chelan. His friend Tom is a nephew
of Grady Auvil, an innovative grower who is best known for introducing
the Granny Smith to America and whose vision and links to New Zealand varieties have had a huge impact on the entire industry. The Auvil
family orchard includes more than fifteen hundred acres in the heart of
the Wenatchee Valley and a large packinghouse. Mark watched what his
friends the Auvils were doing and told his dad he wanted to tear out part
of their orchard and plant a new variety, Gala.

Mark says his dad "just about went nuts" watching him pull up five
acres of beautiful old Reds. But Mark will never forget his look of disbelief after the first harvest. "I mean, we made $600 a bin! Dad was
like, 'Naawww!!!'" That five acres made 50 percent more than the other
twenty-three acres of the orchard combined, and that year and for many
after, Galas financed the rest of their operation. "I used to look at them
and say, this two-acre block just paid for picking costs. That five-acre
block just paid for production on everything else."

Mark put in more Galas, followed by Fuji and Braeburn, and began
transforming the fundamental structure of the orchard from old trees to
new dwarf varieties. One year they spent $100,000 on replanting, pulling
up everything, roots and all, Mark says with a hint of bravado. They cut
trees by hand with a chain saw until a friend told him an excavator could
have two acres pulled and burned in an afternoon. By the next day, the
old trees were stacked up and two burn piles were taking care of the
branches. After that, Mark says, "We were on our way."

Once the block was cleared, they set about replanting in an entirely
new way based on high-density planting then being developed in Europe. "Posts, wires, three thousand trees per acre. You can take this system and the rootstock on it, and you've already got the superstructure
for the next variety." Mark got started early with the shift to Galas, and
once he had set up his orchard to adapt, followed the lead of Auvil and
others who were adopting new varieties as they came out. Mark threw
his lot in with ENZA, a New Zealand breeder and marketing company
that licenses and markets the club variety Jazz™. Other growers took sim-

ilar paths with Cameo and other varieties. As consumers rushed to try the latest new variety, the whole apple market expanded. It was hard to tell whether the new varieties were really pushing the old ones out or just rising with the tide of overall increasing sales, but they sold well and stores began looking for more to excite their apple displays.

Mark visited orchards in other regions and countries as a board member of his marketing co-op in the mid-1980s and early '90s, which solidified his decision to follow the trends. "It wasn't because they were better apples; it was all just because it was new."

It was a few years before growers began to talk about flavor. Apple eaters in the United States, increasingly adventurous and curious about their food, responded enthusiastically. Public and private breeding programs began to search not only for taste but for another elusive quality that might make people willing to try a new apple: a satisfying crunch.

The University of Minnesota fruit-breeding program is a big player in developing new apple varieties; along with Cornell and the University of Washington, it's one of only a few major public apple-breeding programs in the United States. Minnesota's program began in 1878 and moved to its current facility and test orchard in 1908, during the heyday of the emerging field of pomology. Finding varieties that could live through harsh Minnesota winters took fifty years. Once naysayers had been proven wrong and growing apples in northern mid-continent climes was no longer a question, the focus shifted to finding a better-tasting apple. The search for the perfect eating experience is the Holy Grail for apple-breeding programs these days. For now, the Holy Grail is named Honeycrisp.

Honeycrisp spent its early years in the University of Minnesota orchard as MN1711. When Dave Bedford started work as an apple researcher there in 1979, he saw "Discard" scribbled in the notes for the test trees. He was about to do just that but, as the legend goes, noticed the trees were in a low, wet spot and decided to try them in a better location. Like the stubborn Red Delicious a century before, MN1711 rewarded patient loyalty. Its "explosive crispness," as the university's website describes it, combined sweet, juicy flavor with a crunch that surprised and delighted almost

everyone who tasted it. It was released in 1991, registered by the university as an open variety, meaning anyone could plant trees and market
the fruit. It has been an astounding success.⁹

Aaron Clark of Clark Brothers Orchards in Massachusetts remembers
their first test of the new apple. "We had a whole orchard of Liberty—it's
scab resistant, doesn't need spray, it's a good tasting apple, but there's
no market for it. My brother Dana wanted to graft them to something
else, so we got some Fortunes and some Honeycrisp. We did half of each,
and now the Honeycrisp are selling like crazy and we can't move Fortunes except at our farm stand." Aaron shakes his head. "I've never seen
consumers react that way to another apple. I sent out gift baskets to
everyone I knew with Honeycrisp and three others I liked better, to test.
Everyone liked the Honeycrisp." In 2015, the Clarks pulled up all but a
few of their Fortunes. Aaron points toward a large block of new planting.
"We had six acres of Empires here; we cut a whole block of them off and
grafted Honeycrisp onto them." I look out, astonished at the long rows
of trees, remembering the three little grafts I painstakingly made in my
afternoon at Seed Savers.

Honeycrisp is a hard apple to grow well. It's susceptible to fruit rot both
in the orchard and postharvest, and to bruising and stem punctures in
storage. That's part of what leads to its high price—the wholesale price
of Honeycrisp in Massachusetts in 2014 was $50 to $70 per case while
McIntosh was around $28 to $30—and the high price in turn is why
growers keep planting it in spite of the challenges. For reasons both logical and mythical, consumers continue to be willing to pay two or three
times the price of other varieties, even those bred from Honeycrisp. The
variety warrants its own half day of intensive workshops at the annual
meetings of the Washington State Horticultural Association and the
International Fruit Tree Association.

The University of Minnesota patent on Honeycrisp expired in 2007.
But sales are still climbing, and Honeycrisp has set the bar. With Envy™,
Jazz™, Pink Lady®, and dozens more jockeying to be its successor, the
process of bringing new apple varieties to market is a bit breathless
these days. In the May 2015 issue of *Good Fruit Grower*, Richard Lehnert
cautioned, "The apple industry is planting as if the apple section of the

grocery store is going to look like the cereal aisle—60 plus varieties stacked high on both sides—when it is much more likely to look like it does today: 10–12 specialty varieties at $2–3 per pound, and the standard commodity varieties for less." Fifty-four new apple varieties were introduced that year. A Pennsylvania grower quoted in the same article worried, "The consumer did want something better than Red Delicious. Our industry came up with six or eight different varieties that were considerably better. The consumer is not asking for 50 more."[10]

Everybody agrees they won't all succeed, and everybody is sure the one they are betting on will be a winner. No one thinks it's likely any of them will overtake Honeycrisp anytime soon. Kevin Stennes at Chelan Fresh sees Honeycrisp replacing sales of varieties like Braeburn, Cameo, and Jonagold that used to hold their own in smaller volumes, making it a challenge to keep marketing them even though they're good apples. "There're times we can't keep up with demand. It's $70 to $100 on Honeycrisp, and you can't sell a Cameo for $20." He shakes his head. "That's one of the factors hurting some of the other apples."

There is talk that the thinking behind the New England Seven needs to return some restraint to the whole business, but others say those days are long gone. Consumers may not want fifty varieties, but they have a steady appetite for the new and different.

The interest in something different could be an opportunity to reintroduce older varieties too, but that has its own pitfalls. While consumers haven't increased overall apple consumption, they have increased what they're willing to pay for the latest varieties. Higher prices mean higher profits. Promoting older varieties that typically sell at lower prices might move some extra apples, but if doing so lures customers away from the higher priced branded apples, profits fall for everyone.

New brand names are another strategy for boosting sales. Cripps Pink was first introduced as an unbranded cultivar developed in Australia. Worried about flooding the market, and dodging a vague association with gang names, the variety owners turned it into a managed variety by rebranding it as Pink Lady®. Now it is sold under both names. In 2014, the New England Apple Council began testing JuicyGold, a new name for Jonagold, to be licensed to any grower in New England. They hoped to

generate enough excitement and income to sustain the acres of established trees already producing tasty fruit, although they've been stalled
by trademark challenges from growers elsewhere with similarly named
apples.

Then there is the tried-and-true strategy of turning every apple red.
Despite the cautionary tale of the Red Delicious, nursery catalogs and
trade magazines tout the newest, reddest versions of established favorites. Even the apples that have been the best at differentiating themselves
from the old Red Dels are trying hard to look more like them. Lady in Red
is a sport of Cripps Pink; Crimson Crisp™, Red Cameo™, Red Braeburn,
and RubyMac® are all redder versions of earlier cultivars. One ad crows
"Jonastar® is an exciting new Jonagold sport with virtually 100 percent
red color," begging the question of why a gold apple should be redder.
And then there's the ultimate confusing transformation, the Crimson
Gold. More than a few growers think Honeycrisp is on the same path
to ruin as Red Delicious: Royal Red Honeycrisp® and four or five other
redder versions are already being advertised.

Most of the new varieties come from established breeding programs,
but a few are chance seedlings, putting Red Delicious and Honeycrisp
stars in their owners' eyes. Ambrosia™ is an example of how complicated
things can get. It was found as a seedling by Wilfrid and Sally Mennell in
their British Columbia orchard more than twenty-five years ago. They let
it grow, thought it produced good-tasting fruit, and decided to commercialize it in 1993. They registered the Canadian breeding rights in 1997
and contracted with Summerland Varieties Corporation to manage it
for them. Until the Mennells' rights expired in 2015, Canadian growers
paid them a royalty of $2/tree. The U.S. patent, obtained in 1999, set a
royalty of $1/tree or $1,000/acre, whichever is less, plus a franchise fee of
$1,000/acre. After a few years of interest but no real leadership in devel-
oping the variety outside Canada, an exclusive license was granted to
McDougall and Sons in Wenatchee, Washington, in 2005. All U.S. growers but one now have their Ambrosia™ apples shipped to and packed at
McDougall, which produces most of the U.S. Ambrosia™ crop in its own
large orchards. A separate company, Columbia Marketing International,
is the exclusive marketer of Ambrosia™ in the United States and specified

export markets. The U.S. patent expires in 2017, McDougall's license expires in 2019, and in some other countries the variety is protected until as late as 2034.[11]

It's head spinning. By the end of 2015, Ambrosia™ was the second-highest-selling variety in British Columbia, after Gala. The Washington State Tree Fruit Association reported Red Delicious is still number one by a long shot, with Gala in second place followed by Granny Smith, Fuji, and Golden Delicious, and in much smaller volumes, Honeycrisp, Cripps Pink, Braeburn, and Jazz™. Three decades ago, Gala was a brand-new variety; now it is number two in both production and sales.[12] Ambrosia™ is eager to take its place.

Still, shelf space is finite. Stores used to carry Red Delicious in three fruit sizes, plus multiple sizes of bags. Now most carry only one size of the top sellers, rotating less-familiar varieties in and out throughout the season. The rapidly expanding new brands are steadily pushing the standards and regional varieties off the shelf.

WITH MORE TREES planted in fewer varieties comes even greater risk. As new denser planting methods produced more and more bushels per acre, Mark Gores and his fellow growers in Washington got nervous. How big could the crop get before they started hurting themselves with lower prices? At lunch the day Wynne Weinreb introduced us in Chelan, Mark describes the nagging worry. He was spending big money on grafting, putting in a lot of Jazz™, "and then all of a sudden the price of Jazz™ was doing this," he sweeps his hand like a roller coaster.

"I just thought, my nest egg... I'm self-financed, our nest egg was down to a point..." his eyes grow wild just thinking about it. After a couple of good years, the price for Jazz™ suddenly dropped. Maybe Honeycrisp was already making Jazz™ obsolete. At one point, he even ordered cherry trees to replace his apples, thinking maybe that would be less risky. Then, just as suddenly, Jazz™ was back up to its earlier price, then even higher. The volume was ramping up, and a bad spring freeze followed by summer hail in the East kept West Coast prices high. He settled down, went over the finances, yields, and trees per acre, and realized they could still make it work. He turns to Wynne. "The return on those bins was double anything we've ever done. And it's in the bank, Wynne!" He nods his head like he still can't shake the leftover nerves from those years.

"I believed in this franchise model, and the people that were involved in it were good people." He lists off some big families in the Washington orchard world. "So I hung my hat on the proprietary thing, and we got in it early, and that became the springboard to get the orchard up into a healthy state again." He knew the market on the older varieties was never going to come back to what it had been. He knew he didn't want to be one of those guys who waited for that to happen right up until they had to sell the orchard to the bank. He turns even more serious, looking right at me. "Because that's what happens with farming. I just kept thinking about that. When people ask me, 'Well, you got in on that early, what made you do that?' I tell them it was just flat-out desperation."

He and Wynne share a laugh, and Wynne reminds him that his wife rode out the roller coaster with him. He is quick to credit their marriage and her business sense with keeping his feet on the ground, but there were definitely days she had her doubts. "I had cut down half my Galas, all except three acres, which were a glorious V-trellis on 337 [a special stake and rootstock]. That's when I said to myself I was gonna do it. A couple guys thought I was nuts, but I said, if this apple hits . . . I told Marcia, I'm swinging for the fence."

The Galas are gone, and Mark's orchard is now planted in Jazz™, Envy™, and Pacific Rose™, all varieties he is licensed to grow by ENZA. Wynne points out that even if she wanted to plant Pacific Rose™, "Sorry, baby, you're too late!" The brand owners want to make sure they stay just special enough.

APPLE BREEDING involves painstaking work to cross-pollinate, test, and keep track of each cultivar. Each cross has to be evaluated and tested in a number of regions over a period of years. Texture and flavor have to be above average or the cross doesn't move forward. Thousands of varieties are examined each year, and thousands more are waiting in the wings. Most of them turn out to be "spitters," not destined for the marketplace. Only a fraction of them promise to be commercially successful.

For a private grower or marketer, the formula can be simple: find the next new thing in your orchard, patent it, trademark it, promote the heck out of it, and manage it to maximize your financial return. A growers association or a civic-minded grower might make a new variety freely available and trust the market and fellow growers to make the most of it. For publicly funded land grant breeding programs, with a mission to serve the public good and a funding stream that has been decreasing steadily and relentlessly for decades, the path forward is complicated.

Decreasing funds and steady pressure on public universities to optimize the return on investment of their research has forced researchers to depend more and more on income from their work rather than support from taxes and tuition, as was originally intended. When a public breeding program finds a hot new variety, it has to weigh whether to make it widely available as a public good or to manage it to maximize income so the program can continue breeding apples.

In 2006, just before its Honeycrisp patent expired, the University of Minnesota released a new apple cultivar called MN1914.[13] A cross between Honeycrisp and Zestar!®, it ripens earlier than many other popular varieties. Along with the new apple, the university announced a new licensing model that gave control over propagation, as well as wholesale growing, packing, marketing, and distribution of the variety, to one private Minnesota business, Pepin Heights Orchards. Pepin Heights in turn announced its intention to release #1914 as a club variety with a brand and marketing program to create nationwide demand.

The licensing plans were announced at the December meeting of the Minnesota Apple Growers Association (MAGA), just a few weeks before the apple's release. Pepin Heights owner Dennis Courtier and representatives from the University of Minnesota Horticultural Research Center and the university's Office for Technology Commercialization laid out their preliminary plans for managing the license and their hopes that it would become a high-end specialty item.

Growers anywhere who wanted in were required to join the newly

established Next Big Thing (NBT) Cooperative set up to manage the
project. Each grower had to commit to an allotment of ten thousand
bushels and pay a $1/box fee up front, with a $10,000 minimum. They
would order trees from a designated nursery and pay for propagation
and delivery on top of the fee. The trees would be leased to the grower
and would technically belong to NBT LLC. All of their MN1914 fruit
would have to be shipped to Pepin Heights' packing facility. Marketing,
research, and royalty fees would be deducted from the grower payment
at amounts expected to be around 15 percent of the wholesale value of
the crop. The university and the breeder would receive royalties for each
tree propagated and for every bushel of fruit sold.

A few concessions were made to Minnesota growers: they could band
together to fill a single ten thousand bushel allotment as long as all of the
fruit was shipped and packed by Pepin Heights. Orchards that sold directly to consumers via farm stands and farmers markets could request
up to one thousand trees for the propagation fee plus $1/tree lease. Each
tree would be mapped with a GPS location, and if a grower was caught
selling outside of their own market, the lease would be revoked and the
trees cut down.

Minnesota growers were in an uproar. Even though the apple had been
developed specifically for the Minnesota climate and paid for by Minnesota taxpayers, it would be marketed as a national brand. No grower
identification would be allowed on the packaging. There would be no
opportunity to promote the apple as Minnesota grown, even to local
consumers and distributors. Growers who chose not to join the club
would be competing against it. Other Minnesota wholesale orchards,
competitors of Pepin Heights, were shut out of the new variety entirely.

In an industry where growers have historically provided significant
private support for research through their associations, where there is
a lot of collaboration and connection among growers, university extension and research staff, and where information developed at the state
university is generally understood to be a public good, this new strategy
was especially galling. The new variety had been quietly tested in orchards around the country, and the license agreement was developed
without input from the grower associations. Growers felt insulted that

they were not told of the cultivar and the agreement before it was announced publicly. They didn't think it was proper, or even legal, for the
Board of Regents to be making decisions about which orchards in Minnesota would succeed or fail.

MAGA presented a list of demands to the university. They wanted to
grow and distribute the new apple, paying the same rate as out-of-state-
growers. They wanted direct-market growers to be allowed to sell excess
fruit to other growers, a common practice throughout the industry that
helps both a grower with a surplus crop and a grower with a shortage
due to hail or other issues. They wanted priority over out-of-state growers in the handing out of allotments. They demanded that the university
work closely with MAGA on the release of future varieties.

But the licensing plan went forward mostly unchanged. Apple MN1914,
eventually christened SweeTango®, was rolled out to consumers in limited quantities to much fanfare in 2009. It has its own website proclaim-
ing it "Best Apple Ever!" Aside from two Minnesota orchards (including
Pepin Heights) and one in Wisconsin, most of the licensed orchards are
in Michigan, the Northeast, the Northwest, and Canada. In 2010, two
dozen Minnesota and Wisconsin growers filed an antitrust/unfair competition lawsuit against the university. The case was dismissed "with
prejudice" in 2011, meaning it cannot be brought back to court, and the
growers agreed to a settlement that upheld the arrangement with the
university and Pepin Heights. In exchange, Minnesota orchards were
allowed access to a few more trees only for their own direct markets.

SweeTango® has been a commercial success so far, although nothing
like Honeycrisp. Some of the Minnesota growers who pioneered Honeycrisp say SweeTango® is better in every way—easier to grow, early ripening, long storage life, and beats Honeycrisp in blind taste tests. Better
in every way except to the fickle and illogical consumer, who continues
to buy Honeycrisp at higher prices and greater volumes than ever. The
plan is to market SweeTango® as a limited-time-only apple, available
for only a few months in peak season, like a Starbuck's Pumpkin Spice
Latte. Twenty-two percent of new apple trees planted in Washington in
2014 were Honeycrisp. But in 2015, SweeTango® was reportedly gaining
ground.[14]

As a marketing strategy, keeping control over the production and distribution of SweeTango® is good brand management. Some would say the same enterprising spirit that kept John Chapman going, pushed apples from Iowa to the Northwest, and propelled the Red Delicious to its number one spot has helped secure growers and the university a better position in the competitive global marketplace with SweeTango®.

A more recent addition to the SweeTango® strategy is a second trademark license and fee covering what are called value-added products, like cider, jelly, and sauce. The university has also given control over this license to Pepin Heights, which is inclined to keep it exclusively for the NBT members. That leaves out the small direct-market orchards that were allowed to plant trees. One longtime grower, after sorting through the new process, declared, "I started cutting down my SweeTango® at that point!"

Growers and growers associations are meanwhile in their own search for the Holy variety Grail. Minnesota grower-packer Honeybear Brands holds the plant patent and exclusive marketing right to Pazazz™, a new variety that originated from a seedling in a Wisconsin Honeycrisp orchard. It's being grown by orchards in Washington, Minnesota, Wisconsin, New York, and Nova Scotia, including by some growers who were shut out of the SweeTango® club. EverCrisp®, developed as part of a grassroots grower-funded breeding endeavor, is now licensed to orchards all over the world, including Clark Brothers in Massachusetts, through membership in the Ohio-based Midwest Apple Improvement Association.

Apple breeding has its high-tech proponents too. Arctic® apple is the first genetically modified apple to be approved for registration with the USDA. Its signature benefit is that when cut, the apple doesn't turn brown even hours after slicing. The debate about the use of GMO technology, especially for food crops, is intense and polarized among food and agriculture advocates, and there is struggle around both U.S. and global trade policies over whether food grown using GMO technology should be labeled as such. The Arctic® apple folks aren't at all against labeling their apples GMO. In fact, they are proud to tell you all about it.

For the most part, however, growers aren't enthusiastic about Arctic® apple. Many are worried that public rejection of GMOs will taint the whole apple industry and obstruct access to export markets, such as Europe and Japan. There are reasonable concerns about GMO pollen finding its way into large, uninterrupted swaths of orchard and contaminating non-GMO fruit. Opponents grumble that Arctic® doesn't make the apple taste better, cost less, or need fewer pesticides; in fact, some consumers consider browning a useful sign of freshness. Others point out that varieties including Pink Lady®, Ambrosia™, and Cortland already stay naturally white after slicing.

NEW APPLE VARIETIES still come about in the time-honored ways: an observant grower notices a tree with unusually tasty fruit or especial vigor after a bad outbreak of fire blight. A hardworking horticulturist at a land grant experiment station tastes five thousand apples from the fifty thousand seedlings they've crossed and recorded and nursed along for a decade, and one tree keeps turning out fruit that has that extra zing or crunch they're after. They absolve it for another season and watch how it handles another year of weather, bugs, and competition. They try harvesting it at different times, storing the fruit for different lengths of time, handing a few to friends and colleagues and other growers to gauge their reaction to the first bite.

Eventually, after a decade or two, a few trees make it through that gauntlet and a marketing company or fruit packer or nursery buys the rights to propagate them. Maybe they trademark a new name and license the marketing rights to whoever they think can make it the next big Baldwin or Delicious or Honeycrisp. The apple's polymorphic breeding and profusion means the pool of diverse genotypes is constantly replenished in the foothills of the Tien Shan mountains and in the backyards and fencerows of America. Despite the many forces pressing toward uniformity, apples more than almost any other food crop stubbornly, and a bit subversively, persist in their uncontrollable and ebullient diversity.

Meanwhile, in a makeshift greenhouse like Harold Linder's or a tightly managed test orchard like the Minnesota Agricultural Experiment Station, a scruffy parade of pomologists and grad students hand-pollinate blossoms one by one, carefully mixing the parentage to bring out the best traits of each. They tag the trees, enter their locations into a spreadsheet, and wait. Who knows, Schoolkid could become the next big thing. There are a lot more hands in the pot today, and a lot more ways to make money off this careful poker game, but at the heart of it are still devoted breeders like Harold Linder; enthusiastic public scientists like Dave Bedford at Minnesota, Susan Brown at Cornell, and Kate Evans at Washington State; and devoted apple librarians like Zeke Goodband and Dan Bussey and John Bunker. There are hundreds of new apples to try each year, along with hundreds, even thousands, of old varieties that need saving and savoring.

At the far end of Indian Ladder Farms orchard in upstate New York, Pete Ten Eyck shows me his new planting of SnapDragons®. The trees are planted very close together, just three feet apart, with poles and wires that train them up rather than out. "You want it to grow as fast as possible, so it can't have any competition," he explains. They use herbicide to keep weeds away from the trunks, which are painted white to fend off another kind of pest, a lethal insect called the dogwood borer. An irrigation line runs along each row.

SnapDragon® is a new variety developed by Cornell University, and Pete has been planting test plots for several years. Now they are ready to be released commercially, and he's paid $8 a tree to get in on them early. In the intricate scheme that determines how public universities release new cultivars these days, the size of his orchard entitles him to three thousand trees. He has five hundred already planted as part of the trials, another fifteen hundred on order this winter, and will add more next year. The two-year-old trees in front of us already have fruit on their tiny branches, even though the trunks are no thicker than my wrist and I can touch the top branches without stretching.

Between the pick-your-own section of the orchard and the back acres, a stand of tall old trees lines the top of a small ridge. "Those are Kendalls," Pete says. "I helped plant them when I was in high school." We bump across the grass on Pete's Gator, stopping to look at a stand of Ruby Jons—a dark red version of my favorite apple, the Jonathan—and Redcorts, a red Cortland cross on dwarf rootstock. The trees are short enough that I can pick from the top of the tree without even stepping down from the Gator.

But the small trees just aren't as beautiful as the old giants. Pete is enthusiastic about the new varieties, not afraid to experiment, and he's proud of keeping up with trends that help the orchard stay solvent for the next generation. Still, he looks wistfully toward the Kendalls. "When the last old trees are gone and you're just out here picking bushes, it's time for me to retire," he says, shaking his head ruefully.

CHAPTER SEVEN

Keeping the Farm

SETTING PRICES FOR the apples Red Tomato will market for the northeastern orchards in the Eco Apple program is a nerve-wracking process. Apples are a commodity crop, and prices go up and down with the market. The size of the crop in Washington affects prices everywhere else in the country. Some wholesale customers buy at prices that fluctuate with the market over the course of the season, but some require a contract at a set price for the whole season.

Sales have increased steadily over ten seasons since the Eco program began, but every year is uncertain. What varieties, at what price, will sell this year? Who else is competing for the business? Does the wholesale buyer have the time and experience to consider a decade of good service and quality fruit, or will she just look at the numbers? After all of the careful decisions of the previous months, the prices negotiated before the harvest even starts determine profit or loss for the whole year.

ABOVE: Apple pack line, Clark Brothers Orchards, Ashfield, Massachusetts. Photo by Susan Futrell.

Wholesale growers often have little to no say in the price their apples bring. Setting prices at Red Tomato is different from the way they are set at many fruit companies and brokerages. Growers are involved in the conversation from the beginning. They know what Red Tomato will make, how much the trucking and storage will cost, what prices are offered to customers, and what other growers are being paid.

In July, while the crop is still forming, Red Tomato convenes the first of several weekly conference calls with the growers whose fruit they hope to sell to large wholesale customers. Michael Rozyne, who coordinates the apple pricing, is in a café on his way home from a meeting; one grower is in his office, another in his pickup; at least one person is out in the orchard, judging by the sound of wind blowing across the phone. The agenda is to project the size of the coming harvest and edge toward committing to this year's prices. The goal is to win business without going below what growers need to make or might be able to get elsewhere.

All those numbers are guesswork, but these are experienced growers so they consider all the factors: how big a crop each expects to harvest, the size and quality of the fruit they're seeing on the trees, when the harvest will start. They weigh what they are hearing from customers and reading in the trade press. One grower shares a trade association's just-released crop forecasts for the Northeast, which will affect prices for regional varieties and apples marketed as local. Others add their own predictions about the crop in New York, Washington, and Michigan. They review last year's price and how much they sold.

It's a different equation for every variety. Ginger Gold, Zestar!®, and Paula Red ripen first, so those prices need to be aggressive to get a foot in the door at the start of the season. But it's the prices on Honeycrisp, McIntosh, and Empire that everyone will be living with for months. In a good year, there will be enough apples to sell clear into next summer.

On the call, they work it through, variety by variety. First, they discuss regional specialties such as McIntosh, Empire, Cortland, and Macoun that aren't sold much outside the Northeast. One Massachusetts grower tells the group he's decided to abandon his entire block of Empires. "I've given up on them," he says. "I'm just not making money on them. I cidered over a thousand bushels last year." The lines are quiet until someone asks if he is going to regraft, and what variety he'll put in to replace them. "Whatever the next big apple is going to be," he says wryly. There are laughs all around, but no one offers a suggestion.

Next they work through the high-volume standard varieties that the whole country will have: Gala, Fuji, and finally, Honeycrisp. When the calls finish, not everyone is happy with where things have ended up. One New York grower wants to push for a higher price on McIntosh; Northeast growers expect a good crop this year, and it's a chance to make back some of what they gave up in lower prices last year. Others are nervous about going too high. Washington's crop is going to be good this year too, and being too greedy could lose them the whole deal.

It's as close to informed gambling as anything, with a bit of gut feeling mixed in. In a few days, Michael will carefully compose an email committing the bets for a large customer. He'll tinker with it all day and give it one last read just before hitting Send. When he hears back, it will be just a sentence or two. Within a few weeks, most prices are set for the year, and the picture of what the market looks like for the coming season has come into focus. Everyone starts breathing again. If nothing goes wrong between now and harvest, at least they know what they have to work with.

Setting prices and gambling on your own and your neighbors' crop isn't new to farming or unique to apples. But the stakes have gotten higher, and growers' abilities to influence the outcome to be something other than a "price taker" have steadily diminished over the last century, especially over the past few decades. Global consolidation of the marketing, distribution, and retail sectors has led to more standardization, massive year-round global supply chains, and long-distance relationships that change frequently and are all business. One of Red Tomato's large customers has been through eleven apple buyers in fifteen years. Costs, prices, and individual farm finances have always been challenging, but the shift toward factors outside farmers' control has been steady and relentless.

CHANGES IN AGRICULTURE and the farm economy have put increasing pressure on the profitability of individual orchards for well over a century. The Civil War decimated a generation of farm families, ravaged many of the big plantation orchards in the South, and put the farm economy of the recovering nation in turmoil. After the war, Reconstruction and land speculation fueled a short-lived boom of commercial orchards in the South. A thirty-year expansion followed, fueled by railroads and the barrel-filling Ben Davis apple, the biggest-selling variety for the region. Railroads at first improved access to urban markets for orchards everywhere, but by 1900 trains were shipping large volumes of fruit across the country from the West Coast. Refrigeration, automobiles, and better roads made it easier to ship fresh fruit even to smaller towns and made it easier for people to get to town to shop, all of which made them less reliant on home gardens and farmstead orchards. The railroads also made it possible for big nurseries to ship trees anywhere in the country, accelerating the narrowing of selections to those in commercial demand.

By the turn of the twentieth century, the shift to an urban and industrial economy had put farmers at a disadvantage, one that has continued to intensify. Federal programs such as price supports attempted to take some of the volatility and risk out of farming, but they were directed mostly at a few commodity crops like wheat, corn, cotton, and beans, not fruits and vegetables.

Meanwhile, refrigerated transport affected production patterns all over the country, expanding access to distant markets and encouraging a shift to perishable, high-value fruits and vegetables. But those faraway markets also made individual farms more vulnerable to national gluts and price drops, and left growers dependent on distant and not always trustworthy wholesale agents to find buyers.

Orange growers were the first to respond to these changes by joining together to promote their product.[1] Sunkist growers cooperative introduced the concept of branded fruit in 1907. That same year, the California Fruit Growers Exchange (CFGE), founded in 1893 by a group of orange growers in Riverside, California, tested the first-ever fresh fruit advertising campaign, targeting housewives in Iowa. By the end of the campaign, Iowans were eating 50 percent more oranges than they had before, and by the late 1920s the orange had overtaken the apple as the most popular fruit in the country. Other fruit growers associations adopted the strategy. Marketing—beautiful labels, health claims, contests for retailers to promote and display—became the main, and eventually only, strategy available to growers to influence sales and the prices paid for their fruit.

The trends prompted Liberty Hyde Bailey, prolific horticulturist, author, and the first dean of the Cornell College of Agriculture, to warn would-be fruit growers in 1926 that they would face challenges growing fruit for either a specialty high-end market or for a global commodity market:

> The man who grows fruits for the special markets has a definite problem. The product is desired for its intrinsic qualities; and special products demand special prices. The man who grows fruit for the world's market has no personal customer. The product is desired for its extrinsic or market qualities; and the world's products bring the world's prices.[2]

With some gender updating, his advice still applies today. The long-term shift in economic market power away from growers and local markets toward packers, marketers, and retailers hasn't slowed since California orange growers first ran those ads back in 1907. Advertising promotes the benefits of fruit and loyalty to brands. It also promotes a standard of cosmetic appearance, long-distance durability, and uniformity that encourages ever more perfect, and unrealistic, consumer expectations of the fruit available in grocery stores.

That expectation has pushed fruit markets toward a standard of year-round availability and uniformity requiring global standardization, volume production, quick transportation, and long-term storage. It forces producers to get bigger, or to sell to intermediaries. It has meant year-round access, variety, and beauty for consumers, albeit often in exchange for less flavor and more reliance on chemical management of cosmetics. The rise of a good food, slow food, and local food movement has fostered a more educated consumer who wants to know the farmer and protect the environment, but for the most part those eaters still expect beautiful apples, top-quality crunch, and flavor year-round.

None of which is making it easier to grow apples more sustainably or in more parts of the country. As recently as 1980, half of the apples sold through the Boston Terminal Market were grown in the Northeast. By 1995, the share of regional apples had dropped to 25 percent.[3]

The shift to growing a limited number of crops for faraway markets is especially stark in my home state of Iowa. The Midwest produced significant volumes of apples until the early 1900s. But in the decades after World War I, agriculture across the country shifted further from diversity to specialization. In the 1920s, thirty-four different food crops ranging from corn and apples to cattle and potatoes were produced commercially on Iowa farms.[4] Within a generation, fruit trees had retreated to farmstead backyards as corn and bean fields took over. A big freeze on Armistice Day, November 11, 1940, was the final straw. The weather that day was brutal. A wet year had left the trees and ground full of moisture. Temperatures dropped from seventy degrees at 7:00 a.m. to zero by 7:00 p.m. Sap froze within hours, causing trees to split and die. In one day, commercial orchards throughout the state were wiped out.

Horticultural journals and proceedings had been bemoaning the "industrialization of agriculture, and the dominance of corn"[5] as early as 1918, but the 1940 freeze was the real end of commercial apples in Iowa and nearby states. Concentration in wholesale and retail grocery and an industrial model of production carried over from wartime further encouraged specialization in whatever grew best and fastest in a given area. Post–World War II access to hybrid seed, machinery, and petrochemicals accelerated the shift. Loans to replant apples were hard to get. Loans for corn and hogs were not.

Meanwhile, Washington, New York, and Michigan were producing lots of apples and investing in storage, processing, and other infrastructure to market their fruit. Iowa's deep, fertile prairie topsoil was ideal for nutrient-hungry crops like corn and soybeans, and the hogs and cattle they feed. The many hands needed to harvest apples were replaced by the few needed to drive a tractor through a field. By 1964, only 2 percent of Iowa's farms were producing apples commercially.[6]

As Iowa became king of corn, soybeans, pigs, and cattle, Washington became king of apples. By the end of World War II, the state of Washington was growing 27 percent of all U.S. apples, more than any other state. New York held on to second place, with Virginia, Michigan, Pennsylvania, Oregon, and Illinois jockeying to be in the top five. Most apples in the United States were sold fresh, although in every state but Washington, processing for vinegar, cider, juice, and increasingly for canned apples and sauce was also important. A half-century later, the rankings had solidified even further. Washington increased its share of total U.S. production to nearly 65 percent by 2015, more than all other states combined. Iowa ranked twenty-eighth in apples (out of twenty-nine states still producing enough apples to be reported by USDA) but was number one in corn and beans.[7] If Iowa orchards had produced the same 9.5 million bushels in 2014 that were produced there in the peak year of 1911, the state would rank fifth in U.S. apple production.

THESE LARGER CHANGES in agriculture were reflected in changes at Lyman Orchards in Connecticut. The Lymans had developed a fairly good wholesale business for their fruit following World War II. With a group of neighboring orchards, they formed a cooperative called Laurel State Fruit Growers Association and established a direct-to-store delivery (DSD) service for the First National grocery chain, which John Lyman remembers had a large share of the emerging supermarket business in Connecticut at the time. Each co-op member was responsible for taking orders, packing, and delivering to stores in a designated territory. It was steady business, the chain paid well, and it was a good model for those years, John recalls.

But inevitably, the market began to shift. By the 1960s, First National was having internal problems and became arrogant, a word John uses matter-of-factly but not lightly. Other chains cut into their market. Within twenty years, Stop & Shop had pretty much taken control of the Connecticut grocery market, First National had restructured, and the co-op broke apart. Some of the member orchards continue to sell directly to Stop & Shop and other chains. The Lymans and a few others decided to go a different direction.

Lyman Orchards had always had a few people stopping by asking to buy fruit, so their first move was to refurbish a salesroom and get serious about selling directly to eaters. The farm stand quickly became popular, closing for a few months in spring and opening again in midsummer when peaches were ripe, then selling apples through the winter. It was a prosperous time; gas was cheap, grocery stores were closed on Sunday, people went for a Sunday drive in the country and came home with groceries right from the farm.

John's dad, Jack Lyman, was a major force behind the changes. The only one of his generation who wanted to stay and farm on the family homestead, he had worked summers and weekends on the farm, gone to school and then into the service. "I don't know if Dad ever entertained *not* going back to the farm," John remembers. "The transformation was really under his watch; he was very much a visionary about going direct to the consumer."

The advent of controlled-atmosphere (CA) storage also changed things. By closely controlling the gases, particularly oxygen, carbon dioxide, and ethylene, in refrigerated storage, apples could be kept at near-harvest-quality condition for much longer than apples stored with refrigeration alone. The Lymans adopted the approach around 1963. CA improved the quality of stored fruit, stretched the season, and removed the pressure to sell the full crop right at harvest, when fruit is plentiful and prices low. They had gotten almost completely away from delivering direct to stores and were selling most of their wholesale fruit to distributor warehouses at that point. Those wholesale markets were getting more competitive. Washington apples were taking more and more of the grocery business. Some farmers did well, expanding plantings and increasing production to spread costs over more sales; others struggled to stay afloat in the changing market. The Lymans were pretty diversified in terms of fruit—apples, peaches, blueberries, and pears—which relieved the pressure to expand apple acreage, as some growers were doing.

They also built a golf course. It was a hard, risky decision, a big investment in a totally new venture. A golfing cousin with connections convinced renowned golf course designer Robert Trent Jones to visit the farm and commit to designing a course. They opened the course in 1968. Meanwhile, the salesroom they had built off their packinghouse was doing so well that they were running out of room to handle the crowds.

They opened a brand-new salesroom in 1972. The two major projects back-to-back, golf course and retail store, were a lot for the family to absorb and manage.

Looking back, John says they weren't investing in the orchard itself as much as they should have been during those years. They had begun moving from standard trees to semidwarfs in the late '50s and early '60s, but it took twenty years to get the whole orchard replanted, and each time they had to wait several years for new plantings to bear fruit. They replaced older varieties such as Baldwin, Russet, and Rome with lots of McIntoshes, Macouns, Cortlands, Empires, and in the late '60s, Jona-golds. They also planted newer strains of Red Delicious to replicate what was coming out of Washington. They started a scratch bakery in the early '70s and had "a couple of really good years."

Then the fuel crisis hit. The oil embargo in 1973–74 put a halt to Sunday drives in the country just for fun. Blue laws were repealed, and grocers stayed open on Sundays, becoming competitors. During those years some farms did well, but many were hit hard. Lyman Orchards stayed marginal, helped out by a loyal group of golfers and a general resurgence of the sport on TV that led to a thirty-year period when it seemed there couldn't be enough golf. "It was kind of a roaring time," John chuckles, and it helped significantly to offset the costs of the orchard.

AS THE ECONOMICS of distribution made it increasingly challenging for midsized wholesale growers to compete, the same pressures that pushed the Lymans toward golf have pushed all of U.S. agriculture toward a split into very small and very large. Over the past several decades, the vast majority of farms have become either too small to compete in the global market or too big to survive in direct markets alone. Only two kinds of farms are growing: large commodity production operations and very small, diversified farms selling directly to consumers at their farms, farmers markets, and through community supported agriculture (CSA) ventures.[8] The majority of U.S. farms in the middle, in terms of size and crop volume, have been steadily declining in number for decades. It's a serious loss. These midsized family farms represent diversity in crops, generations of land stewardship and farming knowledge, security from disruption in food supplies, and significant local economic transactions that support local banks, hardware stores, grocery stores, and schools.

The economics of the largest-scale farms tend to be based on the needs of processing and marketing, driven by competition for market share in global supply chains. They are focused on uniform commodities and face relentless pressure to reduce costs of all kinds, which pushes them toward further consolidation and vertical integration into packing, marketing, and distribution. Small, diverse direct-market farms can earn higher prices and keep more of the profits, but they have high, often uncounted costs for getting product to market, and they represent only a fraction of total U.S. food sales. To grow, they must reach more outlets and specialty markets or move into wholesale, trading higher volume for lower prices and greater distance from customers. The 2012 Census of Agriculture shows growth even in the number of small farms beginning to slow.[9]

The 2012 Census of Agriculture defines a farm as "any place from which $1,000 or more of agricultural products were produced and sold, or would normally have been sold, during the census year." That year, the USDA counted 2.1 million farms in the United States. The majority were small; three-quarters of all U.S. farms had sales of less than $50,000 per year, and over half sold less than $10,000 per year. Together they produced only 3 percent of the total value of agricultural products sold. Most of the value of U.S. agricultural production is concentrated on relatively few large farms. Less than half of 1 percent of farms had sales of over $5 million in 2012, but combined they produced 32 percent of the total value of agricultural products sold.[10]

The shift away from midsized farms was hastened by the farm crisis of the 1980s. Then-secretary of agriculture Earl Butz told farmers to "get big or get out" and urged midwestern growers to plant corn "fencerow to fencerow." Pressure to expand left many farmers deep in debt. Costs for fuel and equipment climbed while prices for crops dropped. Land prices stayed high, especially near cities, where housing and commercial development pressure was especially intense. In just one decade, between

1982 and 1992, nearly 15 percent of all U.S. farms went out of business or were sold out of farming.[11] Imagine losing one or two houses on every block, on every street, in every town. Spread out across the countryside, the loss was less visible, but the scars of fallen-in barns and abandoned houses are still a common sight in many rural areas. Organizations such as Farm Aid and American Farmland Trust, both started in the 1980s, have maintained a constant effort to support family farms ever since.

In *Broken Heartland*, author Osha Gray Davidson recounts a 1987 conversation with members of an Iowa farm family who have just learned they will be able to keep their house, two years after the rest of the farm was sold off at a foreclosure auction. It is a bittersweet moment. "What about the farm?" says Kathy Bolin, sitting at her kitchen table. "When we first moved in almost ten years ago, we planted an orchard: apples, cherries, a lot of different fruit trees. The first thing the people who rented the fields did was to bulldoze those trees down—so they could get a couple of extra rows of corn in. You can't describe the kind of pain you feel watching that."[12]

The family farm is still the foundation of U.S. agriculture; 87 percent of farms are operated by individuals or families, and 75 percent of farm operators live right on the farm. In terms of livelihood, though, very few can depend on farm income to support themselves and their families. Sixty-one percent have off-farm jobs in order to earn enough to keep farming.[13] Net farm income across all sizes of farms from 1949 to 2001 stayed relatively flat. Everything else—fuel, taxes, labor, and groceries —kept going up.[14] In 2012, only 46 percent of all farms had positive net cash income—in other words, made money after expenses.

US Apple, the national trade association for apple growers, estimated there were 7,500 apple producers in the United States as of 2016, farming on approximately 322,000 acres. Total crop varies year by year, but it's increasing overall: the annual value of the U.S. apple crop is around $4 billion.[15] The crop keeps getting bigger and the dollars appear to be increasing every year, but food system analyst Ken Meter found that when adjusted for cost of living, the actual annual dollar value of apple sales between 1924 and 2010 has been almost flat.[16] John Bunker of Maine Heritage Orchard points out that in 1860, "top-quality Blue Pearmains could bring up to $1.00/bushel, roughly the same price that Maine farmers were getting for their juice apples 150 years later in 2002."[17]

The number of farms growing apples has been in a steady decline for over a quarter century. In 1983, 41,187 farms reported growing apples commercially. Ten years later, there were 33,879, and by 2007 the number was 25,591, a loss of over one-third in only twenty-five years. States with the largest number of apple producers, for example Washington, Michigan, and New York, lost orchards at rates as high or higher than states with little production to begin with. Some farmers sold out to larger operations, but many stopped growing apples and farming altogether. Over the same time period, the number of acres planted with apples also declined, from 590,541 in 1982 to 398,770 by 2007.[18]

The three-hundred-year-old Stone Ridge Orchard in the Hudson Valley was slated to become a condominium development before Elizabeth Ryan helped raise $1.25 million dollars, some via a Kickstarter campaign, to purchase it in 2015. Ryan, who also owns Breezy Hill Orchard a few miles away across the Hudson River, plans to continue growing a hundred and fifty varieties of apples and other fruits at both orchards. "I've been told by my lenders that it's a bad business decision, not to cash out your land for houses," she told the *New York Times*. "Why do we do this? Because we love it, because we believe in it, because there is a joy and satisfaction in growing healthy food for people."[19]

THE GROWTH IN popularity and visibility of small direct-market farms selling through CSAs, farm stands, and farmers markets has given many people a personal connection to their food and an appreciation for farmers. They may picture the ideal local apple farm as something like the pick-your-own orchards that thousands visit every autumn. Although the challenges for growers who sell direct to consumers are different from those of wholesale growers who rarely see their customers face to face, relying on direct marketing has its own risks. For a PYO orchard or farm stand, higher prices without wholesalers and retailers in the middle can mean more profits on fewer acres. It also means 90 percent of sales must happen during just eight weeks in September and October, and most of that on weekends. It takes a special kind of juggling act to manage an orchard and its expenses all year, hoping for no early freeze, no summer hail, no pest invasions, no crop failures, and sunny weekends just to open that small window of opportunity that pays for it all.

Seeing only those direct-market farms can give a misleading impression of what the rest of agriculture looks like. In order to eat fresh apples for the rest of the year, we depend on wholesale growers. Small and mid-sized local growers are at a disadvantage in the wholesale supply chain. And no matter what size the farm, wholesale prices and crops operate on a thin margin that can fluctuate wildly from season to season.

For example, a record Washington apple crop in 2014 helped sell a lot of apples, but it also brought prices down. When I spoke with Kevin Stennes at Chelan Fresh, he ruefully described the market that year as "a bloodbath." For their orchard, breaking even was the goal, and they looked to sales of pears, cherries, and organic fruit to help tip the balance.

"When you get a hundred and fifty million–box crop that you have to sell in the same time frame that we used to do a hundred, the numbers don't work very well," he explains. "There are a lot of growers with different finances. Say an orchard brought in $5 million; people are impressed, but you'd be surprised at what little percent of that is profit." He shakes his head, then looks out at the row of desks in the sales office and brightens.

"That's just the way it is. You make a living, you love it, some years you make money, and the years you go backwards you just hope it doesn't affect you for too long. Usually one bad year's not going to put you out of business, but it slows you down from where you want to go. If you have too many in a row, then you get nervous."

At lunch earlier that day in Chelan, Mark Gores turns to Wynne and me as we are finishing up our conversation. "I know you've gotta get going," he hesitates, then looks at the floor and barrels ahead. "It's like I've got a stock that has just come off of a ten-year bottom in my orchard and now it's really high. I've had people approach me when I'm out having a beer and say, 'How serious are you about your walk-away figure? Come and talk to us before [you sell].' We might be about to find out retail is ready to yawn again over a new variety. Luckily our foot's in the door with the three we have. I keep telling myself, maybe I should sell when the market's high."

Wynne shakes her head in sympathy. "But what are you gonna do then?" Mark looks past me to the door, trying to picture his life without the orchard. "I just don't know."

He takes a breath. "There's one more thing I want to say, and I'll say it quick. I don't see a future for somebody my size to enter the business." He lets his words linger in the air.

"Really," I respond. It's more an acknowledgment than a question.

THE LYMANS DID a serious review of their operations in the '90s. Realizing they were not going to be able to sustain their production with wholesale, they decided to focus on retail, PYO, and their growing pie business. To do that, they didn't need all of the acres they had planted. They cut back by a third, calling their new strategy "right-sizing." With a hundred acres of apples, they could do well, add other crops, and the input costs were much more manageable than with a hundred and fifty acres. By the mid-1990s they had restructured the farm market as a regional destination and their business started to grow again. They added a corn maze in 2000 and a sunflower maze in 2007.

The farm is now one of the better contributors to the whole operation. Even wholesale is doing better because the overall quality of the fruit is better. "From the early '60s to today, we really transformed ourselves," John Lyman says. "The path started with getting into retail, and over the years we've become a pretty diversified business." When they depended primarily on selling wholesale, they had to guarantee supply whether they had the apples or not. Now, working with a network of growers through Red Tomato's Eco Apple program, they've taken the pressure off and don't have to sell at a loss. With other risk management support, such as crop insurance, that has recently become available, they can even mitigate some vulnerability to weather.

What about golf? "Golf was a helluva ride." It's as close as John comes to swearing. "But it got overbuilt, demand is down. It's going through a tough time, like apples did in the '90s."

Like his father, John is the only one of his generation to stay active with the family farm. When his great-grandfather passed away, the farm was put in a trust that John's grandfather, his two brothers, and three sisters turned into a corporation, Lyman Farm, Inc. The original six shareholders have swelled to 194 with new generations, but only a small number are involved in the farm day-to-day. Five family members sit on the board—cousins and cousins-in-law—and six non-family members, including a grower from a nearby orchard whose family and the Lymans have known and respected each other for a long time. When John's dad retired in 1997, the Lyman Orchards board decided for the first time to hire an outside CEO. Their current CEO is a man John's dad hired as comptroller, and who is "close to family."

John's nephew and a second cousin are now the ninth generation working in the orchard. John is teaching them about the business, trying to be proactive in helping them generate knowledge and interest so they can transition into management of the orchard over the next ten to fifteen years. "My dad always used to say part of the secret of our success is we've never been that successful," John laughs. "There's no big fortune for the family to fight over."

CHAPTER EIGHT

The Enterprise of Apples for Sale

TODAY IT'S POSSIBLE to buy groceries without ever interacting with another human. You visit a sprawling store that has everything, select packages from the shelves, check yourself out with a scanner and a credit card, and carry the bags out the door. Or maybe you go online, click on your selections, and have someone else deliver them to your doorstep. A century ago, provisioning your kitchen for the week meant giving a list to the local grocer, who selected your items from the shelves behind a long counter and assembled them in your shopping basket while chatting about the latest news. Bulk items were displayed in bins and barrels for you to scoop out and bring to the grocer to be weighed. Once you'd bought your dry goods, you went next door to lean over the meat counter while the butcher packaged up your order, and then to the bakery, where you once again perused the display and were handed your loaves.

ABOVE: Apple display, Rogers Orchards, Southington, Connecticut. Photo by Susan Futrell.

Then in 1916, southern grocery chain Piggly Wiggly opened its first store in Memphis, and in 1930, Michael Cullen opened a large-format self-service one-stop shop in northern New Jersey, King Kullen. No more waiting for the grocer to hand items across the counter; shoppers could pick out their own! Within a few years, more than twelve hundred supermarkets had opened in eighty-five U.S. cities. By 1950, there were fifteen thousand of the newfangled stores, offering more and more products.[1] Competition drove standardization in packaging, products, and promotion, which in turn led to consolidation. Companies like A&P and Giant Food Stores built regional empires that sourced products from all over the country and world. Before long, they supplied groceries to the majority of Americans.

The push toward bigger and more efficient led to larger and larger stores, and perhaps inevitably drew large consumer goods companies to start selling food. In the 1980s and '90s, supercenters like Walmart, Costco, and Target emerged, offering everything from groceries to car parts. By the 2000s, cost cutting, volume, and convenience were driving the industry, bringing cutthroat pricing and distant supply relationships to apples just like they had to clothes, plastic containers, and lightbulbs. Supermarket share of food sales (produce, meat, cereal, etc.) went from 82 percent in 1992 to 62 percent in 2007, while sales at warehouse and club stores like Costco and Sam's Club (a division of Walmart) exploded from 4 percent to nearly a quarter of all groceries sold. Supermarkets' share of produce sales dropped to 80 percent as warehouse stores' share rose from 13 percent to 20 percent.[2] The drive to offer everything under one roof led at first to larger stores carrying tens of thousands of items. The drive to cut costs at every point in the supply chain has ultimately forced a move back toward limited variety and centralized decision-making and management.

Burlington, Iowa, has had a front-row seat to all of these changes. A busy river town on the western bank of the Mississippi River in the southeast corner of the state bordering Missouri and Illinois, Burlington is a longtime shipping hub. Multiple railway lines and barge routes connect there, midway along storied U.S. Route 61, which follows the river north to Duluth and south to New Orleans. It's the closest major town to Harold Linder's farm and a few miles from the orchard I heard sell at auction.

Enterprising young Andrew Lagomarcino left his home near Genoa, Italy, for the United States in 1867, just after the Civil War. After a few years selling fruits and vegetables in West Virginia, he headed to Burlington to open the first retail fruit store in the booming frontier town. He went on to become an enterprising wholesale dealer in domestic and imported fruits of all kinds. His bookkeeper, William Grupe, soon became a business partner, and over the next century, Lagomarcino, Grupe, and their families built one of the largest wholesale fruit companies west of the Mississippi.

Lagomarcino-Grupe's downtown warehouse was a block from the river.[3] A railroad switch came right to their building, which had enough cold storage for ten railcar loads of fruit and ripening rooms for five carloads of bananas, the first to be imported to the region. They bought and sold local apples from Iowa, at that time a major apple-growing state, and a 1901 bill of sale for their Cedar Rapids, Iowa, branch also boasted Baldwins, Russets, and Common Cookers from New York. They became a major local employer and community booster; in 1903, the Lagomarcino Lemon Squeezers posted a 14–0 season against the Copeland Banana Peelers and other teams in the local baseball league.

Andrew Lagomarcino died in 1907, and his oldest son, Paul, became president of the company while William Grupe continued to head the Burlington office. In 1915, they were reported to be "the largest fruit house in the middle west outside of Chicago," with two hundred employees and sixty traveling salesmen. They processed fifteen hundred carloads of fruit and vegetables annually and had started selling ice cream, soda, beer, and oysters as well as produce. Over the next fifty years, they opened as many as eleven branches in various towns across eastern Iowa, all less than one hundred miles apart, supplying customers in Iowa and neighboring states. When Burlington's first airport opened in 1927, they could ship in produce overnight from all over the world. They continued to be known as a steady buyer of apples from Iowa orchards. But they also saw the production center shifting west, and after the turn of the century, the company bought a large orchard in

Washington. From there they shipped their own fruit to markets across the country.

The post–World War I years and the Depression were tough on Burlington. Two of its four banks closed in 1929, and many wholesale industries were hit hard. But Lagomarcino-Grupe held on, diversifying further into grocery products to serve their retail customers. Family members, brothers, and cousins all worked for the company and were active in the founding and leadership of regional and national trade groups in the wholesale fruit industry, among them the Iowa Fruit Jobbers Association and Western Fruit Jobbers Association.

Nationally, chain stores and supermarkets emerged from World War II into a fifty-year growth curve that slowed only with the rise of big-box discounters. Supermarkets accounted for a mere 3 percent of all grocery stores in 1946 and only around 5 percent in 1954, but their sales grew from 28 percent to 48 percent of total grocery sales through this period. Traditional neighborhood grocers, supplied by small local wholesalers, felt the pressure from the chain stores at the same time they watched their neighborhoods, small towns, and rural areas became suburbs. The owners of chain stores could source products of all kinds directly from suppliers, setting up their own distribution centers and cutting out the wholesalers in the middle. Away from the dense population centers on the coasts, strong wholesalers like Lagomarcino-Grupe helped independent grocers thrive for a while longer, but the pairing of growth and consolidation was relentless.

Lagomarcino-Grupe celebrated its seventy-fifth anniversary in 1950, trumpeting its original "Fresh to You" tagline even though produce was by then only a small part of the business. A fleet of 116 modern trucks including semis, refrigerated trucks, and small pickups helped them match every need and schedule. Trains continued to deliver daily boxcars of products from all over the world. Company leaders were active in state and national industry trade groups such as United Fresh Fruit and Vegetable Association and International Apple Association. The company was still family owned and run, but the founders were aging and competition intensifying. In 1952, the Grupe family sold their share to the Lagomarcinos and the company began closing branches. Other grocery companies around them were centralizing and consolidating too.

Then the structure of grocery wholesale shifted again. Suppliers began looking for ways to reduce the costs of selling direct to so many retail locations. They wanted middlemen again, but this time around only the largest could provide the service and efficiency the big chains required. Lagomarcino-Grupe merged with Benner Tea Company, a Burlington retailer, combining two of the oldest remaining food companies in the region. The merged company went on to acquire others. It made an attractive and little-noticed foothold when it sold in 1976 to a West German grocery company named ALDI.

ALDI was founded in 1948 by a family that had been in the grocery business since before World War I and had made a name for itself as secretive but innovative. In 1961, Theo and Karl Albrecht divided the company started by their mother into two divisions, North and South, allowing each to pursue his own growth strategy while taking advantage of the benefits of working together.[4] Brenner Tea Company was the first U.S. venture for ALDI South, introducing the "limited assortment" concept to the United States by offering fewer items, many of them generic or store-branded, in exchange for lower prices. In 1978, ALDI North bought another small, limited-assortment U.S. chain, Trader Joe's. ALDI US now has more than fifteen hundred ALDI stores and still keeps its U.S. headquarters across the river in Batavia, Illinois. They closed the Burlington distribution facility in 2011.

The Lagomarcino to ALDI story is a classic immigrant tale, instructive not because it's unusual but because it is so common—a microcosm of how fruit selling became the global industry it is today. The same story has played out many times in towns and cities all across the United States. A wholesale fruit grower once sold directly to a jobber or distributor, who would then bring the apples to a retail grocer. A few pickup truckloads were moved a few miles to the nearest branch warehouse to be sold to independent grocers within a hundred miles or so, most serving communities they had been part of for generations. Then train cars and semi loads began moving fruit long distances to a handful of central locations, to be redeployed to thousands of chain stores.

Those stores were opening, closing, and changing banners and hands constantly, their managers and fruit buyers staying only a few years in any one location before transferring to the next best tax-incentivized business park.

WHILE ALDI WAS OPENING and closing stores and warehouses in the Midwest, Clark Brothers Orchards in western Massachusetts was doing its best to keep up with similar changes in the Boston-area market. The Clarks typically started the season with a call to take an order from Bread & Circus, a regional natural food grocery chain. The orchard workers would pack what was ordered, then they would place a second call to a giant national distributor, C&S Wholesale Grocers, to sell whatever apples they had left at a lower price. In 1999, they never made the second call. Bread & Circus took everything they had. It was the largest crop the Clarks had ever grown, and they packed and shipped apples until the following June.

Aaron Clark had just come back to help his brother Dana on the farm that year. The last time he'd packed apples was as a kid, looking out the window and wishing he were anywhere else. Back then, the crew sorted by hand as the fruit rolled past on a conveyor belt. One person picked out the smaller apples (called 100s because they can be packed a hundred apples to a bushel), another picked out the larger 80s, which sell for a better price, packing them all into bushel boxes to be stacked on pallets and moved into cold storage. The best fruit was carefully nestled into separate boxes in layers separated by cardboard trays, to be sold right away. The larger the apple, the better the price, and prices drop as the year goes on.

When Bread & Circus sales slowed at the end of the season that year, Aaron tried calling C&S, but it was hard to get back in. The brothers continued to sell most of their crop to the natural food chain over the ensuing years, even as it was sold and became part of national chain Whole Foods Market. Whole Foods customers will pay a bit more for quality and appreciate the Clarks' regional varieties like Macoun, so that has been a good relationship for the most part. Still, Aaron says it's scary to see Whole Foods getting bigger too. Will there be room for a sixty-five-acre orchard like the Clarks' to compete with standard wholesale varieties? The extension service marketing folks keep telling him to get big, get niche, or get out.

The Clarks' experience too has been repeated over and over at orchards across the country. A small to midsized family orchard has gone from being a reliable part of someone's supply to being a tiny, almost unnoticeable fraction. You might cooperate to combine your fruit with a few hundred other growers to hold on to some meaningful percentage of sales, as the Washington growers have done. You might go after the latest, newest variety to make your fruit stand out, which growers like Mark Gores have done. You might diversify your markets and become a family entertainment destination, like the Lymans and hundreds of direct-market orchards all across the country. Or, you might just hang on and sell your fruit at whatever price you can get until you're ready to retire, the city moves closer, the taxes rise, and the price of your beautiful rolling farmscape becomes too compelling for you and your family to ignore. You can only sell the farm once, so you'd better make sure the time and price are right.

In Washington State, midsized family orchards have followed the "get big, get niche, or get out" maxim by planting more trees, acquiring more acres as other orchards are sold, or by joining co-ops where they can pool volume and share costs of equipment and marketing. The Stennes family has tied their future to Chelan Fruit Co-op and to the salespeople and marketers at Chelan Fresh.

"I think the average consumer would be surprised what goes into getting fruit on the shelves," Kevin Stennes laughs. "Every step of the way there are a lot of challenges and a lot of smart people making it all work. The growers don't know how much goes into selling their fruit; the consumers don't know how much work goes into getting it there. And a lot of the guys in the office here don't know what goes into growing, either." He laughs again. "Like I said, every step of the way has its challenges."

He goes on to describe the investments the co-op must make to stay competitive. "The fruit-packing technology has gotten really extensive, and expensive. Our sales group here is always reminded of all of our packers' investments in new orchards, equipment, packing line; the co-op spends millions every year to keep us modern. And we're just trying to make a buck a box or something, you know."

Stemilt Growers, one of the largest grower-packer-shippers in the industry, has taken the "get big" path, steadily adding orchards and packing facilities and building a strong, aggressive brand, including an organic line. They market fruit grown on their own farms as well as contracted from other orchards. Founded by third-generation fruit grower Tom Mathison and family owned since 1964, Stemilt's mission reads: "Maximize long-term return to the land by building consumer demand." They've been pioneers in adopting and marketing new varieties, modern technology, and sustainable farming practices.

Mike Taylor, vice president of sales and marketing at Stemilt, told fellow growers at the 2014 Washington State Horticultural Association show that he sees more change ahead. The industry has been through vertical integration; changes in capital, labor, and length of harvest; and retailers' adoption of big-data strategies to manage their shelf space. They are seeing better pre- and postharvest treatments, better quality apples, and a welcoming environment for growing and selling. But it's not enough. "The primary customer, the retailer, is focused on what's good for them and the bottom line. Selling more expensive apples is good for them—40 percent of $1.99 is a lot better than 40 percent of 88 cents."[5]

The branded club varieties have helped apples compete with other fruit, and Taylor sees retailers moving to new varieties more and more quickly. "There is going to be a massive struggle for shelf space. All the apples are going to be good. It's how we execute on marketing that will make the difference." What he doesn't say is that no small or midsized orchard can execute that kind of marketing on its own. Taylor goes on to caution: "We've moved into a situation where we don't sell everything we grow; we sell everything we can. So keep the low demand items out of the bins."[6] Meaning, don't even bother to pick and pack the varieties that are no longer top sellers.

Matt Milkovich, reporting in *Fruit Growers News*, pointed out "Large, well-coordinated supermarket chains require large, well-coordinated apple suppliers."[7] According to Steve Lutz of Columbia Marketing International, although there are thirty-three thousand retail grocery stores nationwide, just thirty grocery chains represent nearly two-thirds of total U.S. food dollars. Supermarkets purchase 77 percent of the entire U.S. apple supply. There are fewer and fewer apple suppliers big enough to command the bargaining power it takes to compete in that market. Competitive pressure on retailers trickles down the whole supply chain: "There's no room to make a mistake anymore," says Lutz.[8]

The number of apples eaten per person in the United States has been declining for thirty years (it's now around nineteen pounds per person per year), but the apples being eaten fresh are more expensive, which helps to keep sales steady despite the drop in consumption. A tremendous amount of shelf space is devoted to apples in the produce section, often more than any other single produce item. Apples are differentiated by a barrage of strategies including local farm posters, organic certification, Red Tomato's Eco certification, Whole Foods Responsibly Grown ratings, and Stemilt's distinctive ladybug logo and kid-sized fruit. Every retailer is looking for ways to make its apple selection unique: varieties, brands, and new packaging all compete for space. Taylor's advice echoes the same refrain as others: get big, get niche, or get out.

AT A FARM STAND or farmers market, growers can sell most of their crop; small sizes and blemishes can be explained face to face. Wholesale buyers, however, won't accept anything that's not perfect. Fruit that doesn't meet the cosmetic and quality standards of the retail market can be sold for processing. It was once common in some regions to grow certain varieties specifically for processing. But these days, few commercial orchards grow only for the processing market. The costs of land, labor, and growing fruit don't leave room for profit at the low prices paid for processing apples.

Still, many Northeast apples, especially in New York, go straight to processing to become newly trendy hard cider, or apple slices for snacks and salads-to-go, or the apple juice and applesauce that parents feed their kids year-round. In 2005, McDonald's Corporation became the largest user of apples in the United States, purchasing over fifty-six million bushels.[9] All those pies and Happy Meals! Refrigerated juice blends like Naked, Odwalla, and Bolthouse Farms, sold everywhere from grocery coolers to convenience stores to airports, use apples as the base for millions of bottles of fresh blended juice. Big processors with familiar names such as Mott's, Musselman's, and Tree Top buy tons of apples from the growers in their regions. When the price for fresh apples drops too low, farmers try to trim their costs for packing by sending even more fruit to processing. But the price paid to growers for apples that go to processing is a fraction of that paid for fresh apples.

The revival of hard cider and craft cider production has also boosted the market for apple juice, spurring renewed interest in heirloom varieties and apples grown purposely for cider. Craft cider, like craft beer, is a point of entry for small artisan makers with a local following. It has been adopted just as quickly by the big guys: Boston Beer (Sam Adams) has Angry Orchard brand, and MillerCoors has rolled out Crispin and Smith & Forge. *Fruit Growers News* reported consumption of hard apple cider grew 89 percent in 2014.[10]

Although orchards across the country are gambling on planting special varieties to supply the cider market, the trend is new. It will take a few years to get good fruit, and no one really knows yet what varieties to plant. Cider apples are a forgiving crop in terms of cosmetics. But these are not the hard ciders of John Chapman's day, pressed from whatever seedling fruit was available and as likely to be turned into vinegar as celebrated at the table. These makers emulate calvados apple brandy, Basque cider decanted from huge wooden barrels, and Normandy *cidre* carefully developed over centuries from just the right blend of apples from just the right orchards.

The move to reintroduce heirloom and cider varieties is complicated by shortages of rootstock and graftwood. Many French and English cultivars are not available in the United States. There are plenty of recommended domestic varieties, but not much experience growing them. The eighty-some varieties considered good for quality hard cider don't grow well everywhere, and there are too many for nurseries to invest in expanding the supply of all of them. Some think it makes more sense to develop new varieties for American tastes rather than trying to duplicate European ciders.

Prices for the right cider-variety apples can be quite a bit higher than for juice apples in general. But again, these are trees, not cornstalks; changing apple varieties takes years, not months. Trends come and go faster and faster all the time. Investing in cider trees takes confidence that the taste for cider isn't going away soon. And this new market opportunity may already be outgrowing itself as a sustainable option for smaller growers. In the marketplace, the "get big, get niche, or get out" cycle has to start over whenever the niche gets big enough. When port disputes in Seattle left a bumper crop of western apples to rot in spring 2015, the market for apple juice concentrate was booming with the big-name hard cider brands. But their supply of concentrate didn't come from excess West Coast apples or from the also large eastern crop; it came mostly from China. Not only is Chinese apple juice concentrate cheaper and available year-round, but one New England cidery claims to require such huge volumes that there are not enough apples in the entire region to fill their need.

Apple growers in China began investing in large plantings of apple trees in the 1970s and have continued planting varieties like Fuji for the expanding Asian and Pacific Rim market. By the 1990s, China had become the top apple producer in the world and now grows over half the world's apples. The large crop also means plenty of apples for processing. Government-supported infrastructure now produces huge volumes of concentrate, and low prices make China tough competition for U.S. growers.

The share of U.S. apples sold for processing dropped from about 40 percent to about 20 percent in 2007, according to USDA.[11] Because prices for new varieties of fresh apples are rising while processing prices are flat, that might seem like a good thing. But those apples that used to go to processing have not shifted to the more profitable fresh market; they've gone unharvested. When prices for Chinese concentrate are so low, the U.S. market for seconds and culls disappears. It becomes cheaper to dump the oversupply than to add the expense of picking and transporting. It's another spectacle of our out-of-balance food system: apples going to waste in one part of the country while concentrate is shipped from around the world to supply cider makers in another.

It isn't only apple juice that's gone global. In 2015, Secretary of Agriculture Tom Vilsack announced a new trade deal to open the U.S. market to Chinese fresh apples and allow U.S. growers to export all varieties from all states to China. Red and Golden Delicious have been allowed into China for twenty years. About half of Washington's Red Delicious crop is currently exported, mostly to Mexico, Canada, and other Asia Pacific countries. China had not been a major export market, so the deal to allow more varieties was welcome. Washington growers, battered by port strikes, an anti-dumping lawsuit from their largest export customer, Mexico, and the pressure of ever-larger crops, crowed happily about the agreement. Growers in the Northeast and Michigan were feeling pressure from Washington with or without China, and eventually supported the deal too.[12]

Many in the industry think that China's fresh apples are not an immediate competitive threat and will still be mostly sold inside China because U.S. customers don't trust their quality as far as chemical residues and food safety are concerned. U.S. growers are already looking beyond China for markets to supply in other large developing economies, such as India and Indonesia. Some expect that the biggest new markets in ten to twenty years will be in Africa.

IN EARLY SUMMER, Michael Rozyne and I travel to Maine for a Red Tomato appointment with the corporate fruit and vegetable category managers at Hannaford supermarkets. We've been building a successful local sourcing program for some of their Massachusetts stores and have arranged to present the program to their corporate office in hopes of expanding to more stores and more items, including, we hope, apples. The person we'd worked with the previous year had been promoted and was now in charge of meat and seafood. The fruit category manager was a company veteran, but she had been in her new position for only five days; before that, she'd been in charge of bakery. This isn't unusual. The fastest way for talented buyers in most big grocery companies to advance is by moving to another category or to a bigger region or store.

The corporate offices of Hannaford handle sales calls the way most large conventional supermarket chains do. Salespeople dressed in logo-wear congregate in an outer waiting area with their sample cases and cell phones. A receptionist checks ID, records the time of arrival and who you are there to see, and hands over a visitor's badge. Sometimes there is an inner waiting room where the buyer can dispense with your sales pitch without even sitting down. More often, buyers come from somewhere on an upper floor and wave you inside to an office or conference room. Hannaford is friendlier and much less stuffy than most. Joe, our contact, rushes out with his hand extended and quickly ushers us up the stairs to a conference room, offering lunch from the company cafeteria and filling us in on the latest plans.

The new apple buyer listens carefully to our description of the Eco Apple program and the marketing support we've put together. She asks intelligent questions and is willing to consider bringing our fruit into a few stores. We move quickly to practical details, always a good sign that you've gotten past "yes" and on to "how."

The details are a good window into what makes local produce challenging even in the best of companies. Local apples fit perfectly with their marketing goal to sell more produce from the states where their stores are located. Eco Apple certification would appeal to their target shoppers, who want to know where their food comes from and how it is grown. But the stores we would serve are supplied by two different warehouse divisions. Not all the stores that would carry our apples are served by the same distribution center, and not every store served by either warehouse would carry our apples. The rest of the apples in the produce section are sold companywide, from all warehouses into all stores, with matching promotions, display signs, and ads in the company flyer.

We haven't even gotten to pricing yet, but already it is clear that as much as they like us and our apples, buying from us will require extra management and communication every step of the way. If we can narrow down the varieties and the number of farms, that would help. We could supply fruit from a dozen orchards with ten varieties among them, but we agreed to narrow the options to five varieties from the two largest orchards. That will limit variety in the stores and add pressure (and sales) for those orchards, but with hard work on everyone's part to make the season go smoothly, it just might work.

On the drive up, Michael and I had been talking over the latest industry news. Hannaford is a longtime Maine-based company, started as a fruit cart on the Portland waterfront and family owned until they were bought in 1999 by the Belgian company Delhaize. Delhaize had just announced plans to merge with giant Dutch company Royal Ahold, which already owns several major U.S. supermarket chains including Stop & Shop. The Hannaford buyers had heard the same news but deflected our curiosity, saying they didn't really know how it might affect them, at least in the short term. As Michael and I head back to the parking lot, enthusiastic about how well the meeting had gone and excited about having a new customer for apples, our talk turns again to the pending merger.

"It's already so complicated for them to manage a local program, or anything else for that matter, with six divisions and hundreds of stores," I worry. "It's hard to see how the merger will be good for anyone, shoppers, employees, farmers, or suppliers. It's more likely to mean fewer management jobs, fewer stores, higher prices, more complicated procedures."

I'm remembering our last sales call to the headquarters of another large globally owned retail chain a couple of years earlier. We had spent months cultivating an encouraging relationship with the regional warehouse and thought we had done what we could to pave the way for a trial program with a few stores. But we'd been told in no uncertain terms that the decision was not up to the regional guys, it had to be "approved by corporate." So we made a daylong drive to their office three states away, visiting a couple of farms on the way. Their waiting-pen is an outer lobby where buyers come via elevator to escort you into upstairs conference rooms as they maintain stern faces that can be seen through the glass walls by their coworkers in the cubicles outside. After an hour of grilling and combative questioning, we walked out knowing we would not be selling them local produce any time soon.

Now we wonder if the merger will push our current good-to-work-with account to become more like its counterparts. "Do you ever think we might be watching the last lumbering lurches of late-stage capitalism before it all crumbles?" I ask Michael, only half joking. Despite the surge in shoppers who want to buy local, it's getting harder and harder for any remaining local orchards to find a way in.

CHAPTER NINE

Working Apples

WORK ON APPLE ORCHARDS today is done by a multitude of hands: orchard owners and family members; year-round and seasonal employees; local residents, immigrants, and migrants who will soon move on; U.S. citizens, those without documents, and those on H-2A guest worker visas. All of these categories intersect in multiple ways. With differences of race, gender, economic class, language, country, and community of origin layered in, the picture of farm labor on orchards is complicated.

Visiting a pick-your-own farm gives a superficial feel for what it takes to harvest a crop. But strolling through an orchard on a cool, sunny fall day, darting from tree to tree as you spy an even better piece of fruit, and filling a bag or two to carry back to your car is as much like a professional apple harvest as opening the hood of your car and nodding your head is like building an engine, or sewing on a button is like making a shirt out of whole cloth.

ABOVE: Jamaican worker at harvest, Lyman Orchards, Middlefield, Connecticut. Photo by Diane Rast.

Orchard work isn't easy. Grafting, planting, pruning and staking trees, scouting for insects, spraying, managing a pack line, packing apples into boxes and bags, fixing equipment, filling out forms, taking orders, making deliveries, making sales calls, escorting pick-your-own visitors to the doughnut line; there's work to be done all year round. Trees dictate when physical labor is needed most. Seasonal crews pick and pack during autumn harvest; some stay the winter to prune and clean up the orchards. Packing crews start with harvest and may work into the following summer. Year-round employees manage the pack line and orchard, maintain equipment, handle marketing and paperwork. It's all demanding, requires skill and responsibility, and can be done better and faster by someone with experience.

Orchards can be good places to work for both owners and their employees, and many year-round and seasonal workers stay with the same orchard for years, even generations. Orchards can also harbor the same poor practices that plague farm and service work throughout the U.S. economy. Seasonal workers' experiences are especially variable, as I learned in talking with fruit workers in the Northwest.

THE ROAD FROM Pasco to Sunnyside, Washington, passes through a wide, dry basin surrounded by bare hills. On my visit in early December, the land is mostly brown and tumbleweed clings to the fences. Angelica Ruiz-Rodriguez, a young woman from Pasco who's agreed to translate for me, is animated and talkative as we drive. She once picked apples for a few weeks herself. She liked working outside, especially when the boss let someone bring a radio or player for music—Mexican, sometimes Cuban—while they picked.

In Sunnyside, a low, dusty town with wide streets and sparse shade, we pull up to the public library and go inside to an inviting room of bookshelves, computer stations, and comfortable chairs. The local organizer for United Farm Workers (UFW) has arranged for me to meet with Jose Onate, a longtime resident who makes his living doing seasonal farmwork. Jose arrives soon after we do. He shakes hands but doesn't smile.

Jose came to the United States from Mexico when he was fourteen. A U.S. citizen, he's lived in Sunnyside for twenty years. He's forty-eight, stocky, and handsome, but careworn. During harvesttime, he is up early in the dark, driving to farms all over southwest Washington to find work. When he goes back to places he's worked before, they are glad to have him, but when I ask if he gets paid more for his experience, he laughs. "No, the pay is low no matter who you are. It is a little bit higher, around $11–$12 an hour, at the smaller farms, even though they may not give as many hours. The bigger places pay only minimum wage. It's much better —*mucho mejor*—on the small places."

The work starts before dawn, seven days a week during harvest. He's picked apples, pears, cherries, cut onions, dug potatoes, pruned trees, and worked on pack lines. Sometimes he works on contract, so much per bin, and sometimes by the hour. In a full day, he can pick twelve or thirteen of the big wooden bins that take fifteen bags to fill. Some apples, like Pink Lady®, are slower; they pick with "scissors" and fill only four or five bins a day. But consumers pay extra for those tender varieties, so the owners want every one perfect.

Farmwork has allowed Jose to raise a family and own a home, but it has cost him more than his labor. Some of what he's experienced is unfair, dangerous, and illegal—wages stolen, safety issues ignored, medical care refused. Some of it is crude racism, disrespect, and unkindness. Often it all goes together.

One boss stole blatantly from the workers; if a worker picked fifteen bins, the supervisor would take credit for five of them. Some companies say they pay time and a half for overtime, then don't pay for even the regular hours. At one company, Jose kept track of his hours in a notebook and his paychecks never matched. One supervisor pointed a gun at him when he showed how much he had actually worked, threatening, "Don't come around here complaining."

The conditions echo familiar stories of the worst kind of worker abuse: portable bathrooms never cleaned, hot dirty "drinking" water full of sludge, and even worms in watercoolers filled only once a week for a hundred people to use. Jose wore pants with big pockets so he could carry his own bottles of water. He's been fired for complaining, one supervisor claiming, "You say there is no water, but here's a video of you washing your hands."

Jose sees it as prejudice, pure and simple. "Wherever you go, you lose a lot of money. It's a lot of suffering. You barely have enough to keep your family fed and clothed." He has never qualified for government programs such as food stamps because they say he makes too much money, and he's proud of getting by without it. "*Duro*," he says again. It's hard.

Jose fell from a ladder last July and hurt his left shoulder. He's filled out the paperwork, but so far nobody has paid for his medical bills or lost wages. All workers in Washington have money deducted from their paychecks for a state program that provides coverage if they are injured. But the system doesn't always work the way it is supposed to. "Supervisors say you fall on purpose, and you don't get paid, not even for the medical.

"They say you have to wear goggles and you can't eat the apples because of the spray, but they don't give you the right equipment for protection. They give you training, but they don't keep up with it. Some companies don't meet the requirements." He laughs again without humor and shrugs.

Angelica tells him about listening to music while picking fruit and he shakes his head vigorously. Years ago, when he was working long days for only $3.36 an hour, he carried a little radio. The owner asked to look at his radio, then smashed it to bits. No more music. He sees younger people with their phones in their pockets listening to music; that's how they get fired. Some owners forbid people talking with each other or even singing to themselves. So everybody just stays quiet. "Why not put a piece of tape across my mouth?" he says, raising his eyebrows for emphasis.

Still, when I ask if he likes to eat apples in spite of all that, he says enthusiastically, "*Sí!* Sometimes you are working so fast, even one bite of a juicy apple is really good. But when a supervisor comes you have to drop it because they don't want you to stop and eat." Some companies give workers gum to chew so they won't eat. One owner would bring a whole box of gum to the orchard and give every worker just one piece. Jose shakes his head incredulously. "We picked thousands of bins for her, and she wouldn't even give us a soda. Not even water."

Picking fruit would be good work, Jose says, if he were paid better and treated better. He'd be even happier if they paid a bonus for long hours and said, "You're doing a good job" now and then. He tells me he's poor but happy with his life, and how proud he is of his children and grand-children. As we stand up to leave, he grins. "Next time, tell Martin [the UFW organizer who introduced us] to have us meet at my house, not at the library." He promises a meal, and describes the food he'll serve—turkey, chicken, chicharrónes, tamales—until Angelica and I both pro-test, "Enough!" This time the laughter is genuine.

FARMS AND FARM LABOR have a long and tumultuous history fraught with contradictions. Nearly every family that settled in the eastern United States in the 1700s was involved in farming. Relatives, children, and neighbors helped early farm families keep self-sufficient homestead orchards. Slaves and sharecroppers tended large plantation orchards from colonial days. By the start of the Civil War in 1861, there were 384,884 farms keeping slaves in the sixteen states and three territories where slavery was legally allowed. Most were smaller farms with fewer than twenty enslaved workers. There were 3,953,742 men, women, and children in bondage doing the work of agriculture that year.[1]

By 1850, fewer and fewer families were working in agriculture, and many farmers were tenants or laborers without land of their own.[2] The Industrial Revolution and the coming of railroads shifted farmwork further toward commercial production, and as farming required more seasonal labor it became harder for local residents to rely on year-round farmwork for income. Migrant laborers following seasonal crops filled in the gaps. The economic distance between landowners and workers increased.

In the Hudson Valley, Italians and other immigrants arrived steadily through the end of World War I. Many stayed, bought farms of their own, or moved on to other jobs. From World War II until the 1970s, African Americans from the South and Puerto Ricans, Haitians, and Caribbean islanders began filling most seasonal jobs in eastern orchards, working their way north after picking cane, tobacco, and other crops.

On the West Coast, Chinese workers initially brought in to work on the railroads began picking fruit in the 1870s, followed by Japanese and Filipino immigrants in the 1900s. Workers from Mexico came north in growing numbers during the 1920s and 1940s through the Bracero program, sponsored by the U.S. and Mexican governments, which brought temporary workers into the country under often abusive conditions. Migrants of all ethnicities from Arkansas and Oklahoma trekked west to escape the Dust Bowl in the 1930s. In the early days of California's fruit industry, boosters promising endless profits crowed without shame or irony: "The fact that Chinamen can be had for the disagreeable parts of the work makes fruit growing more profitable and easier to carry on than if such were not the case."[3] Over many generations these workers from diverse backgrounds, sometimes pitted against each other by owners, unions, and policy makers, have continued to make fruit growing possible in the United States.

There are employers in every industry, including agriculture, willing to exploit the vulnerability of their workers for their own gain. But most farms and orchards, like most small businesses, do their best to follow laws and regulations, collect the required documents, pay employment taxes and wages, and submit to labor audits. Growers privately acknowledge that some of the documentation they've been given is likely false, but they are not interested in making trouble for or losing good employees. All along the Canadian border, from Maine to Washington, apple growers and their employees worry about Immigration and Customs Enforcement (ICE) raids that upend long-standing relationships. The dysfunctional system currently in place blurs the line between what is legal and what is humane.

Unauthorized immigrants and their families face constant vulnerabilities of the most intimate kind. They are caught in an underground economy that exists not just in agriculture but also in low-wage jobs throughout the United States, in meatpacking, egg processing, restaurants, and hotels. Although they pay taxes, raise families, and spend money in local communities, they are easy to forget, often talked about as abstract political footballs. The fear of deportation that uproots lives and separates families is only one small part of a constant grinding reality of limitations and multiple identities that ripple out well beyond their own families.

Most immigrants who come into the United States without authorization do so for economic reasons, when they are unable to work or support families in their home countries, and because gaining legal work status can often take years of waiting and denials. Crossing the border without papers is dangerous and difficult. So, although farmwork is mostly seasonal, once here it is safer for immigrants to stay year-round. Because they may not find other work once harvest and packing are done, many unauthorized workers live far below the poverty line even when they're paid above minimum wage, and they usually earn no overtime or sick pay. For those living in labor camps or housing provided by employers, it's risky to complain or make demands about wages, hours, or conditions. Finding other housing, transportation, or pursing education or other work are near impossibilities.

Many immigrants provide crucial money for food, shelter, school, and medical care to extended family back home. They're often separated for many years, unable to return home to tend sick parents or even go to funerals. While their kids attend school, make friends, and live very American lives, the threat of deportation keeps parents isolated. The lack of a driver's license (and too often the likelihood of being pulled over for "driving while brown") makes it risky to go anywhere, even for essentials such as groceries and medical care. Even those with authorization or citizenship have friends and family without. Homesickness, mistrust, and anxiety are an unrelenting undercurrent even for those with otherwise full and successful lives.

Red Tomato has talked with growers for years about how to promote what they believe are good working conditions and fair pay on their farms without calling so much attention to the farms that it brings unwanted risk to employees. At dinner after one such discussion, a conservative grower from a wholesale orchard sat down beside me, leaning in so he could speak quietly. He told me about attending a wedding celebration for the daughter of a man who had worked for him for nearly twenty years. After hearing other guests repeatedly call his host by an unfamiliar name, the grower was stunned to realize his friend was working under another name and living at constant risk.

A second grower came around the table a few minutes later to sit on my other side. Although she is among the most politically liberal and outspoken members of our network, she too leaned in to speak quietly. Her orchard is highly visible at area farmers markets. A local Mexican American family has worked for her for many years. The husband is the farm manager, his wife runs the busy kitchen and wholesale baking operation, and their daughter, who grew up on the farm alongside the farmer's children, is the office manager and bookkeeper. A few years ago, hers was one of several farms in the area visited by ICE. Scouring files and upending the busy office routine for several days turned up a social security number on forms for a man who had worked for her several years earlier that didn't match up in ICE's database. Despite thinking they had followed all the rules, the farm was fined tens of thousands of dollars. Now the farmer worries that her employees and their community are even more visible and at even greater risk.

If I hadn't worked closely with both of these growers, I might have suspected them of couching concerns for themselves as false concern for their employees. But both of them ended their stories with the same firm and fervent words: "You need to understand something about the labor issue. You don't want to shine a light on it, and it's not for the reasons you think." It's not an issue they can afford to air publicly, but they wish their customers understood that farmers and workers are both caught in a bad system.

R. Karina Gallardo, economist at Washington State University, points out that for U.S. agriculture as a whole, labor represents around 17 percent of the variable costs for producers; for tree fruit growers, it is a whopping 48 percent. The demand for labor to produce apples in the United States is projected to grow 1.7 percent each year for the next twenty years; over the same period, the supply of available U.S. farm labor is projected to drop by 1 to 1.5 percent per year.[4] That is, for every 100 farmworkers today, agriculture will need 138 in 2036. Yet the labor supply is projected to be short by 25 farmworkers for every 100 over that time. It's not hard to see why having reliable workers to pick fruit is a huge issue for apple growers.

John Lyman has seen many changes in Connecticut's farm workforce over the years. There was a strong pool of local labor available for New England apple growers up until the 1960s, as well as a migrant labor force, mostly Puerto Rican, that worked the South's tobacco fields and moved north. By the mid-'60s, most of those workers had moved into cities and out of agriculture.

"Agriculture is a pretty tough job, and there was a generational shift in the work ethic too," John observes, surmising that the younger generation preferred indoor work with regular hours. Even high school kids who used to work summers are scarce. Lyman is a major employer for first-time jobs, but not usually picking fruit. "We get a lot of good high school kids as cashiers and other retail jobs. To watch their work ethic, focus, dedication, it's really inspiring," says John. But most of the harvest takes place in autumn, after kids are back in school.

Lyman Orchards' overall employment has grown to more than two hundred during the busy season and fifty year-round. They hire the same number of seasonal apple pickers, around twenty, as they did twenty years ago. Those workers are a small percentage of their total employees, but they fill jobs that locals can't or won't do. Apple growers everywhere find few local applicants interested in farmwork. Every farmer has a story about a local who shows up at the farm, works half a day, and never comes back. Fears about immigrants and guest workers taking away local jobs misses the big picture of how many other jobs in the pack house and retail store depend on seasonal workers who pick the fruit, John points out.

As local workers became harder to find, the challenge of harvesting a crop and having experienced workers at the right time has become a serious issue for fruit growers across the country. Over the last twenty years, John has seen a new infusion of Hispanic workers in the region, many undocumented. Immigration reform would significantly improve the situation for everyone, but no one in agriculture is optimistic about that happening anytime soon.

WHILE IMMIGRATION REFORM has foundered in a partisan, polarized political environment and crossing the U.S. border without documentation has become riskier and more dangerous, the federal H-2A guest worker program operated by the Department of Labor offers legal employment for workers from outside the country and allows growers to fill crucial seasonal jobs with experienced employees. Apple growers in the Northeast have relied extensively on guest workers from Jamaica to help with picking and other orchard work. As local workers get harder to find and the risk of hiring from outside the United States grows, apple growers in other parts of the country also increasingly look to H-2A for seasonal workers.

The H-2A program began during World War II, aimed at bringing workers from Puerto Rico and the West Indies to cut sugarcane in Florida and the Southeast. Cutting cane is dangerous, arduous work, and conditions in southern cane fields and labor camps were brutal. The H-2A program has been called a form of slavery by some human rights and farmworker advocates, especially in some regions and for some types of farms, and because workers in the program are not free to change jobs or move from farm to farm once they are in the United States. Many of the worst abuses of the program can be traced back to the practices of the early sugar barons, and they still exist in some places—wretched housing, stolen pay, unscrupulous overseers, and high risk of injury.

But for many workers from outside the United States, and the farms that employ them, H-2A is currently one of the safest, most reliable legal sources of jobs in agriculture. After the cane was cut, some workers moved north to pick fruit, making Northeast apple orchards among the other early users of the program. Working conditions, housing, and fair treatment were better in the orchards. Many Jamaican H-2A workers return to the same orchards year after year and have become important contributors to the success and stability of those farms.

The program offers workers guaranteed wages, travel, and housing and a safe, legal way to return home at the end of the season. They can make enough in a few months to pay for kids' schooling, to improve housing, and to buy appliances and clothing in the United States at more affordable prices for families back home. Farmers provide training and can request the same skilled and experienced workers, and sometimes their sons, nephews, and cousins, to return year after year.

However, it's a complicated program and not without problems for both workers and employers. U.S. farmers must apply months in advance for workers to fill specific jobs at specific times, and no changes in job duties can be made once the jobs are approved. They must advertise for and hire any available U.S. workers, even those without experience or skill, before being allowed to bring in H-2A crews, even those that are skilled and experienced. Employers must provide housing and transportation to and from the home country. Wage rates are set annually based on a formula called Adverse Effect Wage Rate (AEWR), which varies by county but is usually well above minimum wage. The same rate must be paid to any domestic employee doing similar jobs.

People seeking H-2A work apply for permits through agencies in their home countries. Once in the United States, workers are prohibited from moving to other jobs or farms. Orchard workers are away from their families for months, living in shared housing with a group of others they may or may not know from back home. They cook together and sometimes sleep in bunk beds ten or more to a room. Off work, their time is their own, but they are dependent on the farmer who hires them for transportation. There is reportedly corruption among the labor brokers who work the system in some countries.

And there are profound differences in economic conditions between the home communities and the United States, which both motivates and complicates the process for everyone involved. Men and women from Jamaica, Mexico, Thailand, and elsewhere come here to work, women more commonly in processing, men in farming. H-2A workers are now a significant labor pool for many parts of U.S. agriculture, especially in labor-intensive fruits and vegetables, where the work can't be delayed when it's time to harvest.

Geoffrey L. has been coming to the United States under the H-2A program since 1992, working in sugarcane the first year, then tobacco for three years. Aside from one year on a flower farm, which he says with a smile was the best, he prefers orchard work. For the last twenty years he's picked apples at the same family-owned orchard in Connecticut, since the owner who is now his boss was a young boy. From April to December each year, family members take care of his cattle and vegetables on his own farm in central Jamaica so he can come here to work. Several of the other crewmembers live near each other back home, and many of them have worked together for many years. "I used to come in February to help with packing," he tells me during a break in picking. He made more money working those extra months, "but it was too long to be away." I tell him that I often work away from home for a week or two at a time and find even that can be hard. "You do what you gotta do," he says mildly.

Pete Ten Eyck at Indian Ladder Farms in upstate New York hires an H-2A crew from Jamaica, many of whom have worked for him for decades. Minimum wage in New York was raised to $9 an hour in 2016. Indian Ladder paid H-2A workers and any local worker doing a similar job the Albany-area AEWR rate of $11.76. For the H-2A crew, transportation to and from the United States, housing, and various fees add another $3 per hour.[5] Pete can sometimes find local help for less, but they are never as reliable or as experienced. He's distressed by the misperceptions about farm labor that persist in the New York legislature and among mostly urban consumers.

"It's hard for people whose only experience is a job with regular hours and a ten-minute commute to understand what seasonal farm jobs are like," Pete explains. During harvest, for example, long hours and extra days are not always considered a hardship. The Jamaican men who work for him are here to work and earn as much as they can. They're not interested in being idle around the farmyard when they could be speeding along the harvest until they can return home. Every fall, when groups of local schoolchildren visit the farm, Pete makes sure that one of the stops on their tour is a session with a longtime Jamaican crew member who talks about picking apples and why he is here so far from home. Pete hopes the kids leave with a bit more understanding and appreciation of the dignity of the men and their work.

Pete spends a lot of time in meetings with state officials and labor advocates, trying to carve out a sensible approach to farm labor issues. At the Farm Aid concert in nearby Saratoga Springs a few years ago, he sat quietly with a group of farm labor and fair trade activists discussing proposed state legislation on overtime hours for farmworkers. At the end of the meeting, when someone asked for his thoughts, he said bluntly that he doesn't want to be given a pass or to treat his employees unfairly, but he struggles to figure out how he's expected to hire unreliable locals over his experienced H-2A crew, pay time and a half for overtime during harvest, and yet sell his apples and doughnuts at a price that attracts consumers and supports his family. "It's not an issue of sustainable agriculture; it's a question of sustainable cuisine," he concluded fiercely. "I don't like saying this, but the reality is, in our current food system I can't make enough to pay either myself or my employees what they deserve."

In Washington State, growers are just beginning to use H-2A more extensively. The Washington Apple Commission estimates thirty-five thousand to forty thousand pickers are employed statewide during peak apple harvest. In 2004, fewer than five hundred were H-2A workers; by 2014, that had grown to over nine thousand, most from Mexico and Central America.[6]

The workforce for the Stennes family orchard near Chelan is a mixture of local and migrant workers. "A lot of them live here, some are from Northern California and work their way up through farms in Oregon and Washington. There's a big population of full-time year-round people. So it's a mix of everything," says Kevin Stennes. "You just hope you can get enough people to pick the crops."

The Stenneses started with twenty H-2A employees in 2013 and the next year doubled that number to half of their harvest workforce. They paid an estimated $3 to $4 over minimum wage before housing and transportation were figured in, and their year-round workers also got a bump in their usual pay because of the requirement to match the H-2A wage levels. "It's definitely not perfect," says Kevin. "But the labor's there when you need it. Our payroll jumped in a huge way by joining the program. But we also didn't have the stress every morning of hoping we get some crops picked that day. So it's a balancing act."

The Stenneses, Lymans, and others have turned to local growers associations like the New England Apple Council (NEAC) and Washington Farm Labor Association (WAFLA) to help navigate H-2A paperwork, regulations, and legal challenges over their right to bring in guest workers, in spite of having to advertise repeatedly for local workers. Kevin says, "WAFLA has a full-time staff just doing those things; if we had to use it as a grower on our own, with the border and Department of Labor, it would be way too daunting. We wouldn't be able to do it."

John Lyman, who's had an H-2A crew from Jamaica on his farm since the late '60s, thinks harsh rhetoric and pressure to tighten borders and persecute owners who hire undocumented labor will push more growers to rely on H-2A. He worries that an already inefficient, bureaucratic system will bog down further, slowing the process of getting workers when they are needed. If guest workers are going to be agriculture's way to address hiring needs legally, John wants the program to be streamlined to handle a much larger group. When the fruit is ripening on the trees, the timing and reliability of people to pick it is crucial. Uncertainty about the future of H-2A adds to an already volatile, emotional situation.

John usually discusses farm labor issues in his typical steady, reasoned manner, in words he's used many times before at meetings, with reporters, and with curious visitors like me. But talking about his own employees, his voice becomes uncharacteristically emotional. "Those relationships that grow over the years are pretty powerful," he says after a pause. He goes on to say that in the midst of the loud arguments about getting all the "undocumenteds" out and sealing the border, we need to give other voices enough room, give guys confidence to speak out. "It has to change," he says adamantly. "Not because most people have thought a lot about it; they haven't had to. When they understand the issue more, they have a different position. It's not just agriculture—there is a much larger impact. It's part of your community."

MOST APPLES ARE PICKED by workers who have climbed a ladder, a heavy canvas bag strapped across their chest. They reach, twist, gently but quickly pull each apple before setting—not dropping—it into the bag, already reaching for the next piece of fruit with the other hand.

Once the bag is full, the picker climbs down and walks a few yards to a large wooden or plastic bin between the rows of trees. She or he rests the bag inside the edge of the bin and releases a clasp, opening the bottom of the bag so the apples roll gently onto the pile. It takes many trips up and down the ladder to fill each bin.[7]

Narrow or pointed at the top and wide at the bottom, orchard ladders are designed to fit up into the branches while staying secure at the base. Ladders are moved by hand from tree to tree. Aluminum is lighter, but the old wooden ones are more beautiful, polished smooth by hands and boots and years of rubbing against tree limbs. They are ladders, nonetheless: spare, narrow, open, sometimes slippery. Most orchard injuries involve ladders.

The Pacific Northwest Agricultural Safety and Health Center (PNASH) training video on ladder safety reports, in Spanish and English, that there are two hundred injuries a year in Washington due to accidents with ladders; they represent 36 percent of all injury claims in the tree fruit industry.[8] Falling twelve or more feet to the ground with a heavy bag of apples tied around your body can result in a broken neck or back, head injury, years of chronic pain, or total loss of ability to work. Average time out of work after a fall is a hundred and fifty days.

Accidents happen for dozens of reasons: the worker is standing on the top steps, the ladder is not in good repair, the ground is wet or icy, the worker leans too far to one side. Experienced workers who tend to get overconfident actually have a higher accident rate than novices. But every worker on the video describes their fall with the same words: "I was reaching for that last piece of fruit. They don't want you to leave any apples behind."

I heard firsthand about the danger of picking from ladders at a United Farm Workers (UFW) training meeting a few blocks from the library in Sunnyside, where I met with Jose Onate. UFW and other labor organizations have a long history here in the valley, organizing grape pickers in the '70s, and more recently workers in the dairy industry. I spot the iconic red-and-black UFW flag taped to the stair rail of a single-story church a few blocks from downtown. Martin, the UFW organizer, and Angelica, my translator, are there along with a dozen other men and women listening intently to a presentation on legal rights for workers injured on the job.

Rosa Torres stays after the meeting to tell me her story. She picked fruit for twenty years, and for most of those years it was good work. Then, in 2012, she fell from a ladder while carrying a full bag of apples. There was snow on the grass, and she slid downhill in the mud and rocks, trying to grab on to something to stop herself until the side of her legs slammed into a tree. The seventy-five-pound bag of apples landed on her stomach. She was working alone, and it took an hour before someone came, even though she yelled and yelled for help. At first she couldn't move and was afraid she wouldn't be able to walk again. As she lay there, she asked God to allow her to move so she could keep taking care of her children.

Rosa hasn't worked since the accident. She has seven kids, five still at home. Her husband is injured as well, and disabled. His small Social Security payment is their only income. Nearly three years after the fall, her knees and back cause constant pain and limit her movements. Even the touch of clothes and blankets hurts. She needs stomach surgery. She's getting some medical coverage from the Washington Department of Health and Social Services, and a month ago they paid some of the doctors' bills, but she's adamant that the employer, not the state, should be held responsible. She has a letter approving surgery for her knees, scheduled for next week, but she still isn't sure the bill will be covered.

Rosa has worked for a half-dozen fruit companies over the past twenty years; none treated her as badly as the company she was working for at the time of the accident. She was hurt once before at another orchard, and people there ran to help her. The owner made her go to the hospital even though she didn't think she was injured, and the company gave her a check right away for her medical expenses. To this day, the owner calls to ask how she is doing. The company where she was recently injured hasn't called once. As she leaves to pick up her daughter, Rosa implores me to tell her story—she's not sure she will ever be compensated for her injuries, but she hopes she can make a difference for other people.

Back in the meeting room, the training session has ended and coffee and pizza are set out courtesy of UFW. Three women, Maria, Marta, and Yolanda, linger at the table, Yolanda balancing her son, Pedro, on her lap. He's slept through the meeting and now he's bubbly and cheerful, sporting a UFW pin on the strap of his jumper. "It's a good thing you're writing about the apple industry," Marta says pointedly.

They've all picked apples. Their stories are much like Jose's and Rosa's. Most owners pay cheaply, and if you bruise apples they fire you. Marta once fell from a tall ladder, and she knew another girl who fell and died a few months later. Yolanda boasts that she picked fruit last year when she was pregnant, moving the bag around when the baby would kick, because she wanted to work.

I ask if the baby likes apples, and they all laugh. Yolanda and Angelica have an animated discussion in Spanish about their favorite music and discover Angelica's favorite band is from the same village in Michoacán as Yolanda's family. Amid the laughter, I'm struck by all the barriers these women face so routinely. There is a long way to go, in agriculture and in general, to address the physical, economic, and political challenges they experience.

IT'S IMPOSSIBLE to separate the issues surrounding treatment of agricultural workers from the greater intersection of race, economics, and immigration politics in the United States. A few years ago, the vice president of United Farm Workers met with some of the farmers in the Red Tomato network to exchange perspectives on farm labor issues. In spite of the historic mistrust between labor unions and farm owners, several of the growers welcomed him to visit their farms. An unusually frank and intense discussion went long into the evening. The sobering consensus was that until there is progress on immigration reform, it is going to be very difficult to shift the dynamic that exists for farmworkers, in apple orchards and anywhere else.

As I write this during the summer of 2016, hopes for immigration reform have faded despite broad support from the political left and right among agribusinesses, farmers, and farmworkers. A 2014 study commissioned by the American Farm Bureau Federation, generally considered a somewhat conservative organization representing U.S. agriculture, concluded that immigration policies focused on deportation and border closings would result in significant losses in production and revenue for most of U.S. agriculture and could lead to a 5 to 6 percent increase in food prices for consumers. The hardest hit sectors will be fruit, vegetables, meat, and dairy: the report estimates fruit production could drop by as much as 61 percent.[9]

Meanwhile, coverage of farm labor abuse in Mexico by the *Los Angeles Times* and others, campaigns in Florida tomato fields led by the Coalition of Immokalee Workers, and widespread movements for higher minimum wages and better treatment of food and service workers have brought conditions for farmworkers, especially immigrants, to the forefront of public awareness.

Publicly, farm owners—vulnerable to labor shortages, entangled in regulations, and worried about crop losses—defend their industry and warn that without large numbers of immigrant workers, their ability to produce food in the United States is in danger. Farm labor advocates, hoping to motivate consumers, politicians, and donors to support the important services and advocacy they provide, focus their public campaigns on the worst situations, calling upon scandal and outrage to make their case.

In private, I've spoken with both worker advocates and growers who readily acknowledge there are problems immigration reform won't fix. One large grower admitted with disgust that if all agricultural employers would obey the laws that already exist, conditions for workers would improve significantly. A longtime legal advocate for farmworker rights conceded wearily that it took a long time for bad practices to take root and fester, and it is going to take time to find solutions.

Amid the highly charged, polarized public debate, leaders from farmworker advocacy groups such as United Farm Workers, Farmworker Justice, Farm Labor Organizing Committee (FLOC), and Oxfam America have met quietly over the past few years with some of the most thoughtful progressive leaders from both large-scale and small-farm agriculture. Many have begun to turn attention to what can be done to improve working conditions and sustain long-term livelihoods in agriculture, to fill jobs and reduce risk for farmers, and to call attention to positive changes as well as to problems in farmwork.

A renewed focus on common goals for workforce development and farm sustainability is emerging as a result. One such effort, Equitable Food Initiative (EFI), is developing culturally appropriate training in Spanish and several other languages to provide communication skills, lean-management philosophy, and worker engagement in problem solving in addition to the food safety and pesticide safety training many farms already provide. Washington Farm Labor Association offers a range of worker training programs as well as human resources training for owners. The Agricultural Justice Project works to bring awareness and promote fair labor practices on small organic farms. Stemilt Growers provides free health clinics for all employees across their extensive large-scale operation. The Domestic Fair Trade Association has developed a set of criteria to promote fair practices for both farmers and workers. Farm labor advocates are partnering with businesses to promote these practices to consumers.

Farm owners and their employees often work side by side, especially on farms with only a few employees. They keep the same long hours, doing hard physical labor, fixing equipment, dealing with weather, and maintaining crop quality as it goes to market. These become personal as well as business relationships, especially when workers, and sometimes their families, live on the farm year-round or return year after year.

Many orchard owners are proud of what they do to make their farms good places to work. They offer fresh produce and help with doctors' appointments, applications for green cards, and getting children into schools. They provide space for soccer fields and make sure the housing, even if it accommodates many guys living together, is clean, comfortable, has some privacy, and offers a good place for cooking. At the end of harvest in November, many farms in Red Tomato's network host a big party before the crew returns home. The Jamaicans cook a huge meal, and there is music and dancing and mutual celebration of another season of hard work and a good harvest.

It's unrealistic to think that these relationships will be completely open and equal. Still, I find it puzzling that farmers aren't viewed in the same way other employers offering the same kinds of benefits might be. Consumers and activists, attuned to barriers that prevent workers from organizing or speaking up, sometimes see these gestures as paternalistic: cynical, manipulative, a way of motivating and controlling workers. They fear owners are reinforcing a debt the workers can't repay or are making workers afraid to criticize a kind boss because they don't want to be seen as ungrateful or to be punished by losing favors or a chance to return next year. Yet sports fields, support for education, and shared meals are considered socially responsible business practices at places like Google, Patagonia, or the artisan bakery down the road.

Agricultural work is unique in some ways, driven as it is by weather and ripening crops that require long days and little time off, but it is also like low-wage work everywhere. Many of the things that make farmworkers' lives difficult are beyond the scope of individual farms: immigration policies, economics at home or in a home country, distance from families, loneliness and depression, racism, both specific and systemic. A farmer who treats workers well and with dignity can make a difference. But race, poverty, and legal status all feed into a power dynamic that permeates relationships, even in the best of situations.

FARM OWNERS DON'T usually count their overtime hours or sick leave or days off; they are compensated by whatever profit is left at the end of the season. Still, farm owners have something their employees often do not: land. Taxes and encroaching urban development can make that land harder and harder to hold on to, but the land—and the trees planted on it—are the farm owner's savings account, at least as long as he or she keeps farming. Farmers in the United States, no matter how much they struggle, generally have access to clean water, public schools, paved roads, and an array of public services and legal protections. The majority are white and enjoy the daily privileges that brings. At the same time, growers who pay their workers $10, $11, or $15 an hour are competing against growers in other countries paying a fraction of that and driving produce prices in the supermarket down.

A few years ago, Red Tomato helped organize a speaking tour called "Voices of Fair Trade." Three Hispanic banana farmers from Ecuador, an African American pecan grower from Georgia, a black African coffee farmer from Ethiopia, and several white apple growers from New England combined voices to share the challenges of getting fair prices for their work and goods. John Lyman was one of the growers who spoke, and the whole group came to his Connecticut orchard for a visit.

As we stood on a ridge looking out over the Lyman farmscape, all the differences of race, class, nationality, and family history came into sharp focus. Used to thinking of John and the other family farmers I'd worked with as the ones needing support, I realized how hard it might be for our visitors from outside the United States to see them as peers sharing the same challenges. Surrounded by the rolling orchard with the graceful farmstead beyond, we followed the angle of John's arm as he pointed downhill to the bunkhouses where his Jamaican crew was housed. Everyone was quiet. John didn't offer to take us any closer, whether out of deference for the privacy of the workers living there, or hesitation at what we would see, or because there wasn't time; I still don't know.

For the rest of the week, John and the others spoke at churches and colleges in Boston, in Manhattan and Yonkers, in Connecticut and New Jersey. They were well spoken, respectful, and not defensive about their positions as farm owners. They were also blunt about the challenges of making a living and paying decent wages when the taxes on their land, unreliable weather, and prices beyond their control could drop them below breakeven in the space of a few hours. One apple grower told of scrambling to provide health insurance for his workers while unable to afford it for himself and his family. Others, like John, spoke of how farming has allowed them to provide a good life for themselves and their families, and why they don't take that for granted. Diane, the pecan grower, recounted discrimination faced by the African American women in her co-op. Banana farmers shared their concerns as employers on their own farms. They all listened with humility to each other. Common ground and vast difference co-existed in a microcosm of how the food we eat is grown.

Farm labor is one of the most challenging, personal, and divisive aspects of farm survival, and the hardest to portray clearly and honestly. I helped petition for the UFW grape and lettuce boycotts in the '70s and '80s. I've participated in many meetings about labor issues within the good food movement. It is rare, although getting less so, to sit in meetings with food and labor activists and find among them real depth of understanding of the profound tensions and dilemmas facing family farmers. I've also listened to farmers talk privately about their concerns, frustration, and commitments, with compassion and a sense of powerlessness and betrayal at the way they are perceived. In public, farmers and workers are often portrayed as antagonists—boss and employee, white and of color, citizen and immigrant, owner and tenant. In reality, there are many tangled intersections and a mutual desire for change.

Near the end of my conversation with Jose Onate, the man I met in Sunnyside, we talked about the then-recent shooting of Michael Brown in Ferguson, Missouri, and other shootings in the news, including a young boy who had been shot and killed on the street in Sunnyside just a few weeks earlier. *It's not right*, one of us lamented with each recounted story. For Jose and Angelica, these are more than news stories; their communities are where these shootings happen, often, and the vulnerability of their children and friends isn't speculative, it's real. It is tempting to think of these issues as separate from how food is grown. One of the lessons of apples is that we don't have the luxury of thinking that way. Racism and immigration reform are profoundly and inextricably part of what we need to grapple with if we want to have fair food, sustainable farms, and locally grown fruit. It's another aspect of apples in which finding the intersection of common ground and common good is the only way forward.

CHAPTER TEN

Pests and Public Science

THE USE OF CHEMICALS to manage insects, fungi, disease, and crop quality in fruit isn't a modern phenomenon, or even a twentieth-century one. While it has intensified in the past one hundred years, the turn toward chemistry dates back to the mid-1800s when U.S. fruit production began to shift from a mostly backyard endeavor to a commercial one and a whole array of poisons, some mild and some incredibly toxic, began to be deployed to protect apples.

Sprays recommended in horticulture manuals of the early nineteenth century were an earthy collection of materials: copper sulfate; sulfur and lime sulfur; miscible oils made from petroleum; "whale oil" soap made from fish oil; kerosene and soap emulsion for aphids; and tobacco extracts for sucking insects, chewing insects, and fungi all in one. Along with the hard stuff, growers used whatever else was available that might slow down voracious bugs: vinegar, soap, clay, lye, salt, urine, alcohol, turpentine, and an extensive arsenal of decoctions made from every

ABOVE: Spraying the old way, Lyman Orchards, Middlefield, Connecticut. Photo by Lyman Orchards.

kind of plant including herbs, onion, and cayenne pepper. Some treat-ments, such as oil, soap, and sulfur, are so effective they're still in use, but many pests and diseases remained unchecked, causing consider-able damage as new crops were introduced region by region across the country.

As early as 1820, sulfur compounds were used against mildew on fruit crops such as peaches and grapes, but the biggest shift toward harsh poisons began in the United States around the time of the Civil War. As with planting systems, and apples themselves, many of them were first adopted in European orchards before being brought to the United States. In Europe, fruit growers experimenting with a variety of chemi-cals to battle fungi in vineyards and orchards eventually found success with a combination of copper and sulfur known as Bordeaux mixture, still used today. Hundreds of similar combinations and formulations were tried and used over the next decades.

Around 1860, U.S. farmers and researchers followed the lead of their French counterparts and turned to combinations of sulfur, copper, and an especially toxic element, arsenic, to save their crops. Currant worm was ravaging eastern crops, and the particularly voracious potato beetle was inflicting great damage in the West. Desperate for effective controls, farmers widely adopted the new formulas. Paris green, a mix of copper oxide, arsenic, and acetic acid, became the go-to solution for crops of all kinds, including apples. Among the most destructive apple pests, then as now, were plum curculio and the dreaded codling moth, responsible for ruining as much as 30 to 40 percent of a crop in some years. Until horti-culturists in the Midwest discovered that timely spraying of Paris green for cankerworm would also destroy codling moth, the recommended treatment was "the use of bandages upon apple trees to prevent insects from ascending the trunks . . ."[1]

A 1910 volume titled *The Spraying of Plants*, by E. G. Lodeman (part of a series of farming guides edited by the eminent Liberty Hyde Bailey) offers an exhaustive history of the discovery and use of arsenic, lead, sulfur, and copper in combinations including Bordeaux mixture, Paris green, and another arsenic compound, London purple. Lodeman notes reassuringly, "Since very nearly all the arsenic found in Paris green is practically insoluble in water, it is true that this poison is the safest insecticide now in general use."[2] Some compounds, like Paris green, were even advertised as human medicines before being adapted to agriculture. Within a few years, orchards throughout the United States were being routinely dusted with various formulations of arsenic powders. Pictures of Wenatchee orchards from the 1930s show them white with lead arsenate.

The new sprays necessitated a varied and inventive procession of new devices. Handheld sprayers and small barrel devices that could be pulled along by a single man were advertised alongside the latest horse-drawn outfits. Flatbed wagons with wooden towers constructed above the spray barrels let the human applicator stand as high as possible to reach the tops of the trees, but also put people in close contact with whatever they were spraying. Advice for cleaning the sprayers was more concerned with reducing waste of the valuable materials than protecting either operator or the surrounding soil and water.

Even as the newfound formulas were revolutionizing pest control, arsenic poisoning was a growing public health concern for orchard workers and anyone exposed to it in soil, water, or air. Arsenic's controversial use was fought over by consumer advocates and growers associations for decades. It was the most widely used pesticide in agriculture until being replaced by new chemistry after World War II. Due in part to its success, the amount of insecticides used in the United States almost tripled between 1919 and 1929.[3] Soil contaminated with lead and arsenic on old orchard sites is still a health hazard and must be cleaned up as land is converted to housing, schools, or other crops.

DDT, the pesticide banned in the United States after Rachel Carson's *Silent Spring* awakened the public to its dangers, was first synthesized in 1874. But not until World War II was it used as an insecticide, to combat carriers of typhus in Italy and mosquitoes in the Pacific. Wartime production created a surplus that was available for civilian use after the war, including to spray neighborhoods for mosquitoes. Other pesticides developed for wartime use, including organophosphates and herbicides such as 2,4-D, were also put to agricultural use after the war, ushering in a new era of synthetic pesticide use.[4]

Farm chemical advertising from the 1950s and earlier has a "down the rabbit hole" sensibility that is almost comical today. Du Pont de Nemours, Sherwin-Williams, Corning Glass, any company that made products using chemistry seemed to have a pesticide division. Lurid cartoon drawings of bugs being blasted by clouds of spray or pounded with giant hammers were especially popular.

Many of these chemicals are still in use in various forms, albeit with significantly more regulation and protective practices. Because synthetic substances are not allowed under organic regulations, substances such as copper and sulfur are important options for certified organic crops. They're still highly toxic, and alternatives would be welcome.

BIOLOGICAL AND ECOLOGICAL pest controls have a history at least as long as the use of chemistry. Many farming practices important to organic and integrated pest management (IPM) are based on a deep understanding of plants, insects, and ecology going back to the earliest days of agriculture. As early as 300 BC, the Chinese recognized the role of climate in the timing of pest attacks and were using natural methods of control such as herbs and natural predators.

Mating disruption as a strategy was first identified by Jean-Henri Fabre, a French naturalist and entomologist who observed insect chemical communication in peacock moths in 1870. After noticing male peacock moths attracted to a single female that had hatched in his study, he made a trap baited with a piece of flannel on which a female moth had been resting. Dozens of male moths found the trap instead of the female. "I had devised a trap by means of which I could exterminate the tribe," he wrote.[5]

The first highly successful biological control program in the United States, using vedalia beetles to control a type of citrus scale, began in 1888, the year after land grant experiment stations were established under the Hatch Act. The development of IPM has roots in the publicly funded land grant institutions. That's no coincidence; these more holistic methods are meant to reduce and eliminate toxic treatments, and while that benefits both farmers and consumers, it's less interesting to most companies trying to sell a product.

In the late 1950s, research using insect hormones to interfere with mating was under way at the same time as widespread spraying of DDT was becoming a public concern and Rachel Carson was beginning work on what would become *Silent Spring*. The term *integrated control* was first used in the 1950s at land grant institution University of California. Later, researchers began using the term *integrated pest management* (IPM) to emphasize a focus on management rather than control.

In 1962, with the publication of *Silent Spring*, awareness of the impact of widely used broad-spectrum poisons helped shift research priorities toward finding less toxic alternatives. Carson offers extensive examples of biological control methods in the last chapter of her book. The first U.S. field trial of insect mating disruption was conducted at University of California, Riverside in 1967. President Richard Nixon was the first president to use the term *integrated pest management* when he asked several federal agencies to commit to developing and promoting the concept. In 1972, the USDA funded its first major IPM research effort, the Huffaker Project, and in 1978 the first pheromone for use in mating disruption was registered with the EPA.[6]

Consumers Union published a comprehensive study in 1989 heralding IPM practices as the most promising way to reduce pesticide use in U.S. agriculture and food:

> IPM strategies are specific to each pest, local soil, vegetation and climatic conditions, and other local factors. It requires multidisciplinary research, often years of it, to develop successful IPM methods, and unlike chemicals, once developed, IPM strategies can't be packaged and sold everywhere. In addition, many chemical pesticides cost comparatively little to use, in large part because the risks and social costs associated with their use are not included in their price.[7]

At the same time IPM was developing in land grant institutions, organic farming philosophy was emerging in the nonacademic, noncommercial realm of philosophers and practitioners. There was considerable overlap in thinking between the more advanced approaches to IPM and the most holistic pioneers of organic methods, such as Sir Albert Howard, Lady Eve Balfour, and Jerome I. Rodale. Natural food colleagues Joe Smiley, Grace Gershuny, and many others advocated soil health and ecosystem diversity as foundations of good orchard and fruit health long before *organic* became a regulated term.

The organic philosophy was so much outside the dominant thinking about agriculture that for decades little research on organic methods was done, even at land grant institutions. IPM and organic research are often complementary, and there were early voices inside these institutions and government agencies advocating for a wide range of organic and sustainable practices. It took urging from consumers, farmers, and emerging associations such as the Organic Farming Research Foundation to press for more funding before organic practices began to show up in mainstream agricultural research.

In the West, one of the greatest successes of IPM is the widespread use of mating disruption for codling moth on all kinds of orchards, organic and not. Codling moth comes from Kazakhstan, the original home of apples, and it has traveled with apples to every region of the world. A far-reaching endeavor combining IPM, organic agriculture, and chemical pesticides has brought it under nearly complete control in the vast orchards of the Pacific Northwest.

Dr. Jay Brunner, a Washington State University entomologist, his colleague Dr. Larry Gut, now at Michigan State University, and others began working early in their careers on pheromones to disrupt mating behaviors of codling moth. Over time, they have developed some of the most significant advances in IPM for apple production. In the 1980s, they received federal funding to test an area-wide codling moth management program in Washington. The program worked; growers who tried it told other growers, leading to widespread adoption of the technique. "If a scientist tells you, that's one thing; but if your neighbor can do it, you can do it too," Brunner acknowledged to an appreciative audience of growers and scientists at the 2014 Washington State Tree Fruit Association meeting.

Pheromone technology has become a foundation for the Northwest fruit industry. Eliminating sprays is almost a side benefit; the big bonus is how well the pheromones work. Before the introduction of the program, it was common to have to spray a dozen or more times a year for codling moth. Around 90 percent of all apples and pears in Washington are now treated using mating disruption. The average yearly application of pesticides in orchards has steadily declined over the past twenty-five years.[8] With pheromones deployed over vast, uninterrupted acres of orchards (rather than only here and there on isolated orchards, such as Lyman's, in the Northeast), codling moth is now controlled by mating disruption throughout the Northwest.

ORGANOPHOSPHATES (OPs), an especially toxic class of pesticides linked to neurological and other diseases, especially in children and farmworkers, were introduced in agriculture after World War II and were at one time sprayed routinely to combat a variety of pests in apple orchards. Their use in orchards has dropped significantly in recent years as concerns about their long-term health consequences continue to mount and as alternatives become available. Many fruit growers, including those in Red Tomato's Eco Apple network, are phasing out OPs entirely. But one of the difficult balancing acts faced by growers and regulators is whether completely discontinuing an entire class of substances such as OPs is the right approach for the long term. Researchers and growers in Washington point out that the codling moth pheromone program would not have been able to get a foothold if OPs had not been used in the beginning to knock the insect population down to levels that could then be controlled by pheromones.

In 2010, the growers and scientists advising the Eco Apple program agreed to eliminate all but one OP, chlorpyrifos, from the production protocol. Chlorphyrifos is a broad-spectrum insecticide, meaning it is effective against a variety of different pests. Like other OPs, it is a neurotoxin that has been shown to be dangerous to humans and other vertebrates both in water and on land. It is also one of the only effective treatments available for a species of trunk borer that can damage not only a season's apple crop but also the trees themselves. For five years, the Eco Apple orchards managed successfully without any use of OPs, including chlorpyrifos, and were ready to remove the last OP from their protocol for good. Then, in the summer of 2015, an outbreak of dogwood borer struck several orchards. Two orchards made the difficult decision to use targeted treatment with chlorpyrifos in order to save acres of trees and many bushels of apples. In December of that same year, although there still were no good reliable alternatives to combat borers, the EPA announced plans to permanently phase out chlorphyrifos use on all food crops.

The decision to eliminate all other OPs from the Eco Apple protocol in 2010 meant that growers also lost the option to use another treatment, phosmet. Phosmet is highly effective against some of the worst apple pests, including codling moth and plum curculio; it is also highly toxic to bees, although less toxic to mammals and less persistent in the environment than other OPs. Replacing phosmet meant adding a whole regimen of more frequent though less toxic treatments.

Clark Brothers Orchards in Massachusetts has been Eco Apple certified since 2005. They haven't sprayed anything on their orchard before bloom in more than twenty years and have a healthy population of native pollinators. They use very few sprays in their orchard season-long, but until it was eliminated from the Eco protocol, phosmet was one of them. Without it, they must spray other treatments more often. But using phosmet would negate their Eco certification, one of the few ways the Clarks have to promote the many positive things they do in the orchard. It's not a trivial trade-off, and it is not yet clear whether the net impact on humans and the environment will be an improvement over the long term.

David Granatstein, sustainable agriculture specialist at Washington State University, points out that lead arsenate used to be the recommended treatment for codling moth. Then codling moths began to develop resistance to arsenic, and the rates of application needed to control them kept getting higher and higher. When DDT came around it was a miracle—it worked, you didn't need to spray as much, and it wasn't as poisonous as lead, to humans anyway. It looked like progress in terms of sustainability. Then *Silent Spring* pointed out the flaws in that thinking. Around the same time, in 1965, OPs became widely available—they were highly toxic, but not as persistent in the environment as DDT. Remarkably, codling moth didn't become resistant to OPs, at least not right away. But some of its natural predators did, which was even better because it meant growers could treat with OPs and still maintain effective biocontrols and beneficial insects too. Once again, it looked like progress in terms of safety and sustainability. Then came research on the effects of OPs on human health.[9]

Over and over, substances have been introduced and promoted as certainly safe only to be discovered, often a decade or more later, to be extremely toxic in ways not predicted or at least not advertised. Substances such as lead arsenate, DDT, and OPs have all followed that same pattern. We have enjoyed the beautiful, bountiful fruits of their use, but we will be confronting their effects as neurotoxins and endocrine disruptors on agricultural workers and eaters, especially children, for many years to come. Will we find out in twenty years that there are unintended problems with pheromone use too? "It's not likely, but never say never," says Granatstein.

Externally imposed changes have also helped drive development and adoption of IPM in the apple industry. In 1996, the Food Quality Protection Act was passed unanimously by both houses of Congress. It requires that pesticides be reregistered on a risk basis only rather than using the risk-benefit evaluation that had previously been the standard. It also requires regulators to consider aggregated risk of multiple pesticides for all uses, a big step forward in understanding and limiting use. Although there has been some increase in the cost of pest management as a result, for the most part outbreaks and losses haven't been as bad as feared.

There are both encouraging and risky signs for the future. Two insecticides based on natural substances with low to no toxic danger to humans, oil and kaolin clay, are now used extensively in Washington and elsewhere. Researchers are developing new technologies for monitoring pest levels and new attractants to speed up trapping. They've created new models to predict pest development based on weather, which help growers reduce both risk to their crops and overuse of the most toxic substances. These approaches also tend to promote sharing of information among growers, researchers, and others in the industry. One such model, the Washington State University Decision Aid System, a database and network of weather stations, helps growers see what pesticide is most effective and evaluate health and ecosystem effects and other factors so they can make better decisions.

But with significant funding cuts to public research and extension service positions, growers are left to rely more and more on chemical company sales reps and suppliers for advice and information on new treatments. The concentration of economic power in large chemical and farm supply corporations means research on environmental and health effects, and on alternatives for growers, still lags behind research on the benefits of chemical use. Tools like the Washington State University database, accessible to all and not tied to a specific manufacturer, are the kind of crucial support growers need to maintain their orchards and continue improving practices. The success of codling moth mating disruption is a good example of why integrated, carefully targeted strategies using a variety of approaches make sense, and why it takes time and research to understand the best options and the full consequences of various approaches.

FOR FARMERS AND anyone who wants more sustainable and ecological ways to grow food, public science as it is practiced at land grant institutions is a crucial resource. Wendell Berry, farmer and essayist, wrote a scathing critique of the land grant system in 1977, charging that over time it had abandoned its original mission. In *The Unsettling of America: Culture and Agriculture*, he invokes the Morrill Act's original intention "to promote the stabilization of farming populations and communities and to establish in that way a 'permanent' agriculture, enabled by better education to preserve both the land and the people . . . The land grant legislation obviously calls for a system of local institutions responding to local needs and local problems."[10]

Berry went on to deplore how far land grant institutions' priorities had strayed from this vision, shifting away from a broad foundation in liberal arts entirely toward the practical, and then from practical to careerist, bought and paid for by large corporations that fund research that benefits them economically. The same transformation has continued inexorably throughout much of higher education. But despite Berry's warning, in the ensuing decades, land grant and extension research has to some extent come to reflect the same broad range of approaches as the rest of agriculture. While corporate chemical research still dominates in the cornfields, many public employees who do the day-to-day work of the institutions are leading the way in providing alternatives.

Growers associations supported land grant institutions from the very beginning and advocated for passage of the Morrill, Hatch, and Smith-Lever Acts. Today they lead the private fundraising that is more and more necessary to fill the gap as public support declines. Farmers like John Lyman, the Eco Apple grower in Connecticut, worry about the long term. "Support for research is a concern. There's less money available, and I'm not sure where it's going to come from. We need to make applied science more cost effective and build on existing research more effectively, but it's a continual challenge."

The centuries-long search for effective, safe, nontoxic approaches to insects, disease, weeds, and fungi is constantly evolving as new chemistry and new pests enter the orchards. There is a need for basic science exploring the biology and chemistry of organisms and substances, and for applied research to make that knowledge useful in practice. Quick, seemingly simple solutions such as chemicals and sprays, even organic and biological ones, compete for attention and funding with longer-term, more complex approaches like building soil health and nurturing beneficial insects that feed on pests. Growers willing to try the newest methods take a risk that the science won't work in the orchard the way it does in the lab. Growers willing to try long-term approaches risk this year's crop while they test a slower approach. Decisions about funding for research and practical use are influenced by the needs of the biggest players, by companies that profit from selling new products, and by pressure from consumers who worry both about spots and poisons on their apples and don't realize that agricultural research addresses both.

For growers like Lyman, the dedication to alternatives is as much about philosophy as it is about economics. The economics might pay off in the long run if there is a reduction in spray costs, for example, but often, especially in the early stages, the biological approaches cost more and add more labor. Those costs are not shared by everyone who benefits.

Dr. David Rosenberger, a respected Cornell plant pathologist, retired in 2015 after a long career as a public scientist. He's seen firsthand the steady decline in public support for research and the steady reduction in state and federal funding that has resulted. Research dollars, once allocated through a range of programs, now mostly come through competitive grant processes that pit one project against another, requiring short-term results and time-consuming proposals that must be resubmitted every year or two. As extension land grant scientists who began their careers in the '60s and '70s retire, they are not being replaced. In 1978, Rosenberger points out, there were 36.5 full-time employees in pomology and tree fruit pathology research in land grant schools east of the Mississippi. As of 2013, there were twelve.

Another trend is the erosion of funding for research and research facilities authorized by Congress and provided through the USDA. A 2016 report by a consortium of land grant institutions notes with alarm:

> Few programs illustrate the challenges in science funding better than Agriculture and Food Research Initiative (AFRI). Established as part of the 2008 Farm Bill, it is open to all universities and institutions. Although Congress authorized AFRI for $700 million annually, it has received less than half of this amount to date. As a result, only $270 million of the $1.4 billion in projects recommended for funding by AFRI's review panels in FY 2014 received support. The funding shortfall discards innovative solutions as well as support for a new generation of researchers.
>
> University administrators are also struggling with securing adequate funding to maintain the facilities that are the bedrock of their invaluable research. A 2015 report found $8.4 billion in deferred maintenance at the agricultural schools of 91 universities, many of which were state land grant institutions.[11]

When public funds aren't there to support research, growers and private philanthropists pony up as best they can. The fruit industry in Washington recently agreed to contribute $32 million to support Washington State University's Research and Education Centers in Prosser and Wenatchee. The largest gift in WSU history, it will support endowed chairs, information and technology transfer, and research. The Hudson Valley fruit lab associated with Cornell University received a grant from the private New World Foundation in 2014 to fund seven extension positions that had been eliminated.

Cold Spring Orchard, the University of Massachusetts Research and Education Center in Belchertown, Massachusetts, was purchased in 1962 for fruit research by the Massachusetts Fruit Growers Association (MFGA) and later donated to the university. The University of Massachusetts Amherst, a premier land grant horticulture research institution and one of the early leaders in developing IPM programs for fruit,[12] has not had a tree fruit entomologist on faculty since Ron Prokopy, who died in 2004. Prokopy was a mentor to many of the fruit growers and scientists working in the field today, and one of the people most responsible for developing apple IPM in the United States and around the world. At the end of the 2014 MFGA annual meeting, a small grim-faced group convened in a classroom to discuss fundraising for a position to be named after Prokopy. Growers from all over New England were there. They had already raised a quarter of a million dollars from among their members, but needed at least half a million to create an endowment that would support one position at a cost of around $80,000 to $90,000 a year. Whoever was hired would still have to raise his or her own money for research, attract graduate students, and help them raise money to support projects and publications.

Not many of the farmers in the room would be called wealthy. While they may live comfortably, they aren't part of the small economic class that we in the United States usually think of as philanthropists. Yet future access to new research and education that supports fruit production and benefits farmers and eaters in this region rests almost entirely on their generosity. Twenty-some men and a couple of women, sun-dark faces shaded by trucker hats with the logos of their farms or their favorite suppliers, sat in rusty metal chairs, leaned on folding tables, and rubbed their heads with rough hands in frustration. These are the kind of people who can get things done and who don't brag about what they do. They looked serious, and worried. It might not be reasonable what the rest of us are asking of them.

THE CRUCIAL NEED for research doesn't end when one problem is solved. Responsible growers throughout the country push the standards of ecological stewardship well beyond what is required, adding labor and costs to their orchards with little return in the form of consumer appreciation or higher prices, mostly because it is the right thing to do. A new invasive pest has put all of their hard work at risk.

Tracy Leskey, an entomologist who was a graduate student under Ron Prokopy, is now head of the USDA-ARS Appalachian Fruit Research Station tucked into a historic fruit-growing region in the West Virginia mountains. In 2009, she gave a presentation to a group of about fifty fruit growers, scientists, nonprofit marketers, and funders at the annual Eco Apple growers meeting. Tracy sounded like she was narrating a B-grade sci-fi movie as she described an invasive insect from Asia that first showed up in the United States in the late 1990s. She spoke in what could be called lurid terms, but she had the charts, photos, and matter-of-fact delivery to show that the threat from brown marmorated stink bug (BMSB) is real.

The first U.S. sighting of BMSB was in Pennsylvania in the late 1990s, and it has since been detected in at least forty-two other states. The pest was hitchhiking and chomping its way steadily north and west into the prime apple-growing regions of New York and New England, and had already leapfrogged into the orchards of Washington and Oregon.

BMSB is voracious. It eats every kind of fruit and vegetable it encounters, from hot peppers to sour cherries, and a bevy of ornamental trees and flowers too. It overwinters under tree bark or leaf litter on the ground and also inside houses. Tracy showed a slide of someone sweeping big piles, tens of thousands of the bugs, off a front porch into a five-gallon bucket. The walls behind the sweeper were crawling with more. They smell horrible when squished, hence the family name. They're sneaky, too. Researchers and farmers attempting to count brown marmorateds in orchards observed them dropping to the ground, moving to the opposite side of trees to hide, and playing dead when humans approached.

Pesticides that work on native stink bugs didn't work on BMSB, and traps didn't catch them. There were no pheromones or attractants yet developed to lure them, and scientists didn't know what colors, lights, shapes, or other features attracted them. They travel in fruit bins and on truck tires. They don't seem to mind refrigeration or even freezing. They also exhibit Lazarus-like powers. A chart of morbidity rates after spraying with a variety of highly toxic pesticides looked like a backwards check mark: the bugs died off over a period of days, the graph bottomed out at an encouraging 100 percent morbidity on day six, but on day seven some of them miraculously sprang back to life. As her final slide appeared, a teeming mass of white BMSB larvae hatching out at a blinding rate wiggled on the screen at the front of the room and everyone let out a collective "Eewww!"

As the lights in the room came back on, an apple and peach grower from Pennsylvania stood up. A sturdy, serious man with the weathered hands that show he works outside year-round, he held up a glass jar. "I brought a few with me," he drawled in a slow voice with a note of amusement in it, a hint he knew he had everyone's full attention. The jar was half full with a sluggish, stumbling mass of brown bugs, their fat bodies shaped like a shield about the size of the fingernail on his little finger, with thin, spidery legs. Gingerly, with a tinge of respect given the apparent supernatural powers we'd just seen assigned to these things in Tracy's slides, the jar was passed around the room. Some people handed it along quickly, as though they'd rather not even touch it; some stared fixedly through the glass, trying to match what they were looking at with the report we'd just heard. When the jar of stink bugs had made it around the room, someone set it on the window ledge. Chilled after being driven for several hours in the snowy early March cold, the bugs looked ugly but almost benign.

For the next hour, the growers and scientists at the meeting discussed what BMSB meant for Eco Apple growers. What spray, eliminated after years of diligent effort, would need to be allowed again if a grower found BMSB in his or her orchard? What qualifiers would be needed in marketing claims? Could they still say that no organophosphates were used on the apples? If not, would buyers consider their fruit any different from the tons of other apples that flood the market every fall? What about the carefully nurtured predator insects, beneficial mites, pollinators, and all the other creatures that make up a well-balanced orchard ecosystem grown with an IPM philosophy? Would the same sprays needed to kill the nasty stink bugs also kill off the friendly insects, butterflies, and bees that make these orchards so unique and that are so crucial to a sustainable future for the farms in this region?

At the end of a long day, the group agreed on a special emergency protocol for BMSB, allowing a grower who found them in the orchard to use treatments that were otherwise prohibited, but only if the level of infestation reached an agreed-upon threshold and only in sections of the orchard infested at those levels. No one was entirely sure that would be enough, but it walked the line as well as could be. The hardworking group was still talking as they walked out to their cars and trucks for the drive home.

Three of us stayed behind to tidy up the room and load papers and supplies into our car. As we scanned the room one last time, we all saw the jar on the windowsill at the same time. Now in full sun, it teemed with bugs crawling, flying, falling, and squirming over each other in a mass of constant motion. They seemed indeed to have special, dangerous, evil powers. We reflexively checked our clothes, not wanting to be the vector that carried them back to Massachusetts. Tracy's research showed that even the most toxic poisons don't always work on BMSB, but if we'd had a bottle of insecticide handy, I swear we would have sprayed it, no question. It was suddenly easy to imagine the things playing dead and springing to life again.

Produce industry newspaper *The Packer* reported that apple growers in Pennsylvania, Virginia, West Virginia, and Maryland suffered $37 million in damage from BMSB in 2010.[13] The BMSB project, a massive federal grant project involving ten universities and dozens of researchers in as many states, with funding from the USDA and Tracy's leadership, became a national effort a year later, in 2011. Over the next five years, scientists around the country investigated everything about the bug: biology, mating cycle, overwintering habits. They tested different colors and shapes and pheromones for trapping so they could monitor movement. They visited China, where BMSB originated, and learned that in its native ecosystem it doesn't do much damage, so there's very little information on how to kill it. The USDA researchers tested tall netting at orchard borders and "trap trees" to lure the bugs away from the center of the orchard so they can be targeted without having to spray the entire block. They tested every common pesticide allowed for use on apples, and some that were not, and found that the most toxic were not always the most effective. They found one pheromone that worked. Tracy's lab became its sole distributor, sending supplies out to labs all over the country.

Each December, the scientists and project advisors gathered in a small conference room at the USDA lab in West Virginia to compare notes, discuss results, and plan strategy. In year four, someone found a small, unfamiliar parasite attached to the back of a BMSB that appeared to be deadly to its host, and they started monitoring for that too. It's the most hopeful sign yet that ecosystems here in the United States will eventually adapt to this new invader the way they've adapted to so many others, and that BMSB will eventually be kept in check as it appears to be in its native ecosystem. It has taken a massive collaborative effort to arrive at this point. Thanks to the team of scientists beholden to no one but the tax-paying public and the people directly affected by their work—farmers, home owners, and eaters—effective control of BMSB looks like a real possibility. In 2016, the USDA approved funding for another five years of research.

DANA CLARK of Clark Brothers Orchards turned to me one summer when I was visiting the orchard. "I *hate* to spray," he said vehemently. "I just hate it. Especially close to harvest. But we don't see any alternative." That captures succinctly the challenge of growing commercial fruit. Consumers, like many farmers, want the least possible use of chemicals, preferably none, on their apples. But most eaters are squeamish about bugs in their fruit and associate blemishes, spots, and imperfect shapes with low quality. Finding a way to produce near-perfect fruit with near-zero use of chemicals is a centuries-old challenge. It's where the paradox of finding a path that is good for the environment and good for farms intersects with the challenge of growing local apples in diverse places.

Farming is becoming ever more complex: advances in technology, new regulations, marketing channels, and expanded options for varieties and pest management are compounded by climate change, rapidly traveling invasive species, labor and immigration issues, and food safety concerns. The need for cutting-edge publicly supported research is greater than ever.

The collaboration around knowledge, tools, and helping hands that has made good apple-growing possible for the last several centuries is public in many senses of the word. People make up government, schools, and businesses, knit together by voluntary associations, a well-informed press, and a sense of obligation to keep making things better. Decisions about the future of public science take shape in winter meetings and conversations at the gas station or café in town, among growers active in their local and state associations, extension agents in close contact with all kinds of growers, and equipment dealers as familiar with their challenges and thinking as are growers themselves.

This public-private web of collaboration has shaped the fruit industry for centuries. If we want our near-perfect apple grown with near-zero chemical use, we need this whole system intact and thriving. We won't achieve that near-perfect bowl of fruit without it. We can't expect farmers alone, in shrinking numbers, to bear these costs, nor can we rely on a few conscientious entrepreneurs willing to stake a long-term future on solutions that may or may not be profitable. This isn't radical new thinking; it's old-school democracy. We owe our selection of beautiful year-round apples to a couple centuries of just that kind of civic-mindedness.

Dana Clark ended our conversation about spraying by telling me about a news report he had heard on the radio. Researchers in North Carolina were investigating the use of hummingbirds to control another invasive pest, spotted wing drosophila (SWD). The scientists were hanging feeders among blueberry bushes to attract both birds and SWD. The hummingbirds were eating the flies. "Wouldn't that be something," Dana mused, "if we could hang hummingbird feeders in the orchard and that would take care of it?" He chuckled like he doesn't expect to see it in his lifetime. It's delightful to think about; who wouldn't rather spend their days filling bird feeders instead of spray tanks?

CHAPTER ELEVEN

Marketing the Ideal

"WELL, THERE WAS ALAR . . . " John Lyman shakes his head, looking down as if he'd rather not be talking about it. But whenever someone asks why he has invested his time, energy, and a good share of his apples helping to develop a program to certify and market ecologically grown fruit in the Northeast, he has to start there.

In 1989, a study linking the chemical daminozide to a range of health conditions was released by the nonprofit advocacy group Natural Resources Defense Council (NRDC). One use for Alar, the trade name for daminozide, was to treat apples to prevent early drop—apples falling before they are ripe and red. The research tied residue in tested fruit samples to quantities of fruit typically eaten by children, who, because their body mass is smaller, often eat proportionally higher amounts of vegetables and fruits than do adults. However, regulations governing acceptable levels of pesticide residues in food are typically based on adult consumption levels. The report indicated that at those legal lev-

ABOVE: John Lyman III checking the harvest, Lyman Orchards, Middlefield, Connecticut. Photo by Diane Rast.

els, children's risk of health problems linked to Alar and other chemicals used in crop production was many times higher than for adults. And, children's primary source of exposure was fruits and vegetables. Especially apples.

The study hit the news like a tidal wave. Parents, suddenly afraid to feed their kids fresh apples, applesauce, and apple juice, stopped buying everything with apples in it, purged applesauce from their cupboards, and dumped apple juice down the kitchen drain. Almost overnight, the bottom dropped out of the apple market, prices fell, harvests went unsold, and products were pulled off grocery store shelves. The wholesale market for apples tanked.

Alar use on U.S. apples was legal and within guidelines established by the Environmental Protection Agency (EPA). NRDC's criticism was largely directed at the EPA and a weak regulatory process. The peer-reviewed, data-dense report charged, "Current federal regulation of pesticides fails to protect the preschooler. EPA has virtually ignored infant and child food consumption patterns when regulating pesticides."[1] The release was part of a well-planned public relations campaign intended to pressure the EPA to enact stricter guidelines for agricultural chemicals like Alar.

Apple growers, law-abiding and caught by surprise when the report was released, were the ones who actually felt the body blow. Thousands were hit hard financially, whether they had ever used Alar or not. In the aftermath, some never recovered and many orchards, already vulnerable, went out of business.

The Lymans had started a pick-your-own operation at their Connecticut orchard in 1969, and their retail sales had been stable for a few years. John had come back to the farm with new ideas from Dutch orchards; he'd started replanting with dwarf trees and had added small fruits such as blueberries so they had a solid five-month harvesting season. They'd had good growth all through the '80s.

Then the Alar scare hit. "It was really devastating to a lot of growers," John says soberly. Alar had helped address a lot of problems in commercial orchards. Improving the quality of the fruit and keeping apples on the tree longer so they would turn red but stay firm made varieties like

McIntosh a viable wholesale crop. Macs were a popular regional variety and along with Macoun and Cortland were important for Northeast growers. Without Alar, fewer apples made retail grade, more went to processing, and Macs especially were not profitable to grow. Acres of trees were cut down, and orchards were closed and sold.

Even more damaging, the perception of apples shifted from an emblem of health and wholesomeness to a bearer of poison. "It was pretty devastating," John says again, in his understated way. "It was a well-orchestrated campaign with some truth to it, but a lot of exaggeration." For growers it meant disillusionment and a sense of betrayal. They felt unfairly targeted by data taken out of context and painted as villains in the environmental cause.

"It was frustrating. You could talk all the science in the world, it did not matter," remembers John. "How do we address it? We're a small industry, a minor crop, all the guns are aimed at us. There was a lot of soul-searching." He pauses. "PR is a powerful thing."

Organic food was still a young and mostly invisible industry in those days. There were no federal regulations defining organic practices or labels, and dozens of private certifiers set and verified standards for organic production. A network of specialty manufacturers, small producers, and regional distributors supplied natural food stores all across the country, and a few organic products were finding their way onto regular supermarket shelves. Organic marketing was increasingly sophisticated, and organic sales were growing by double digits annually. R. W. Knudsen, Cascadian Farm, and Santa Cruz Organic, juice brands with national distribution, were small companies at the time, owned by individuals who had worked hard for years to promote the benefits of their certified organic products. A few smaller regional brands made up the rest of the supply of wholesale organic apple products, mostly sold through natural food stores, co-ops, and buying clubs.

Fenton Communications, the public relations firm that worked with NRDC on preparing the media campaign against Alar, was well connected in the natural and organic industry. They had worked behind the scenes for months to land the *60 Minutes* television segment that propelled Alar into the national spotlight, hoping to boost the visibility of organic foods. Certified organic crops were grown without the use of Alar. Although national standards were not yet established, the voluntary certification agencies that monitored and inspected organic products maintained restrictions and guidelines similar to one another. Organic apple companies quickly checked their certifications and put out press releases announcing their products were Alar-free and safe for children.

In 1989, I was director of marketing and sales for Blooming Prairie Warehouse, a cooperatively owned regional distributor of natural and organic foods based in Iowa City, Iowa, with a second warehouse (formerly DANCe Cooperative) in Saint Paul, Minnesota. We were a major supplier of organic brands and had built a steadily growing customer base among the co-ops, natural food stores, and buying clubs of the upper Midwest. Our phones started ringing off the hook. Did we carry organic apple juice? Could we ship some right away? Our regular customers ordered extra cases and began to stockpile supply. Stores we had never heard of, and a few that had sent us away empty handed when we'd knocked on their doors over the years, suddenly wanted to do business with us. It was a bit like being the bookish kid in school who is suddenly surrounded by all the popular kids when they hear you've brought cupcakes for lunch: exciting, flattering, but not entirely to be trusted.

Within days, organic juice companies were running out of everything apple. At the warehouse, we huddled around the intersection of loyalty and opportunity. Here was a tremendous chance to get a foot in the door with new customers; they were calling *us*! But our longtime customers had new shoppers and organic converts at their doors too, clamoring for something to give their apple-loving kids. Everyone wanted organic apple juice.

After much deliberation, we crafted a policy to allocate product by prioritizing regular customers but limiting the number of cases they could order. We opened a few new accounts, but decided not to create new delivery routes for those that wanted only apple juice. Our suppliers did the same. The news eventually quieted down; a few new customers stuck around, and once the organic supply ran out and conventional retailers and many consumers retreated to their old buying patterns, organic apple juice sales slowly returned to steadier levels of growth. Amid the uproar, Alar was voluntarily withdrawn from the market by its manufacturer, Uniroyal, a few months later.

The Alar story was a watershed moment for the organic industry and a nightmare for apple growers. The marketing response on the organic side veered between those playing to fears of poisoned food and those focusing on the larger environmental benefits of organic farming. There was a confusing mix of claims—no Alar, no residue, no spray, certified organic—and not much more than nerves to help consumers and retailers sort through it all.

For the organic movement, on its way to becoming the organic industry, Alar spurred efforts to strengthen the integrity and consistency of organic marketing claims and helped organic players, from farmers to retailers, come together and see the scale of the opportunity ahead. This realization eventually coalesced around a far-reaching decision to pursue federal organic standards based on production practices rather than pesticide residues. The news reports validated concerns about pesticides and food that had motivated many of us to get involved in natural foods to begin with and echoed the warnings of *Silent Spring* and earlier debates over lead arsenate. The attention on analysis that connected farming practices to the health of eaters was welcome and needed.

For apple growers, the story had more splintering and damaging repercussions. It's still a sore subject that can provoke harsh memories. "As an apple grower," one longtime orchardist told me wryly, "I completely understand how someone else's misfortune can be a windfall for you." Freezing weather or hail a few counties away, a bad crop in another part of the country, or news about a chemical you don't use can mean your apples are suddenly in demand at a higher price through no fault or credit of your own. He recalls the anger and frustration as if it were yesterday.

Elizabeth Ryan of Breezy Hill Orchard in the Hudson Valley refers to that time as "During Alar." Like many smaller growers following organic practices, she had never used Alar. She wanted to reassure her customers but didn't want to speak badly of growers who had made different choices. She relied on answering her customers' questions directly at her farm stand in the busy Union Square Greenmarket in Manhattan. One morning a woman approached her table, picked up an apple, and smashed it violently onto the box of apples in front of her. "You're poisoning the children of America!" she screeched.

"Are you talking about Alar?" Liz's voice quivers with emotion even now.

"Yes! I'm a schoolteacher. I give apples to my students!" When Liz assured her that she did not use Alar and was sympathetic to her concerns, the woman retorted, "You would say that!" and stalked off.

"There was no dialogue there," Liz finishes. We're both quiet for a minute. I can almost see the betrayal on the face of the woman at the stand, the powerless sense that she'd been had, maybe even been an instrument of harm toward the schoolchildren she cared about. It had to be someone's fault, and the farmer in front of her looked like a target.

Media coverage of Alar brought needed attention to the risk of agricultural chemicals to children's health. The target of that attention, Alar, was used on less than 11 percent of apple orchard acreage at the time, according to NRDC's own information, and it faded quickly from use. The unintended targets, apple growers—even though many were already working hard at implementing IPM—were collateral damage.

NRDC's report included a lengthy set of recommendations on how the government should support apple growers faced with the implications of their research. They called for Congress to "assist growers in reducing pesticide residues; provide credit assistance, crop insurance and other financial protection for growers who are changing from conventional, high-chemical agriculture; impose a tax on pesticide use; . . . establish national definitions of 'integrated pest management' and 'organic' farming techniques and develop a national certification process for commodities grown using these techniques." They also called for "modified federal farm support programs to reward growers for using fewer chemicals, and modified agricultural supply-control systems to ensure that they do not create demand for cosmetically perfect produce which requires excessive pesticide use."[2]

All of these were well-reasoned, tangible ways to help farmers weather the change in pesticide policy that was the primary focus of the report.

They were also mostly pie-in-the-sky given the policy thinking that dominated at the time (and, with a few exceptions, still does today). There was no time for any such policies to go into effect fast enough to save the immediate livelihood of apple growers. Their plight was lost in the drama of coverage about vulnerable children. Every action recommended at the time to support farmers remains largely unrealized twenty-five years later, except one: national organic standards. A powerful grassroots movement of consumers helped make that happen and continues to defend its existence and integrity. The other equally crucial changes needed to support growers and move the food system toward more sustainable practices remain mostly unrecognized.

A wedge between the environmental community and family farmers was hammered even deeper in the Alar aftermath, and repercussions still resonate. At the time, I exulted along with others in the organic community without ever thinking about whether there were other, less positive consequences for farmers. The concerns about health, pesticide residues, and vulnerable children were real and have not disappeared. The need to support apple growers in meeting those challenges is also persistent, and in many ways more urgent than ever.

ALAR CERTAINLY WASN'T the only reason behind the growing support for organic foods, but it was a catalyst that helped crystallize a powerful cultural shift. The link between organic farming and human health—one of the most powerful motivators of shopping behavior— lodged firmly in the public mind. Sales of organic products grew at double-digit rates for the next two decades. Conventional food companies began to pay attention to the organic market, putting in small specialty sections and adding their own organic brands, determined not to be left out in the next big wave of publicity.

The Alar story was a huge opportunity for the activist community as well. Their message that toxic chemicals in the food supply needed to be reduced finally hit home where it counted: with parents and their kids. Some of those parents were famous. One of the most passionate, articulate, and visible of the celebrity moms, actress Meryl Streep, helped found a new organization, Mothers & Others, to advocate for stronger regulations to protect children's health.

In New England, John Lyman and other longtime apple growers, even those who weren't using Alar, were caught in the downdraft. Lots of research on alternatives to broadcast spraying had been done through the '60s and '70s. Extension reports and grower meetings were already very focused on how to reduce pesticides. Many growers had begun adopting IPM practices in the '60s to cut both costs and pesticide usage. Frustrated that their efforts were unrecognized, a couple of New England growers reached out to Streep and her organization. To John's continuing amazement, they agreed to meet. Mothers & Others acknowledged they had wanted to bring attention to something they felt was harmful, not put farmers out of business. They'd never heard of integrated pest management. A dialogue started, and they began to work toward mutual goals.

Out of those conversations about finding a way forward, Core Values Northeast was formed, a coalition that included the New England Apple Institute, IPM Institute of North America, and others. Core Values was seen as a way to increase understanding of environmentally conscious farming practices already in use and to build up the public image of apples again. Similar efforts were under way in other parts of the country, including a joint project of UMass, the USDA, and the Massachusetts Department of Agricultural Resources called Partners with Nature. These laid groundwork for programs such as California Winegrowers' Lodi Rules and Stemilt's Responsible Choice program, all aimed to reassure consumers and provide an incentive to growers to reduce the use of toxic chemicals.

The attempts to promote sustainable farming practices garnered mixed support among organic and conventional growers alike, but none of the efforts moved the dial much with consumers. Retailers were scared of anything referring to pesticides, and "certified organic" was the simplest way to reassure their shoppers.

The Lymans decided it made sense to become part of Core Values Northeast. "We were trying to find ways to be proactive and not be a victim," says John. "It was a very defining moment for the apple industry."

Lyman Orchards was still having difficulty making the orchard profitable, and the Lymans were looking seriously at how to keep the farm. Their wholesale volume was too small to have much influence, but they needed wholesale outlets in order to sell all their fruit. They couldn't keep doing what they were doing. If they were going to stay viable, they had to be more than just a redder apple or a better price.

Mothers & Others went on to build a tenuous bridge with many of the most progressive commercial apple growers in the Northeast, including John Lyman and Pete Ten Eyck of Indian Ladder. The program they created together helped educate consumers about eco-friendly fruit production and was an early promoter of the idea of buying local. But eventually, without a coordinated logistics and sales component or a big marketing budget, there was not enough infrastructure and funding to keep Core Values Northeast going, at least not enough to influence the food market in time to make a difference for apple growers.

The program faded away. But at one of those Core Values meetings, John Lyman met Michael Rozyne, who was just starting a new organization, Red Tomato. John started selling peaches to Red Tomato at first, but they both kept thinking about apples. John had always felt it would be good to market fruit based on his orchard's growing practices. "It seemed like we could have a different edge by growing a different way." He also knew they couldn't tackle a wholesale marketing program on their own. As Core Values faded, Michael, John, and five other growers began working with a team of scientists to develop what eventually became the Eco Apple program.

The rapid expansion of organic production after Alar brought challenges to longtime organic growers like Scott and Wynne at Jerzy Boyz Farm in Washington, too. Thousands of new acres converting to organic caused prices to fluctuate and put small growers in direct competition with large-scale orchards as their tiny organic niche went mainstream. At that point, they were selling to a few health food stores around the country, doing a good business with gift boxes, and had just begun to think about selling at the Seattle farmers market. The price of organic Braeburns, a variety Jerzy Boyz had been able to sell at high prices, dropped precipitously. When a recession hit on top of the rising organic supply, the direct sales were the only place they could make a profit. "We basically started out small, and we've just been getting smaller and smaller," laughs Scott.

Mark Gores, their neighbor in Chelan, agrees. "Like Scott said, all of a sudden, everybody's starting to go organic. That market picks up, except the market is only so big, so how do you set yourself apart?" Mark didn't have the commitment to organic philosophy that motivated Scott and Wynne, but he was watching new apple varieties attract attention. His priority was sustaining his farm. "All I can do is to recognize where the market's going. I can't be involved in trying to out-produce the big guys in Reds, Goldens, Grannies; I've got to follow the money with new varieties." Scott nods in sympathy. "We both have some of the best locations in the whole world. He has fifty acres, but still, Mark's competing against farms that have a thousand to ten thousand acres. He has to produce a high volume of high-quality fruit."

Support and growing demand for organic has helped sustain orchards like Jerzy Boyz, but for growers who follow other production practices, it's hard to find a way to tell their story.

IPM AND ORGANIC share many common roots and cultural influences, but they have had very different paths into the marketplace because of the nature of each approach and because of strategic choices made by practitioners and advocates. IPM has never been a strong market position on its own; IPM scientists and growers sometimes wonder enviously at the steady growth of organic sales.

There have been efforts to promote IPM in the grocery store, some in the background, some as part of labeling and promotional campaigns, and still others as part of broad efforts to define sustainability. In the days before organic standards were established, produce sold in natural food stores was sometimes labeled as IPM or naturally grown. Because IPM lacks a consistent definition and covers a broad continuum of practices, including some adopted by so-called conventional agriculture (not to mention the disconnect of using the word *pest* to promote food), the term fell out of favor for marketing. The national organic standards and a desire to promote and safeguard the still-new shelf space for organic pushed natural food retailers to adhere to that stricter definition. For a time, the term *transitional* was used to indicate growers who were moving toward organic certification, but even that designation was eventually discouraged in favor of an either/or approach: products and farms were either certified organic or they were conventional.[3]

Conventional is still used unthinkingly to mean "everything else." The term lumps IPM practitioners using advanced practices aligned with organic into the same category as commodity producers relying heavily on chemical practices. It also means that while organic agriculture has painstakingly reached just under 1 percent of the value of U.S. agricultural production, the other 99 percent remains largely misunderstood by the food-buying public.

In many ways, the elements that are strengths of an IPM approach when it comes to production are its bane when it comes to marketing. The wide spectrum of practices included under the IPM continuum encourages adoption and movement toward better practices. IPM allows for the use of the full range of strategies, including synthetic chemical applications. Most growers, no matter their production philosophy, monitor pests and weather, considered basic practices in IPM. Far fewer growers use highly advanced soil and ecosystem management plus a wide array of nonchemical, biointensive strategies, including mating disruption, predator insects, and trapping. Yet despite this extra effort, they too are included under the umbrella of IPM.

IPM-based practices can also vary within a single farm, between crops, and from year to year depending on pest pressures and other factors. A set of one-size-fits-all standards based on specific substances and requirements is in many ways antithetical to the philosophy of IPM. It's an approach inherently designed to be applied differently depending on specific conditions, climate, location, crop, pests, and time. This makes sense for farmers, but it doesn't lend itself to strict guarantees for consumers. Farms using IPM have quietly kept progressing along the continuum in nonstandard, complex, and trial-and-error ways, but continuous improvement does not translate well into advertising copy. And an inquiry-based middle ground doesn't fund-raise as well as the rallying cry of the certain.

Organic growers have always used practices consistent with IPM, including cultivation methods, maintaining soil biological activity, rotating crops, and the selective use of elemental chemistry such as sulfur and copper. When the organic regulations were being drafted and debated in the early 1990s, a controversial decision was made to base organic labeling standards on a prohibition against all synthetic substances. It is a clear-cut standard for consumers based on a need for certainty that doesn't always have the same logic on the ground.

The prohibition against synthetic substances in organic production remains one of the major divisions between some proponents of organic and those advocating other forms of advanced IPM/sustainable farming. It cemented organic growers' reliance on older chemistries, making the need for noncommercial research into alternatives even more crucial. The synthetic-nonsynthetic divide also encourages a false expectation of purity in everything organic, and it led to an approach to organic standards that in some ways has made it easier for large-scale producers to comply with the certification requirements. There are leaders in the organic community who strongly believe it is antithetical to a more holistic approach consistent with organic philosophy.[4]

The prohibition against synthetic substances can lead to some surprising choices for ecologically minded growers, especially in regions like the Northeast where weather, pest pressures, and variety preferences can make the amounts of copper, sulfur, and clay needed for commercial organic production questionable in terms of ecological impact.

"Would you grow apples organically if you could?" I innocently ask a grower in the Eco Apple program on my first visit to his orchard. An experienced apple grower and dyed-in-the-wool New Englander with an exceptionally strong, proud commitment to ecological values and environmental stewardship, he fixes me with a hard-eyed look. "What I'm doing is better than organic," he declares, enjoying my startled look of surprise.

HENRY WARD BEECHER, in an essay on the subject of whether books about farming are useful, wrote in 1859, "Unquestionably, there are two sides to this question, and both of them *extremes*, and therefore both of them deficient in science and in common sense."[5] That sentiment could apply as well to the fierce divisions that have developed around farming practices over the past several decades.

For years, the main critiques of organic and sustainable agriculture came from representatives of chemical-based, industrial, so-called conventional agriculture. Lately, however, the darts are from folks who consider themselves guardians of organic philosophy. One might expect such kindred thinkers to be grateful that more than forty years of hard-fought activism, dedication, and persistence have made organic foods something nearly three-fourths of consumers say they buy at least occasionally. Instead, some complain that organic has become too big while others argue that the standards don't go far enough. The grievances are several. Too much regulation places an unfair burden on small farmers. Big Ag has adopted only the organic practices that can be scaled up, leaving behind the cherished values of family farms, fair labor practices, and healthy soil that once seemed inherent in the term. Most damning of all is the complaint that *organic* has become meaningless.

Organic foods represent a proud though meager 5 percent of food sold in U.S. grocery stores.[6] That suggests a fight not yet won. But the circular firing squad within progressive causes is a timeworn phenomenon. When issues and enemies are too overwhelming, it's simpler and more satisfying to go after those folks closest to you—their faults and failures are familiar, and if your standard is perfection or purity, there's no shortage of targets. So while the barrage of criticism from conventional agriculture has softened to grudging acknowledgment that organic agriculture has a place and might even offer solutions to serious problems, some of the harshest critiques of organic are coming from the environmental and local food side.

At a 2013 meeting of the National Organic Standards Board (NOSB), the USDA-appointed body that approves updates and changes to the national regulations, activists outraged by overuse of antibiotics in agriculture (a serious issue in animal agriculture) campaigned for a blanket prohibition on antibiotic use in organic production. Antibiotics are already prohibited in organic meat and dairy; the proposed change forbid all uses, including as a targeted treatment for fire blight in fruit growing. Organic growers and scientists alike argued unsuccessfully that responsibly managed antibiotic use was valid and safe on fruit crops, that research on alternatives had not progressed enough to give growers a reliable alternative, and that thousands of growers were at risk of having to abandon their organic certification in order to save their orchards. One consumer activist was arrested while protesting for the ban, and those who argued for a less drastic move were painted as enemies of good health and organic values.

The ban was adopted and has since gone into effect. Research on alternative treatments for fire blight continues, and as of 2016 there has been some progress, but it remains a big issue. Organic growers are seeing bacteria become resistant to the one available treatment they are allowed, fire blight damage is increasing, and some orchards are abandoning their certified organic status.

Kevin Stennes at Chelan Fresh is among those in the organic community who think the move was a mistake. "Most of the time fire blight comes through an open blossom when it's warm and moist. You have a ten-minute rainstorm or all the right factors for a few days, you get fire blight. On a fifty-acre orchard that took $20,000 an acre to get producing, you've got a million dollars invested, and that's in a relatively small orchard. If it's threatened by fire blight, are you going to spray the antibiotic and save the orchard or just cut down the trees? If you spray and lose your certification, it will take at least three years to qualify again. Not many will go through that. You're going to have a conventional orchard instead of no orchard." He's hopeful that research and the industry will come up with a good alternative. But the reaction of the activists is puzzling to him.

"When you and I get sick, we take antibiotics. But a consumer doesn't want to eat a pear or apple from a tree that may have been treated with an antibiotic two or three years ago. I mean, a lot of things sound good, but in practice they don't work. I think a lot of important topics get decided by the 5 percent who are the loudest, and maybe not the most up to date on those issues."

Antibiotics offer a useful parallel to the role of synthetic pesticides in the context of IPM. Few argue the value of targeted antibiotics in human or animal health. They are sometimes the only effective treatment for a life-threatening illness. And yet, broad and extensive overuse across many kinds of agriculture, including meat and dairy production, has resulted in bacteria resistant to the most common antibiotics, which ultimately led to calls for banning use in all agriculture. The arguments about use and overuse pit growers against each other and against their customers. Research is slow, and the biggest research dollars, public and private, go to corn, cotton, and soybeans, not apples. An all-or-nothing approach doesn't always align with the real interests of farmers or eaters. Instead of pointing everyone toward a process that might more quickly reduce the most egregious harm and find workable solutions over time for the rest, the need for certainty pushes decisions toward extremes of all or nothing.

Neonicotinoids (often called neonics) may be on a similar path. This class of pesticides was introduced as an improvement to harsher, older forms of nicotine and as a less toxic alternative to organophosphates (OPs), promising low risk to mammals and vertebrates such as songbirds, wildlife, and people. Neonics have allowed many apple growers to reduce or eliminate OPs completely. But new research indicates that neonics are toxic to bees. Their heavy use, especially to a massive degree as seed treatments for corn and soybeans, has polluted waterways throughout the Midwest. Every advocacy group with a remote connection to environmental issues is calling for a ban on neonics to "save the bees."

Even strong advocates for pollinators like the Xerces Society recognize that carefully targeted neonicotinoids on tree fruit can be consistent with an IPM approach to pest issues and might make more sense than a complete prohibition, at least until research finds alternatives or consumers are willing to buy resistant varieties or apples with spots. Issues such as the role of neonicotinoids in agriculture and pollinator health take years to sort through before effects show themselves, research catches up, and the mechanisms of market economics, alternative solutions, and public opinion collide and produce a shift to another substance or another approach. It seems simpler just to ban all neonics now.

Research, grower needs, and consumer desires align more often than they get credit for. Researchers are continuously learning more about pest biology, looking for better and more options, and finding ways to target treatments more effectively. But that long, slow, deliberate process doesn't match the few hours or days a farmer has to make a decision about treating for an infestation of borers or codling moth. And it's nearly impossible to sort out the impartial data from the hype in a research, funding, and regulatory environment fraught with polarization and profits at stake. All of us have a vested interest, whether we recognize it or not, in finding solutions that truly serve the health and sustainability of the environment and the livelihood of farmers and workers who actually do feed the world.

Last year I got an urgent phone call from a Red Tomato customer with questions about pesticides on our apples. "Are they sprayed with Alar?" was her first question. "Wow!" I thought, wondering how she even knew to ask and amazed once again at the power of PR all these years later. I reassured her that Alar was off the market and hasn't been used on apples for many years. I explained the differences between Eco-certified and certified organic apples, such as the use of synthetic treatments. She was floored when I didn't try to convince her to abandon organic. "It's important that you know what you are buying," I said. "For people who really want to support local growers, our apples are a really good option; if you're most concerned about synthetic chemicals, you should buy organic." Those two options don't begin to cover the multitude of choices we have to make about our food. They are shorthand for something that is not an either/or choice. I want us to figure out how to face the next Alar-like conundrum without endangering either the health of children or the existence of local farms.

THE ONLY REAL WAY to measure the long-term value of different growing practices is to measure their impact on the ecosystem and land. Despite various efforts over the years, there is still disagreement over how to accurately measure impact in ways that account for all of the variables that exist in farming. At the same time, "know your farmer" food awareness, along with food safety scares, has made transparency about farm practices a requirement, in part to reassure consumers their expectations are being met. Once farmers who are selling to wholesale customers make their crop management decisions, they must document and justify them for various certifications and labeling programs such as certified organic, the Eco Apple program, state labels, worker licenses, food safety certifications, pesticide regulations, and more. There's a chorus ready to help decide what can and can't be done in each situation.

In midsummer, I visit one of the orchards certified by Red Tomato's Eco Apple program. I'm there to observe the every-three-year inspection so I have a better understanding of what's involved and can help make some decisions about how to structure the program to be more useful and less costly for the growers. I listen as the farmer answers question after question from the inspector, an experienced crop consultant who's visited the orchard before. This grower's family has farmed here for generations. He talks frequently with other growers and is an active member of the state fruit growers association and Farm Bureau. He uses IPM in his orchard because it makes sense and he doesn't like to spray any more than the next guy. He keeps all of the records and paperwork because his customers require it.

When the inspector asks if he's using a gauge to measure wind speed when he sprays and where he's recorded the results, the farmer takes off his sunglasses to look him in the eye. "You know," he says, "I always check. I've been doing this for forty years. But I don't write it down every time. Did you know I'm a pilot too? Know how I can tell how many knots and what direction the wind is blowing?" He waits, sure that we don't. "The leaf on an apple tree." He points toward branches bobbing in a light breeze and continues. "My neighbors on both sides keep bees. I don't want to hurt the bees. Neither of them is complaining to me about drift, so I must be doing okay." The inspector nods without indicating what he thinks about the answer, enters something into the form on his laptop, and moves on to the next question.

When the discussion again turns to pollinators and bees, the farmer mentions he's avoided using neonicotinoids this season because one of his big customers is concerned about them. But because he avoided a neonic spray early in the season, he's now facing a pest issue that he'll have to treat. He stopped using OPs a few years ago along with the rest of the Eco Apple group. Without OPs or neonics, he doesn't have many options. None of the other options is from a different class of substances with different modes of operating, which is what he needs to rotate into his treatment plan to reduce the likelihood of pests becoming resistant to what he's using.

The farmer has been leaning against an apple sorter in his packing shed for this part of the inspection and I've been standing off to the side at the end of the roller belt, trying to stay out of the way. Now he shifts his feet on the concrete floor and turns to me. "If the customers are going to tell me how they want me to grow my fruit, at some point they are going to have to start sharing the risk," he says pointedly.

"You mean financial risk?" I ask.

"I mean, if I do what they want and don't treat a problem the way I think is best, and then I have a problem with that crop, they need to buy my crop anyway and help figure out a way to market it."

He's not just being stubborn. He's already taken a considerable risk by avoiding neonics, not because he has to, but because he knows it will make his customer more likely to keep buying his apples. It's no guarantee they will stay loyal, even then. I ask if he received the packet of information about a new set of standards from a big retail customer, and he just shakes his head.

We're standing in the darkened pack building; it's quiet this time of year but will be full of apples and people in another month or two. We're asking this farmer to justify a whole list of decisions so he can get points on our Eco rating form. The give-and-take here is important—both the farmer and the people who eat the farmer's fruit have a stake in how it is grown and the factors that drive decisions about risk, health, bees, and pretty apples. But it is a bit embarrassing to stand here, looking out the open doorway to the orchard of lush, leafy trees loaded with not-yet-ripe fruit, and try to translate the days and months of attention to those trees into a few pointed questions. "Did you take pollinators into account when making your spray decisions?" The inspector gamely asks the next question on his list. The farmer shakes his head and smiles wryly, as if he doesn't even know where to start.

Later, walking in the orchard, I ask about some branches that stand out among the dense verdant green on a few trees in each row. They are brown and shriveled, almost like someone had carefully applied a defoliant on just that twig and left the rest of the tree alone. "Fire blight," both men say at the same time. I look out at row after row after row of trees, knowing that the picking crew won't start for another month and that there are peaches, tomatoes, and a dozen other crops to tend to in the meantime. The farmer should be keeping detailed records of what he does about the fire blight, too. The brown twigs make me shudder.

RACHEL CARSON is rightfully considered the catalyst for the modern environmental movement and the reason DDT is still banned in the United States. Forty years after I first read *Silent Spring*, her ringing indictment of indiscriminate, ill-advised pesticide use is still timely and relevant, supported by pages and pages of scientific evidence that has only become more compelling in the decades since. After the opening fable that etches the book's title, she compares the use of chemical pesticides to the then-new and rapidly expanding use of radiation, cautioning that both exist in nature but that the speed of human intervention is allowing no time to achieve ecological balance. She points out that synthetics, newly introduced to the world, require generations to be adapted into ecosystems. She considers the irony of using chemicals to bolster a system of agriculture that overproduces so much that the government spends money to store the surplus. She talks about monocropping and the challenges of invasive pests. She is scathing in her indictment of chemical companies, users, and regulators. She condemns "the right to make a dollar at whatever cost" and fiercely defends the public's right to know.

But even as she lays out the problems so clearly, she confronts a far more challenging response than is usually credited or remembered:

All this is not to say there is no insect problem and no need of control. I am saying, rather, that control must be geared to realities, not to mythical situations, and that the methods employed must be such that they do not destroy us along with the insects.[7]

In correspondence with her editor at Houghton Mifflin, Paul Brooks, Carson wrestled with this paradox, referring to the arsenic issues of the 1930s and expressing a fervent wish that none of the harmful substances would ever have to be used. She admits that is impractical, and goes on to say to readers of her book:

It is not my contention that chemical insecticides must never be used. I do contend that we have put poisonous and biologically potent chemicals indiscriminately into the hands of persons largely or wholly ignorant of their potentials for harm. We have subjected enormous numbers of people to contact with these poisons, without their consent and often without their knowledge . . . I contend, furthermore, that we have allowed these chemicals to be used with little or no advance investigation of their effect on soil, water, wildlife, and man himself.[8]

The term *integrated pest management* doesn't appear in Carson's book, but she writes about the benefits of selective spraying to bring things under control so biological methods can take effect. She deplores unnecessary roadside spraying for weeds and the effects of pesticides on honeybees. Her last chapter contains a detailed review of then-current research on alternatives to chemical control of insects—sterilization, mating disruption with pheromones, trapping, sound, viruses, bacteria such as Bt, parasites, and predators. Her critique still ringing true today, she wrote, "Progress on alternatives suffers from lack of support for research."[9]

My worldview is profoundly shaped by Carson's prose, the beauty of her sentences, the clarity and excitement in her explanations of science, the urgency of her call to action. Reading her at fourteen, I absorbed all the outrage in her words. Rereading her as I've turned sixty, I still see the outrage and clarity, but I also find the complexity and measured voice of a realist. Carson chose each word she wrote with excruciating intention. There is no sloppy language, no throwaway sentence, and no qualifying or softening of her cry of alarm. She ends the book: "It is our alarming misfortune that so primitive a science has armed itself with the most modern and terrible weapons, and that in turning them against the insects it has also turned them against the earth."[10]

And yet, she tells us, it's complicated. "In nature nothing exists alone."[11] Everything is connected, including humans and our weight upon the world, our limited understanding, and our endless curiosity and inventiveness. Changing one thing, solving one problem, has its own ripple effect, and that has consequences too.

CHAPTER TWELVE

A Democracy of Apples

"A THING IS RIGHT when it tends to preserve the integrity, stability, and beauty of the biotic community. It is wrong when it tends otherwise," wrote Aldo Leopold, the great conservationist who grew up a few miles from Harold Linder's orchard in southeast Iowa.[1] I'm struck by his choice of the word *tends*. Leopold, like Rachel Carson, studied nature and ecosystems closely and saw few absolutes. He believed humans have an integral and active role to play in sustaining and managing both wild and domesticated landscapes, and he considered conservation and agriculture to be processes, not individual actions. Like Carson, he saw them as connected.

Meanwhile, we are living with an increasingly bifurcated food system. One side is based on giant-scale, industrialized monocrops and short-term efficiencies that result in cheaply priced, uniform goods with externalized social and environmental costs. On the other side is a microscale,

ABOVE: Leaf print on a McIntosh apple, Indian Ladder Farms, Altamont, New York. Photo by Susan Futrell.

highly integrated, and diversified system producing for the dedicated few who can afford the time and money to participate.

If we can't change those relationships, we will lose the land base, the farming knowledge, and the ability to produce food regionally and locally. We will end up with a food supply concentrated in a few vast agricultural zones in various parts of the world, overseen by the few people with the training and knowledge to manage them, employing a few million interchangeable, low-paid workers. It will be supported by a whirring global industrial research and product development complex, moving toward ever more mechanized, technology-dependent processes that will produce 99.9 percent of what we eat. Local farms will be something we visit on weekends.

Years ago, in a letter about the future of the Core Values Northeast program, John Lyman wrote that the single most valuable element of that program to both buyers of apples and the farmers growing them was "our local roots, and our connection to our communities." Strengthening local connections to the food supply is at least as urgent today as it was fifteen years ago. But *local* pushes back on all the big things that drive the growing and marketing of apples: access to the latest variety; a year-round supply; unblemished, reliable quality; fruit grown without pesticides; cheap food. Rebuilding the kind of diverse, community-based local food and farm system that so many people have envisioned and have been working toward for so many years is going to test our assumptions about what *local* looks like, for whom.

Tracie McMillan, in *The American Way of Eating*, concludes her compelling account of the people working in fields, kitchens, and grocery stockrooms by proposing that we will not have a truly sustainable and fair food system until we view the production of food as a public good. I think she has identified a profound way to reframe the way we think about food and farming in the United States.

Building a sustainable local food system as a public good means finding a way to support commercial-scale farming and commerce as well as urban gardens and CSAs. It means finding a way to foster the livelihoods of generations of farmers who are good at what they do, as well as independent grocers who stock the products their neighbors need and want. It means providing access to fresh, fairly priced food for cooking and for eating away from home. It means decent jobs, livable incomes, healthy diets, and money circulating both inside and outside the local economy, based on a production and distribution system that is paced to thrive for many generations to come. It means the massive land base, both privately and publicly owned, that produces food and fiber is providing ecosystem benefits—rich soil, carbon sequestration, clean water, biodiverse plant, insect, and animal communities—that we all enjoy.

We will need to go back to the source, to learn from and respect the growers of apples. Chef Dan Barber suggests in *The Third Plate* that to be truly sustainable, our food system needs to reshape itself around the growing—not the eating—of food. Eaters must adjust their needs, wants, and expectations around all that it takes to farm sustainably and ecologically: around the weeds and cover crops and seconds, not just the perfect harvest; around what makes sense for this tree, on this farm, in this season, in this soil, and on this slope.

If that's the kind of food system we want, we can't abandon our civic responsibility by leaving that public good to businesses under pressure to maximize profits, or NGOs compelled to constantly fund-raise to get their message heard. We can't expect to rely on underfunded government agencies that have become a battleground for competing interests, or the voluntary grower associations and individuals already carrying so much of the weight of protecting the food supply and the land base that produces it. All of these are essential players in keeping a healthy food system, and our democracy, vital and intact. They've been key to sustaining the apple's presence in America for four centuries. But for that to continue requires all of us to think of ourselves as more than consumers. We have to be good neighbors and good citizens, caring about more than what's in our own shopping cart. We have to care not just about where food comes from, but everything it takes to make it possible.

Some people use the word *democracy* to mean a kind of entitlement—the right to have and do what you want and think you deserve. It is partly that, but only if you include the rest of the process: making room for people who think and live differently to have what they want and think they deserve too, and committing the resources and knowledge and time that allow a democratic system to function. As demanding, data-drenched consumers of foodstuffs, our vision of food and farming can't be just about food miles, or knowing the name and face of the farmer, or getting what we want. It has to be about what is true for any thriving, diverse democracy: there has to be room for many voices and many ways to make progress toward common goals. And those goals need to include a rekindled faith in, engagement with, and funding for a public sector to sustain our public good.

All of this points to the need to find a middle way forward. We've gotten used to thinking of the middle as something to abandon, the wishy-washy fence-sitting, the compromise, the safe position. It's tempting to carve a line in the sand between an all-or-nothing definition of good versus bad practices. It's hard to resist a simple badge or checklist that tells us when we are there. But without a middle ground, we have nowhere to meet, to put our unique knowledge, experience, and beliefs to work, together. We have no common ground on which to build a common good.

Deciding how to manage pests and pesticides is an example of why the middle is anything but soft and safe. The presence and use of toxic chemicals in our environment and their effect on human health is a legacy we will be grappling with for generations. Agriculture and food are often a focus of these concerns, and need to be. But manufacturing, industrial waste, fossil fuels, and many other practices that deposit toxins in air, soil, and water have left most of us with an overall body burden, what biologist Dr. Sandra Steingraber describes as "the sum total of these exposures [that] provide[s] a measure of cumulative exposure,"[2] which includes hundreds of different residues for the average American. Decisions about the larger impact of the way we use and develop pesticide technology can't be settled only in the aisles of a grocery store or with voluntary funding of research on pest management. All of these sources of exposure are a result of complex, often competing interests and priorities. Steingraber notes pointedly that "the path that chemistry has taken in the last half of this century is only one path."[3]

Farming and health both involve a series of individual choices, dependent on research that expands knowledge and options over time, with many factors influencing outcomes. Natural systems don't lend themselves to uniformity. What is reasonable or precautionary may vary in the context of a specific orchard block or pest. The right decisions change over time as better information and better options are uncovered.

Can I be fierce about standing in the middle and rejecting certainty in favor of complexity? I think so. Making room for a middle way means facing into, not backing away from, differences and contradictions and difficult choices. It means fiercely defending our own unique needs and values while never losing sight of the good of the whole. It means respect for people whose opinions, choices, and life circumstances are not the same as ours but whose deepest beliefs make us sisters and brothers. Truly embracing the idea that everything is connected uncovers contradictions and paradoxes we cannot dodge. I am tired of *either/or*. I refuse to give up on *yes, and.*

THE SUMMER AFTER my visit to Chelan, wildfires again ravaged Washington State. The 2015 fires, like the Carlton Complex fires the year before, were started by lightning and fueled by long-term drought in much of the western United States. Once again, they devastated vast acres in the heart of apple country. When I first read the news, I thought of the fire that had burned near the Stennes family's orchards only a year before. I clicked on a map and realized that the latest fires were burning all around Lake Chelan, including what I thought was the road to Wynne and Scott's farm. I sent an email and was grateful when Wynne's reply popped into my inbox the next day: "We lost some ground but we're okay."

The fires went on for weeks. One of the Chelan Fruit Co-op packing plants owned by the Stenneses and hundreds of other families burned to the ground. A news photo showed a scorched shell of metal and concrete behind a pile of charred apples. The caption said it was the largest apple packing facility in the world.[4] Thousands of bins of fruit along with over a hundred and fifty thousand wooden bins and forty forklifts went up in the flames.

The co-op managed the crop that year by packing fruit at other facilities in the area. The plant was insured, and the new building will be bigger and more modern than ever, a chance to position the co-op for the future. Photos of the construction progress are posted every few weeks on the co-op's website. Members and customers follow the process with pride and also concern. If the building isn't done in time for the 2016 harvest, it will be a challenge to get the fruit packed because it looks like it will be a bumper crop.

The following spring I wrote to Wynne again. A few weeks later, an email from her daughter arrived gently letting me know that Wynne had died of cancer in March 2016. Remembering her strong face and immense presence in the orchard, it was hard to absorb the news that she is gone. There can be no crueler reminder that doing the right thing is no guarantee. There is still so much more to be researched and understood about human health, just as there is about apples and chemicals in the environment.

Mark Gores's face smiles from the Envy™ apple website, which features him as one of their most dedicated growers. "I'm 58 and I've been in this business all my life. And I'm lucky enough to be involved with the beginnings of new varieties," his profile reads. "Something that is really neat for someone who has been around the business as long as I have: that suddenly you're growing something that has flavor, and it counts."[5]

The Lyman family is tending to the future of Lyman Orchards. In the summer of 2015, they invited members of the ninth generation to spend two days at the farm learning about the finances, the marketing and brand values, and the joys and challenges of the family business. Sixteen young women and men from all over the United States and Canada were able to participate. A nephew and another young relative are working at the orchard; others may become involved or seek jobs there in the future; all of them will be better-informed shareholders. It was a fun, inspiring weekend, John Lyman says, but there are no guarantees about the future. "Every family business has the responsibility to prepare the next generation. Every business has its own unique challenges. Maybe one advantage we have is that we know it won't happen without a lot of work and effort. It's not to be taken for granted. It's the nature of farming that you can't take anything for granted."

His hope is that the family will find enough members to sustain the business for the next decade and beyond. "I think it's a little of 'to be determined,'" John told the local paper. "Nothing lasts forever."[6] In 2016, they celebrated their 275th anniversary, the twelfth oldest family business in the United States.

Dana Clark's son and daughter, Silas and Naomi, and Naomi's husband, Craig, are the up-and-coming faces of Clark Brothers Orchards in Massachusetts. Naomi returned to the farm after a few years away at college and recovery from an accident. After a year of learning the ropes, she did some research, worked the numbers, and called a family meeting to convince her dad and uncles it was time to replace the old pack line with a new state-of-the-art computerized machine. The new pack line was installed in 2016. A large new planting of EverCrisp® and other promising varieties and a solar installation that provides half the power for the farm are helping the fifth generation carry on, and Silas as well as his and Naomi's brother Isaak are already raising a sixth generation of Clarks in the family tradition.

Finding someone to eventually take over the orchard at Indian Ladder Farms has been a worry of Pete Ten Eyck's as he thinks about retiring. A young man from nearby who's worked for him for several years, Joe Nuciforo, hopes to make orchard management a lifelong profession and is gaining experience and confidence every season. I can hear the relief and pride in Pete's voice when he tells me that his two daughters and one son, unbeknownst to him, had talked over the future of the farm and decided they would do what it takes to keep it operating and in the family. His son, Peter, has taken on a management role. His daughter Laura and her husband are growing hops on the land, and a new cidery and brewery have just opened next to the already popular farm stand and café. It's not an easy path, but they'll work with their longtime employees and with Pete to sort out a way forward.

Hundreds of varieties of Kazakh apples are now part of the National Apple Collection at Cornell University's New York State Agricultural Experiment Station in Geneva, New York, the largest collection of apple specimens in the world. They contain genetic material that may offer disease resistance, climate tolerance, new flavors, and more. Dr. Aimak Dzangaliev, now in his nineties, and his wife Tatiana Salova are still busy collecting wild remnants in the Almaty forest and selecting all-wild specimens to commercialize, one way of ensuring they do not disappear.

Eight years after I listened to the auction signal the end of one orchard story and the start of another, I decided it was time to find out what had happened to the orchard in southeast Iowa. I'd been afraid to find out that things had gone awry, that making a living with pick-your-own fruit in an out-of-the-way part of the Midwest just wasn't feasible. Maybe the young couple I'd seen at the equipment auction optimistically buying bins and tractors and coolers had called it quits; maybe "Orchard Estates" houses were going up where the trees had once been.

I found the orchard still listed online and called and made arrangements to visit at the very end of apple season, late October. On my way south, I retraced the road to Harold Linder's place, afraid to see the trees cleared and the orchard gone there too. The house was still there, the yard well-tended, but the doorbell was broken and there was no one around. The orchard was scraggly and overgrown, already turning to wild pasture. I'd brought the pencil-drawn map, rolled up, but with no one home to sanction my trespassing and the undergrowth a tangled mess, I didn't try to go past the wire fence into the orchard itself. A few rows in, even without consulting the map, I could clearly see the long, low horizontal branch of the Burlington Leopold tree.

On the way to Appleberry Orchard, the new name for the state's oldest still-operating orchard, I drove past the state prison at Fort Madison, the casino in Burlington, and acres of cornfields and hog confinement buildings. In downtown Burlington, the old Lagomarcino warehouse is part of a new downtown historic district. Aldo Leopold's boyhood home stands gracefully at the top of a bluff overlooking the Mississippi, with a bronze plaque to mark the spot although the orchard itself is long gone.

On the other end of the phone that icy night of the auction, someone else who had never grown apples was anxious for the bidding to start. Jessica Welch and her husband Ryan lived just down the road. They'd driven by the orchard hundreds of times, knew it had been untended for the past couple years, knew about the family issues over how to manage it. Jessica had an idea that they could make something of it that would be a good life.

They weren't completely unprepared. They were already operating a small berry farm just up the highway. Jessica, an accomplished baker, had been selling baked goods at local farmers markets for several years, and Ryan had grown up nearby and worked around the farming community all his life.

Jessica is in her thirties, a petite woman with red-brown hair and a direct, no-nonsense manner, compact energy, and focus that match her lively eyes. "I was doing the bidding," she told me with a bit of fire in her eyes. "I said if we're going to do this, I want to be the one." There were about thirty people in the room. With seven parcels and Jessica not knowing who was there to bid on which, the atmosphere was tense. Fortunately, the parcel with the house and most of the orchard was up first. She remembers that bidding started with three or four bidders. Two dropped out right away at around $50,000. Jessica and an older gentleman stayed in.

She remembers looking intensely at the auctioneer while the rest of the room fell away. "Is she in?" she heard her mother ask. Back and forth, very fast, the bids edged up, until she started to wish the other guy would "jump the bid" past her top limit just so it would all be over. Instead, he stopped. The auctioneer kept his patter going half a minute longer. "Going once . . ."

"She's got it!" she heard her mother exclaim in disbelief. Then, "SOLD."

When I ask Jessica if they've ever had regrets, Ryan, sitting at the cash register a few feet away, looks up. "Every day," he says, not quite smiling. "Every day." But he joins the conversation as they describe plans to install solar panels, expand the kids' play area, plant new sections, and add more varieties. The orchard is well tended, there is a fresh coat of red paint on the barn, there are pies for sale and a batch of fresh doughnuts on the counter. The place is full of commitment and optimism.

HENRY WARD BEECHER gave his address on the democratic apple in 1864, to an audience of apple enthusiasts and society folk in the Hudson River Valley. In a time and place still embroiled in the carnage and long struggle of the Civil War, which by then had been raging for nearly four years, it must have been a relief, even for the dedicated abolitionist, to turn attention on a lovely afternoon to something as pleasant, comforting, and mundane as the apple. And yet he titled his speech "The Political Economy of the Apple," unable perhaps to completely disengage from the larger forces swirling around their little island. But in doing so, he turned not to difficulty and conflict but to all the ways that apples were a common good, hardy and easy to cultivate, productive, adaptable, available to all. "The apple-tree is the common people's tree, moreover, because it is the child of every latitude and every longitude on this continent."[7]

"Apples were as common as air," he reminisces near the end of his cheery and in some ways whimsical discourse. But underneath the remarks about flavor and virtue and productivity and ease, he keeps returning to something more substantial. Even in the midst of the war so nearby, he chose to focus on what was universal and good. Apples are the fruit of the common people, he said in a variety of ways. "Whether neglected, abused, or abundant, it is able to take care of itself, and to be fruitful of excellence . . . Of fruits, I think [the apple], above all others, may be called the true democratic fruit."[8]

I borrowed Beecher's phrase to describe this most favorite of fruits at first without realizing how aptly it describes the world that nurtures the best apples, a world marked by interdependence, diversity, resilience, respect for difference of philosophy and approach, and public support for the commons.

The lessons of apples are not always what I expected. I've experienced both the power and the limits of a market-based strategy for change, of what politics in a democracy can achieve in one lifetime. I've learned from apple growers that few things about farming are absolute, or predictable. Solutions are incremental, priorities vary with the time and season, weather changes, tactics work for a while and then have to be adapted to new conditions. I believe the future of apples in America lies at the intersection of these contradictions and choices.

The same forces pressing against a positive future for apple growers are pressing against all farmers in the United States. Concentration in retail, wholesale, and packing infrastructure and concentration of production in only a few states threaten the ability of markets and growers to adapt to local needs. Population growth and development are sucking up land. Climate change affecting weather, regional varieties, and invasive insects is compounded by dramatic cuts in funding for public research, extension, and breeding programs. Fewer midsized farms mean fewer growers to support associations, research, public policy, and marketing. Cheap commodity apples and concentrate coming from China and fresh apples from the Southern Hemisphere encourage the consumer fetish for year-round supply, perfection in fruit, and unrealistic expectations of "pure" production practices.

Both the pressures and the positive things that are happening in the world of apples offer lessons for our larger vision of farming and food in the United States. If we want to take apart the current food system and build something better, it's worth considering both what needs to be changed and what needs to be appreciated.

To change the food system, we will have to take apart the things that make it difficult for local farms to thrive. Along with subsidies, price supports, and other kinds of agricultural policy that get attention during Farm Bill cycles, we need to examine the economic structure of agriculture. This includes concentration and control over markets, research, and inputs. Shopping behaviors and market equations concentrate too much economic power in the largest and most consolidated corporations, making it difficult for independent farms to survive.

Civic abdication has allowed a public good—agriculture—to become a business investment for a few powerful entities. Beyond regulations, restrictions, bans on toxic substances, and unsustainable practices, we need to prioritize the kind of research and land use policies that will allow orchards and farms to produce apples and other crops successfully and ecologically. We need business structures and policies that strengthen independent, family-owned farms of all sizes.

These days, the capacity to hold and honor different and often conflicting truths is called up in every arena of life. Farming happens within the context of the biggest social, ecological, and political issues of our time. Climate change. Race and equity. Human health. Hunger. To be able to acknowledge the truth that exists for you without negating the truth that exists for someone else is a matter of survival. Many of the issues facing apple growers are larger than agriculture, larger than food, larger than the United States. These issues will not be solved by agriculture alone, and agriculture will not be healthy and sustainable until we've found ways to address them.

Two of the biggest external threats to the future of independent apple growers in the United States are population growth and climate change. The symptoms are loss of farmland and constant pressure on crops from extreme weather and invasive pests and diseases. The biggest internal threats include the increasing concentration of economic resources into fewer hands, loss of knowledge, loss of genetic diversity, and loss of public funding for agriculture research and education. The big risk to all of us if those forces are left unaddressed is loss of the people, land, and knowledge that give us the capacity to produce food in many parts of the country.

There are many ways to change that outcome that invoke appreciation. Do all the things that connect you to food and farms and community. Shop at farmers markets, CSAs, and pick-your-own orchards. Try new and old varieties. Ask farmers and family members for stories of their own connection to apples. Seek out, support, and advocate for the kind of farming practices that will make the earth better for all of us. The urge to know your farmer, to relish and explore heirloom apples, to shop conscientiously, to plant a fruit tree in your yard or on your apartment balcony, to work to increase fairness, reduce waste, and make fresh fruit available in food deserts — all of that is good and crucial work.

All of these positive actions can make a difference—but none is right in every situation. They are necessary but not, on their own, sufficient.[9] The only ones I would discourage are those that make it harder to work together. Our "food rules," standards, regulations, and labels—all of which are useful and important signposts—will have to soften around the edges. We'll need to adapt and evolve to make progress, accept trade-offs and compromise, and allow ourselves and our fellow citizens to be imperfect. We will have to get better at not confusing methods, strategies, and philosophy with the shared values and goals they can so easily obscure.

I would add a few other things to that list. Be less doctrinaire and more understanding of different approaches to farming and marketing. Be more curious—ask more questions. Don't expect guarantees and certainty from a process as variable as nature. Be more forgiving of imperfect solutions. Support independent, family-owned farms and orchards of all sizes. Thank a farmer but don't stop there. Thank an extension agent, scientist, local grocer, and cook for their part in bringing good, healthy, local food to you. Support funding for public research. Pay your taxes gladly, and then stay engaged to make sure the public servants who represent you know how you think those taxes are best used. Find and defend what is necessary for you. Recognize it is not sufficient for the whole. Think of farming as a public good, of democracy as a right and also a responsibility.

What's at stake? Certainly farming knowledge, the ability to feed ourselves, to have apple orchards, and apples. Maybe even our democracy and our national soul.

To provide delicious, diverse, nourishing, ecologically responsible apples from farms that provide a fair and sustainable livelihood to farmers and their employees and enhance the economy, culture, and land in communities across the United States, it takes a nation, not just a farm. A healthy democracy requires civic responsibility: informed citizens, appreciation of difference, willingness to be good neighbors. Growing apples that feed local communities requires a democracy of taste, diversity, enterprise, science, and civic-mindedness. A democracy of apples.

Harold Linder's collection of trees, the wisdom captured in my collection of old farming and apple books, the crisp tart apples at Lyman, Clark Brothers, Jerzy Boyz and Appleberry Orchards, and the cider doughnuts at the farmers market all bring me great pleasure. So does knowing the mounds of new and old varieties with stickers saying Stemilt, Cascade Crest Organics, or Envy™ came from orchards tended by generations of innovative, hardworking growers. I'm determined that Rosa, Angelica, Jose, and the Jamaican crews I've met on my orchard visits in the Northeast will move toward a more just, safe, and honorable place in orchard work and will lead the rest of us there, too.

The love, loyalty, and emotion that are called up by beautiful rural landscapes and walks through an orchard are as essential to me as breathing. I'm only a generation away from the farm. I have an emotional and intuitive yearning for a connection to the rolling land, a yearning I know is shared by many. These things matter because I believe they deeply affect the kind of ecosystem, economy, and values we are creating for ourselves and for the next generation.

Harold Linder wanted to grow good apples, to feed his neighbors, and to take care of the land. I'm keeping the map of his orchard not out of nostalgia, not as a remnant of something that's disappearing, but as an inspiration for a way forward.

NOTES

Unless otherwise noted, all first-person statements quoted are from interviews with the author.

INTRODUCTION

1. USDA/Department of Justice Public Workshops Exploring Competition in Agriculture, Ankeny, Iowa (March 12, 2010) (statement of U.S. Secretary of Agriculture Tom Vilsack), https://www.justice.gov/sites/default/files/atr/legacy/2010/12/20/iowa-agworkshop-transcript.pdf.

2. Henry Ward Beecher, "The Political Economy of Apples," in *Plain and Pleasant Talk about Fruits, Flowers, and Farming*, 2nd ed. (New York: Derby & Jackson, 1874), 4.

CHAPTER ONE

1. USDA Agricultural Marketing Service, https://www.ams.usda.gov/services/local-regional/farmers-markets-and-direct-consumer-marketing.

2. Rich Pirog and Zach Paskiet, *A Geography of Taste: Iowa's Potential for Developing Place-Based and Traditional Foods* (Ames: Leopold Center for Sustainable Agriculture at Iowa State University, 2004), 7–8.

3. Leopold Center for Sustainable Agriculture, *Iowa Food and Farm Facts*, based on "1998 Survey of Buying Power," *Sales and Marketing Management*, 1998. Craig Chase, Marketing and Foods Systems Initiative program leader at the Leopold Center, cautions that it is difficult to get an accurate percentage because of variations in the way production and marketing data are reported.

4. *Trends in U.S. Local and Regional Food Systems*, January 2015 (Washington, DC: Economic Research Service, USDA), https://www.ers.usda.gov/publications/pub-details/?pubid=428-.

5. U.S. Census of Agriculture, 2012 (USDA National Agricultural Statistics Service).

6. *Overview of Organic Production*, 2013 (Washington, DC: Economic Research Service, USDA), http://www.ers.usda.gov/data-products/organic-production/documentation.aspx.

7. The Lewis Hine quote is reported in a variety of sources, including http://thehumanist.com/magazine/september-october-2011/features/remembering-lewis-hine.

CHAPTER TWO

1. The only apples indigenous to North America are a few wild crab apples growing among forests and brush. Imported seeds tucked into the pockets of immigrants and refugees carved out a place for the apples we know today, and for the humans who carried them. In possibly the greatest burst of genetic diversity and apple evolution ever seen, apples brought to North America became both an agent of domination over land and native peoples, and at the same time a comforting sign of domesticity and stability.

2. Gary Nabhan, *Where Our Food Comes From: Retracing Nikolay Vavilov's Quest to End Famine* (Washington, DC: Island Press, 2009), 121.

3. There is still ongoing debate about the contribution of various species to the modern-day apple and its proper botanical designation.

4. John Bunker, *Not Far from the Tree: A Brief History of the Apples and Orchards of Palermo, Maine, 1804–2004* (self-published, 2007), 21.

5. Creighton Lee Calhoun, *Old Southern Apples* (White River Junction, VT: Chelsea Green Publishing, 2011), 3.

6. Ibid.

7. Alice Martin, *All about Apples* (Boston: Houghton Mifflin, 1976), 15. Martin also notes: "The eastern tribes were skilled agriculturists, and as the colonists learned about the indigenous corn, beans, and tubers from them, the Indians, in turn, observed the foreign plants introduced by the invading English, Dutch, and French, and appropriated what they felt would serve their way of life. The apple tree, whose fruit they mostly dried, became one of the new food plants cultivated extensively by the Indians." She confirms the existence of the Cayuga and Seneca Lakes orchards and notes a number of named apples grown on native orchards in the south.

8. William Kerrigan, *Johnny Appleseed and the American Orchard: A Cultural History* (Baltimore: Johns Hopkins University Press, 2012), 25.

9. David W. Kilbourne, *Annals of Iowa* 2, no. 4 (October 1864).

10. Calhoun, *Old Southern Apples*, 7–8.

11. I owe this delightful description of apple genetics to Dan Cooley, professor of plant pathology at University of Massachusetts Amherst. He explains: In apples, and us, each chromosome is made up of a pair of long strands of DNA. These two strands match up all along the length of the chromosome, working in tandem. A gene is actually a segment of a chromosome, made up of similar

segments of DNA from each of the two strands. Similar, but not the same—each gene is made up of a segment from each DNA strand, an allele from each, two alleles for each gene.

Here's a simplified example. Suppose we have a gene for apple skin color, and there are two possible alleles, one directing red and one calling for yellow. To make the skin color gene, both alleles come together in the chromosome. If both code for red, the gene is homozygous for red, and the apple is red. If both code for yellow, the apple is homozygous for yellow, and we get a yellow apple. But what if the gene is heterozygous, with one red and one yellow allele, what color will the apple be then? Maybe it's red, maybe yellow, or maybe a beautiful orange blush, depending on how the alleles interact. And what if there's another allele for green? Now there are six possible combinations, with the possibility of shades that mix red, yellow, and green. And suppose the color gene interacts with a "stripe/solid" gene, making the apple either a solid color or varying shades of color across the surface? These genes may interact with wax genes and russet genes, and maybe instead of three alleles we have five for each gene, so that the possible combinations get incredibly, wonderfully complex and variable!

12. Howard Means, *Johnny Appleseed: The Man, the Myth, the American Story* (New York: Simon and Schuster, 2011), 8.

13. Chapman is a controversial figure in apple circles, a hero to some and an amateur to others; several historical and recent accounts of John Chapman's life are listed in the bibliography.

14. The account of Henderson Luelling's traveling nursery is drawn from several sources, including Kent Pellett, *Pioneers in Iowa Horticulture* (Des Moines: Iowa State Horticultural Society, 1941); H. E. Nichols, "Pioneers in Horticulture," *The Palimpsest* 47, no. 7 (July 1966); Rosanne Sizer and William Silag, "Fruit in Iowa: A Brief History," *The Palimpsest* 62, no. 3 (May/June 1981); and Patrick A. Hall, "Oregon's Johnny Appleseed," *Frontier* magazine, June/July 1967.

15. Notes and various articles come from the papers of M. Waterman, Salem, Iowa, State Historical Society of Iowa Archives, MS 253, box 28, file 39.

16. Ibid.

17. U.S. Bureau of Census, Census of Agriculture, 1860, USDA Census of Agriculture Historical Archive, http://agcensus.mannlib.cornell.edu/AgCensus /homepage.do.

18. Morrill Act of 1862, Pub. L. No. 37-108.

19. Hatch Act of 1887, Pub. L. No. 24, Stat. 440, Chapter 314, https://nifa.usda .gov/program/hatch-act-1887.

20. Smith-Lever Act of 1914, Pub. L. 63-95, https://nifa.usda.gov/sites/default /files/Smith-Lever Act.pdf.

CHAPTER THREE

1. US Apple website, http://usapple.org/all-about-apples/apple-industry-statis
tics/.

2. According to the University of California, Davis website, "Integrated pest
management is an ecosystem-based strategy that focuses on long-term prevention of pests or their damage through a combination of techniques such as biological control, habitat manipulation, modification of cultural practices, and
use of resistant varieties. Pesticides are used only after monitoring indicates
they are needed according to established guidelines, and treatments are made
with the goal of removing only the target organism. Pest control materials are
selected and applied in a manner that minimizes risks to human health, beneficial and nontarget organisms, and the environment." http://www2.ipm.ucanr
.edu/WhatIsIPM/.

3. U.S. Census of Agriculture, 2012 (USDA National Agricultural Statistics
Service).

4. *Semidwarf* refers to the type of rootstock used for the orchard, explained
further in chapter 4.

5. U.S. Census of Agriculture, 2007, 2012 (USDA National Agricultural Statistics Service).

CHAPTER FOUR

1. Henry Ward Beecher, *Plain and Pleasant Talk about Fruits, Flowers, and
Farming* (New York: Derby and Jackson, 1859), 292.

2. The pheromones Lyman uses for apple maggot flies are not as easy to get
in the East, where there are fewer growers using them. But the more users there
are, the more the supplies will become available, which John hopes will eventually lead to more growers adopting the approach.

3. Monitoring trees by growth stage adds precision, because tree growth,
insect development, and disease infection are driven by the weather, notably
temperature. For example, evolution has synced the development of plum curculio to that of the apple tree so that small new apples, the ideal site for curculio eggs, are ready just when the curculio is ready to lay eggs. Knowing that, a
grower watches out for curculio "just after petal fall and during the few weeks
of fruit set."

4. Art Agnello, ed., *Scaffolds Fruit Journal* 24, no. 6 (May 4, 2015), New York
State Agricultural Experiment Station, Cornell University, Geneva, New York.

5. Some growers are moving away from glyphosate because of concerns
about toxicity and because many fast-growing weed species are developing
resistance to it. New research shows it may persist in the environment longer

than originally indicated, and it may have more serious health consequences for humans and wildlife, adding to the pressure to find alternatives.

6. Orchard owner Pete Ten Eyck explains that fire blight bacteria grow in the trees' conductive tissues and prevent water from getting to the tissue so that shoots dry up and die.

7. Dan Cooley of the University of Massachusetts notes: One recent product of this research is computer-based technology that takes some of the uncertainty out of thinning. Scientists have defined relationships between the weather, specifically the amount of sunlight falling on an orchard and the temperature, carbohydrates produced by the apple tree, and the amount of fruit that trees are likely to set and retain. Weather data and forecasts are fed into the computer model, and the relative impact of a thinning is estimated. Combining this with counts of flowers and later developing fruits, growers can take much of the guesswork out of thinning, making alternative thinners much more viable.

CHAPTER FIVE

1. Liberty Hyde Bailey, *The Principles of Fruit Growing, with Applications to Practice* (New York: Macmillan, 1926), 35.

2. Gary Nabhan, ed., *Forgotten Fruits: Manual and Manifesto* (n.p.: Renewing America's Food Traditions (RAFT) Alliance, 2010), 4.

3. Andrew Jackson Downing and Charles Downing, *The Fruits and Fruit Trees of America* (New York: John Wiley and Sons), 1845.

4. W. H. Ragan, *Nomenclature of the Apple: A Catalogue of the Known Varieties Referred to in American Publications from 1804 to 1904* (Washington, DC: United States Department of Agriculture, Government Printing Office), 1905.

5. Spencer A. Beach, *Apples of New York*, vols. 1 and 2, New York Agricultural Experiment Station (Albany, NY: J. B. Lyon Company, 1905). Beach later served as head of the Horticulture Department at Iowa State College from 1906 to 1922.

6. Melissa Block, "Keeping Heirloom Apples Alive Is 'Like a Chain Letter' over Many Centuries," National Public Radio, September 19, 2014, http://www.npr .org/2014/09/19/349626755/keeping-heirloom-apples-alive-is-like-a-chain -letter-over-many-centuries.

7. *The Illustrated History of Apples in North America* at 3,600 pages in seven volumes is tentatively due out in January 2017 from JAK KAW Press in Mount Horeb, Wisconsin. For more about Dan Bussey and his apple opus, see Michael Tortorello, "An Apple a Day, for 47 Years: Apple Picking Season Is Here. Don't You Want More Than a McIntosh?" *New York Times*, October 22, 2014, http://www .nytimes.com/2014/10/23/garden/apple-picking-season-is-here-dont-you-want -more-than-a-macintosh.html?_r=0.

8. A. J. Downing, notebooks, Parks Library Special Collections, Iowa State University, Ames.

CHAPTER SIX

1. Sources for the story of Jesse Hiatt's Red Delicious include various newspaper articles and announcements archived at the State Historical Society of Iowa and Kent Pellet, *Pioneers in Iowa Horticulture* (Des Moines: Iowa State Horticultural Society, 1941).

2. Pellet, *Pioneers in Iowa Horticulture*, 3.

3. Paul Domoto, professor of horticulture, Iowa State University, quoted in *Des Moines Register*, September 29, 2008, 4.

4. Malinda Geisler, Iowa State University Ag Marketing Center Fact Sheet, revised by Diana Huntford, AgMRC, December 2013.

5. The Wealthy was found growing in Minnesota by Peter Gideon, an eccentric orchardist who had brought some of the parent stock from Maine after learning of it in a dream. Gideon went on to become the first head of the Minnesota Agricultural Experiment Station, which a century later produced an even more illustrious offspring, the Honeycrisp.

6. "The New England Seven," issued by the extension services of New Hampshire, Connecticut, Vermont, Massachusetts, Rhode Island, and Maine, June 1928.

7. Gary Nabhan, ed., *Forgotten Fruits: Manual and Manifesto* (n.p.: Renewing America's Food Traditions (RAFT) Alliance, 2010), 4.

8. Adrian Higgins, "How the Public Lost Its Taste for the Once-Popular Red Delicious Apple," *Washington Post*, August 14, 2005, http://www.sfgate.com/bay area/article/How-the-public-lost-its-taste-for-the-2647967.php.

9. The story of Honeycrisp is drawn from several sources, including "With Honeycrisp's Patent Expiring, U of M Looks for New Apple," Rachel Hutton, *City Pages*, Oct 1, 2008, and "The Apple—Rebooted," May 29, 2014, University of Minnesota website, http://discover.umn.edu/news.

10. Richard Lehnert, "How Many Apple Varieties Are Too Many?" *Good Fruit Grower*, June 1, 2015.

11. Geraldine Warner, "Ambrosia Restrictions to End," *Good Fruit Grower*, June 18, 2015.

12. Washington Apple Commission Crop Facts, http://bestapples.com/wash ington-orchards/crop-facts/.

13. Parts of this account are drawn from Ken Meter, food systems analyst, Crossroads Resources paper on the history of MN#1914, 2001, and "The Minnesota Apple Growers Position on the Release of the #1914 Apple Selection," February 16, 2006.

14. Washington Apple Commission Crop Facts, http://bestapples.comwash ington-orchards/crop-facts/.

CHAPTER SEVEN

1. Susanne Freidberg, *Fresh: A Perishable History* (Cambridge, MA: Belknap Press of Harvard University Press, 2009), 139; J. A. Filcher, California State Board of Trade manager, quoted in Steven Stoll, *The Fruits of Natural Advantage: Making the Industrial Countryside in California* (Berkeley: University of California Press, 1998), 73; original quotation from *Pacific Rural Press* 55 (January 1, 1898).

2. Liberty Hyde Bailey, *The Principles of Fruit Growing, with Applications to Practice* (New York: Macmillan, 1926), 31.

3. Ronald Jager, *The Fate of Family Farming: Variations on an American Idea* (Lebanon, NH: University Press of New England, 2004) 162; *Northeast Farms to Food* (Belchertown, MA: Northeast Sustainable Agriculture Working Group, 2002).

4. Rich Pirog and Zach Paskiet, *A Geography of Taste: Iowa's Potential for Developing Place-Based and Traditional Foods* (Ames: Leopold Center for Sustainable Agriculture at Iowa State University, 2004).

5. S. A. Beach, *Report of the Iowa State Horticultural Society for the Year 1918*, vol. 53 (Des Moines: State of Iowa, 1918).

6. Rich Pirog and John Tyndale, *Comparing Apples to Apples: An Iowa Perspective on Apples and Local Food Systems* (Ames: Leopold Center for Sustainable Agriculture at Iowa State University, 1999).

7. U.S. Census of Agriculture, 2012 (USDA National Agricultural Statistics Service). Of the 915 million U.S. acres in agriculture—over 40 percent of our total land base—only 5.2 million are fruit, tree nut, and vineyards combined; a whopping 163.5 million are planted in corn and soybeans. For the first time, in 2012, these two crops represented more than 50 percent of all cropland harvested in the United States.

8. Thomas A. Lyson, G. W. Stevenson, and Rick Welsh, *Food and the Mid-Level Farm: Renewing an Agriculture of the Middle* (Cambridge, MA: MIT Press, 2008), xi. A thorough analysis of farm size and ownership trends is also included in the appendix: Mike Duffy, "The Changing Status of Farms and Ranches of the Middle," 257–83.

9. U.S. Census of Agriculture, 2007, 2012 (USDA National Agricultural Statistics Service).

10. U.S. Census of Agriculture, 2012 (USDA National Agricultural Statistics Service).

11. *A Time to Act: A Report of the USDA National Commission on Small Farms* (Washington, DC: U.S. Department of Agriculture, 1998).

12. Osha Gray Davidson, *Broken Heartland: The Rise of America's Rural Ghetto* (Iowa City: University of Iowa Press, 1996), 19–20.

13. U.S. Census of Agriculture, 2012 (USDA National Agricultural Statistics Service).

14. U.S. Census of Agriculture, 2002 (USDA National Agricultural Statistics Service).

15. US Apple website, www.usapple.org/all-about-apples/apple-industry-statistics.

16. Ken Meter, systems analyst, Crossroads Resource Center, based on consumer price index and comparisons to wholesale price index, Federal Reserve Board.

17. John Bunker, *Not Far from the Tree: A Brief History of the Apples and Orchards of Palermo, Maine, 1804–2004* (self-published, 2007), 59.

18. *Census of Agriculture* (Washington, DC: Bureau of the Census, U.S. Dept. of Commerce, and USDA, National Agricultural Statistic Service, 1997, 2002, and 2007), http://usda.mannlib.cornell.edu/MannUsda/viewDocumentInfo.do?documentID=1825.

19. Paul Post, "Real Estate Boom Pinches a Produce Supply in the Hudson Valley," *New York Times,* June 1, 2016.

CHAPTER EIGHT

1. Rajiv Lal, Jose Alvarez, and Dan Greenberg, *Retail Revolution: Will Your Brick and Mortar Store Survive?* (Cambridge: Harvard Business School, 2014), 172–73.

2. Ibid.

3. The history of Lagomarcino-Grupe is primarily drawn from National Register of Historic Places Registration Form, Lagomarcino-Grupe Fruit Co, U.S. Department of the Interior National Park Service, 2013, http://www.burlington iowa.org/DocumentCenter/Home/View/257, and Philip D. Jordan, "In the Shade of the Old Apple Tree," *The Palimpsest* 55, no. 3 (May/June 1974).

4. Dieter Brandes, *Bare Essentials: The ALDI Way to Retail Success* (London: Cyan/Campus Books, 2004), 26.

5. Geraldine Warner, "Bigger Crops Ahead," *Good Fruit Grower,* January 21, 2015.

6. Ibid.

7. Matt Milkovich, "Supermarkets Reshape the Global Apple Industry," *Fruit Growers News,* January 29, 2016, http://fruitgrowersnews.com/article/supermarkets-reshape-the-global-apple-industry/.

8. Ibid.

9. Melanie Warner, "You Want Any Fruit with That Big Mac?" *New York Times,*

February 20, 2005, http://www.nytimes.com/2005/02/20/business/yourmoney
/you-want-any-fruit-with-that-big-mac.html?_r=0 .

10. Matt Milkovich, "Rising Demand for Hard Cider Fuels Growing Demand
for Apples," *Fruit Growers News*, February 9, 2016, http://fruitgrowersnews.com
/news/9541/.

11. USDA Economic Research Service, *Fruit and Tree Nut Data* (Washington,
DC: USDA Economic Research Service, 2015), https://www.ers.usda.gov/data
-products/fruit-and-tree-nut-data/.

12. Geraldine Warner, "China Agrees to Accept All Varieties of U.S. Apples,"
Good Fruit Grower, January 26, 2015.

CHAPTER NINE

1. United States Bureau of the Census, Census of Agriculture, 1860. USDA
Census of Agriculture Historical Archive, 1840–2002, http://agcensus.mannlib
.cornell.edu/AgCensus/homepage.do.

2. Margaret Gray, *Labor and the Locavore: The Making of a Comprehensive
Food Ethic* (Berkeley: University of California Press, 2013), 29.

3. Susanne Freidberg, *Fresh: A Perishable History* (Cambridge, MA: Belknap
Press of Harvard University Press, 2009), 137, and William Nutting, *California
Views in Natural Colors* (San Francisco: California View Publishing, 1889), 5.

4. R. Karina Gallardo and Michael P. Brady, "Adoption of Labor-Enhancing
Technologies by Specialty Crop Producers: The Case of the Washington Apple
Industry," *Agricultural Finance Review* 75, no. 4 (September 2015): 514–32.

5. In addition to hourly wages, Pete Ten Eyck paid $1,040 per H-2A worker
for transportation to and from Jamaica to the United States in 2016. For seven
weeks at fifty hours a week, typical during harvest, that adds almost $3/hour
per worker in addition to the cost of housing and various fees and permits. If
New York requires farms to pay time and a half for over forty hours, as has been
proposed, Pete expects he would have to limit his crew to forty hours because
he could not afford the additional pay. He's certain the H-2A workers would
apply to go to farms in other states to be able to work the hours they want.

6. Washington Apple Commission Crop Facts, http://bestapples.com/wash
ington-orchards/crop-facts/.

7. Technology and high-density planting of dwarf trees are ways to address
labor shortages and risks. A grower in Michigan has patented a mechanical
vacuum tube device to carry apples from a picker's hand directly to the bin. On
a self-propelled platform, workers can pick from the tops of trees even at night.
The vacuum hose gently sucks the apples into the bin the way a pneumatic tube
whisks bank deposits to the drive-up teller.

High-density plantings of dwarf trees that can be pruned and harvested without ladders are also driven in part by the need to cut labor costs. Moving from tree to tree becomes more like moving from bush to bush, and the picker's feet stay on the ground. "Ladderless orchards would be huge for our industry," a grower told *Fruit Growers News* in 2014. See "Vacuum Harvester Redesigned to Be Self-Propelled," *Fruit Grower News*, November 2014.

8. Pacific Northwest Agricultural Safety and Health Center, Department of Environmental and Occupational Health Sciences, School of Public Health, University of Washington, "Orchard Ladders: Life-Changing Injury Stories, Real Workers, Real Events," 2014, http://deohs.washington.edu/pnash/orchard -injuries.

9. Patrick O'Brien, John Kruse, and Darlene Kruse, *Gauging the Farm Sector's Sensitivity to Immigration Reform* (Columbia, MO: World Agricultural Economic and Environmental Services, 2014), http://www.fb.org/files/AFBF_Labor Study_Feb2014.pdf.

CHAPTER TEN

1. Ernest Gustavus Lodeman, *The Spraying of Plants*, Rural Science Series, ed. Liberty Hyde Bailey (New York: Macmillan & Co, 1910), 62.

2. Ibid., 121.

3. Ann Vileisis, *Kitchen Literacy: How We Lost Knowledge of Where Food Comes From and Why We Need to Get It Back* (Washington, DC: Island Press, 2008), 175. For a detailed account of the use and regulation of arsenic compounds and DDT in the United States, see pages 173–85.

4. Sandra Steingraber, *Living Downstream: A Scientist's Personal Investigation of Cancer and the Environment* (New York: Vintage Books, 1998), 95–96.

5. Jean-Henri Fabre, *Social Life in the Insect World* (New York: The Century Co., 1914), 214.

6. The Environmental Protection Agency Office of Pesticide Programs formed a Biopesticides and Pollution Prevention Division in 1994. Pheromones must be registered with the EPA just as other pesticides are. There are now about 130 mating disruption pheromones registered, for a variety of insects and a variety of crops, in a category called biopesticides. See https://www.epa.gov /ingredients-used-pesticide-products/what-are-biopesticides.

7. Charles M. Benbrook, *Pest Management at the Crossroads* (Yonkers, NY: Consumers Union, 1996), i–ii.

8. Jay Brunner (presentation, Washington State Horticultural Society annual meeting, Kennewick, Washington, December 2015).

9. David Granatstein, *Sustainability and Tree Fruit Production* (Wenatchee, WA: Center for Sustaining Agriculture and Natural Resources, Washington State University), http://www.tfrec.wsu.edu/pdfs/P2967.pdf.

10. Wendell Berry, *The Unsettling of America: Culture and Agriculture* (San Francisco: Sierra Club Books, 1977), 147.

11. *Retaking the Field: The Case for a Surge in Agricultural Research* (Arlington, VA: Supporters of Agricultural Research (SoAR) Foundation, 2016), www .supportagresearch.org/retakingthefield.

12. Dan Cooley and Bill Coli, "Bringing Scholarship to the Orchard: Integrated Pest Management in Massachusetts," chap. 5 in *Engaging Campus and Community: The Practice of Public Scholarship in the State and Land-Grant University System*, ed. Scott J. Peters, Nichols R. Jordan, Margaret Adamek, and Theodore R. Alter (Dayton, OH: Kettering Foundation, 2005).

13. Andy Nelson, "Apple Stink Bug Damage Totals $37 Million," *The Packer*, May 18, 2011, http://www.thepacker.com/fruit-vegetable-news/crops-markets /apple_stink_bug_damage_totals_37_million_122164094.html.

CHAPTER ELEVEN

1. Bradford Sewell and Robyn M. Whyatt, *Intolerable Risk: Pesticides in Our Children's Food* (New York: Natural Resources Defense Council, 1989), 6.

2. Ibid., 7.

3. As sales of organic food have begun to outpace supply, a "transitional" designation has been established by the USDA with the support of the organic industry in an effort to encourage more growers to move toward organic production.

4. For a detailed first-person account of the debates over the creation of the national organic standards, I highly recommend Grace Gershuny, *Organic Revolutionary: A Memoir of the Movement for Real Food, Planetary Healing, and Human Liberation* (Barnet, VT: Joes Brook Press, 2016).

5. Henry Ward Beecher, *Plain and Pleasant Talk about Fruits, Flowers, and Farming* (New York: Derby and Jackson, 1859).

6. "U.S. Organic Sales Post New Record of $43.3 Billion in 2015," Organic Trade Association, May 19, 2016, https://www.ota.com/news/press-releases/19031#st hash.LIMr7Pvo.dpuf.

7. Rachel Carson, *Silent Spring* (Boston: Houghton Mifflin, 1962), 9.

8. Ibid., 12–13.

9. Ibid., 292.

10. Ibid., 29.

11. Ibid., 51.

CHAPTER TWELVE

1. Aldo Leopold, "A Land Ethic," in *Sand County Almanac and Sketches Here and There*, special commemorative edition (Oxford: Oxford University Press, 1989), 224–25.

2. Sandra Steingraber, *Living Downstream: A Scientist's Personal Investigation of Cancer and the Environment* (New York: Vintage Books, 1998), 236.

3. Ibid., 116.

4. Kirk Johnson and Fernanda Santos, "Western Wildfires Consume Manpower and Acreage," *New York Times*, August 20, 2015, http://www.nytimes.com/2015/08/21/us/3-firefighters-die-in-crash-on-way-to-washington-state-blaze.html?_r=0.

5. Envy™ apple website, https://envyapples.com/en/blog/mark-gores-lake-chelan-washington.

6. Stephen Singer, "Family Cultivates Ninth Generation's Commitment to Connecticut Farm," *Portland Press Herald*, November 28, 2015, http://www.pressherald.com/2015/11/28/family-cultivates-ninth-generations-commitment-to-connecticut-farm/.

7. Henry Ward Beecher, "The Political Economy of Apples," in *Plain and Pleasant Talk about Fruits, Flowers, and Farming*, 2nd ed. (New York: Derby and Jackson, 1874), 6.

8. Ibid., 4.

9. In an October 19, 2015, interview with *Modern Farmer* magazine, "How Has Organic Certification Stood Up to the Test of Time? A Q&A with Mark Lipson," by Brian Barth, Mark Lipson, longtime organic advocate, farmer, and former organic and sustainable agriculture policy advisor in the office of the secretary of agriculture, said: "My formulation has always been, and still is, that organic is necessary, but not sufficient for truly sustainable agriculture in all its dimensions. But the necessary part is absolutely true, and truer than ever. It's still a work in progress."

SELECTED BIBLIOGRAPHY

There are several centuries worth of books and resources available on apples and related topics. What follows is a compilation of those I have found most useful and enjoyable. I have included materials I read and consulted during my research for this book, whether or not they are specifically referenced in the text. News, ongoing research, and digital resources on apples expand and change almost daily. I have included those only as they are specifically referenced in the endnotes, and I have recommended general resources for the most current information.

BOOKS

Allen, Will. *The War on Bugs.* White River Junction, VT: Chelsea Green Publishing, 2008.

Aucter, E. C., and H. B. Knapp. *Orchard and Small Fruit Culture.* 3rd ed. New York: John Wiley and Sons, 1937.

Bailey, Liberty Hyde. *The Holy Earth: Toward a New Environmental Ethic.* New York: Charles Scribner's Sons, 1915.

———. *The Principles of Fruit Growing, with Applications to Practice.* New York: Macmillan, 1926.

Barber, Dan. *The Third Plate: Field Notes on the Future of Food.* New York: Penguin Press, 2014.

Beach, Spencer A. *Apples of New York.* Vols. 1 and 2. New York Agricultural Experiment Station. Albany, NY: J. B. Lyon Company, 1905.

Beecher, Henry Ward. *Plain and Pleasant Talk about Fruits, Flowers, and Farming.* New York: Derby and Jackson, 1859 and 1874 editions.

Benbrook, Charles M. *Pest Management at the Crossroads.* Yonkers, NY: Consumers Union, 1996.

Berry, Wendell. *The Unsettling of America: Culture and Agriculture.* San Francisco: Sierra Club Books, 1977.

Bosso, Christopher J. *Pesticides and Politics: The Life Cycle of a Public Issue.* Pittsburgh: University of Pittsburgh Press, 1987.

Brandes, Dieter. *Bare Essentials: The ALDI Way to Retail Success.* London: Cyan/Campus Books, 2004.

Browning, Frank. *Apples: The Story of the Fruit of Temptation*. New York: North Point Press, 1998.

Budd, J. L., ed. *Transactions of the Iowa State Horticultural Society for 1884, along with Eastern, Western, and Other Local Societies*. Vol. 19. Ames: Iowa State Horticultural Society, 1885.

Bunker, John. *Not Far from the Tree: A Brief History of the Apples and Orchards of Palermo, Maine, 1804–2004*. Self-published, 2007. Available from Fedco Seeds, Waterville, ME.

Burford, Tom. *Apples of North America: 192 Exceptional Varieties for Gardeners, Growers, and Cooks*. Portland, OR: Timber Press, 2013.

Burritt, M. C. *Apple Growing*. New York: Outing Publishing, 1912.

Calhoun, Creighton Lee. *Old Southern Apples*. White River Junction, VT: Chelsea Green Publishing, 2011.

Carson, Rachel. *Silent Spring*. Boston: Houghton Mifflin, 1962.

Cole, S. W. *The American Fruit Book*. Boston: John. P. Jewett and Company, 1850.

Cooley, Dan, and Bill Coli. "Bringing Scholarship to the Orchard: Integrated Pest Management in Massachusetts." Chap. 5 in *Engaging Campus and Community: The Practice of Public Scholarship in the State and Land-Grant University System*, edited by Scott J. Peters, Nichols R. Jordan, Margaret Adamek, and Theodore R. Alter. Dayton, OH: Kettering Foundation, 2005.

Davidson, Osha Gray. *Broken Heartland: The Rise of America's Rural Ghetto*. Iowa City: University of Iowa Press, 1996. First published in 1990 by Free Press/Macmillan.

Downing, Andrew Jackson, and Charles Downing. *The Fruits and Fruit Trees of America*. New York: John Wiley and Sons, 1845 and 1878 editions.

Fabre, Jean-Henri. *Social Life in the Insect World*. New York: The Century Co., 1914.

Freidberg, Susanne. *Fresh: A Perishable History*. Cambridge, MA: Belknap Press of Harvard University Press, 2009.

Gershuny, Grace. *Organic Revolutionary: A Memoir of the Movement for Real Food, Planetary Healing, and Human Liberation*. Barnet, VT: Joes Brook Press, 2016.

Gray, Margaret. *Labor and the Locavore: The Making of a Comprehensive Food Ethic*. Berkeley: University of California Press, 2013.

Griffin, Susan. *Woman and Nature: The Roaring Inside Her*. New York: Harper and Row, 1978.

Griffith, David. *American Guestworkers: Jamaicans and Mexicans in the U.S. Labor Market*. University Park: Pennsylvania State University Press, 2006.

Hatcher, Harlan, Robert Price, Florence Murdoch, John W. Stockwell, Ophia D.

Smith, and Leslie Marshall. *Johnny Appleseed: A Voice in the Wilderness*. 4th ed. Paterson NY: Swedenborg Press, 1953.

Hightower, Jim. *Hard Tomatoes, Hard Times: A Report of the Agribusiness Accountability Project on the Failure of America's Land Grant College Complex*. Rochester, VT: Schenkman Books, 1973.

Hopkinson, Deborah. *Apples to Oregon*. New York: Aladdin Paperbacks, 2004.

Iowa State College and Iowa Agricultural Experiment Station. *A Century of Farming in Iowa 1846–1946*. Ames: Iowa State College Press, 1946.

Jacobsen, Rowan. *American Terroir: Savoring the Flavors of Our Woods, Waters, and Fields*. New York: Bloomsbury, 2010.

——. *Apples of Uncommon Character: Heirlooms, Modern Classics, and Little-Known Wonders*. New York: Bloomsbury, 2014.

Jager, Ronald. *The Fate of Family Farming: Variations on an American Idea*. Lebanon, NH: University Press of New England, 2004.

Janik, Erika. *Apple: A Global History*. London: Reaktion Books, 2011.

Juniper, Barry E., and David J. Mabberly. *The Story of the Apple*. Portland, OR: Timber Press, 2006.

Kallet, Arthur, and F. J. Schlink. *100,000,000 Guinea Pigs: Dangers in Everyday Foods, Drugs, and Cosmetics*. New York: Grosset and Dunlap, 1933.

Kerrigan, William. *Johnny Appleseed and the American Orchard: A Cultural History*. Baltimore: Johns Hopkins University Press, 2012.

Kingsbury, Noel. *Hybrid: The History and Science of Plant Breeding*. Chicago: University of Chicago Press, 2009.

Lal, Rajive, Jose Alvarez, and Dan Greenberg. *Retail Revolution: Will Your Brick and Mortar Store Survive?* Cambridge: Harvard Business School, 2014.

Lear, Linda. *Rachel Carson: Witness for Nature*. New York: Henry Holt and Company, 1997.

Leopold, Aldo. *A Sand County Almanac and Sketches Here and There*. Special commemorative edition. Oxford: Oxford University Press, 1989. First published in 1949 by Oxford University Press.

Linder, Harold. *The Apple: Fruit of the Ages*. Self-published, 2006.

Lodeman, Ernest Gustavus. *The Spraying of Plants*. Rural Science Series, edited by Liberty Hyde Bailey. New York: Macmillan, 1910.

Martin, Alice A. *All about Apples*. Boston: Houghton Mifflin, 1976.

Maynard, S. T. *The Practical Fruit Grower*. Springfield, MA: Phelps Publishing, 1898.

McMillan, Tracie. *The American Way of Eating: Undercover at Walmart, Applebee's, Farm Fields, and the Dinner Table*. New York: Scribner, 2012.

Means, Howard. *Johnny Appleseed: The Man, the Myth, the American Story*. New York: Simon and Schuster, 2011.

Miller, Daphne. *Farmacology: What Innovative Family Farming Can Teach Us about Health and Healing.* New York: William Morrow, 2013.

Nabhan, Gary. *Where Our Food Comes From: Retracing Nikolay Vavilov's Quest to End Famine.* Washington: Island Press, 2009.

Page, Stephen, and Joseph Smillie. *The Orchard Almanac: A Spraysaver Guide.* Rockport, ME: Spraysaver Publications, 1986.

Parsons, Russ. *How to Pick a Peach: The Search for Flavor from Farm to Table.* Boston: Houghton Mifflin, 2007.

Pellet, Kent. *Pioneers in Iowa Horticulture.* Des Moines: Iowa State Horticultural Society, 1941.

Phillip, Leila. *A Family Place: A Hudson Valley Farm, Three Centuries, Five Wars, One Family.* Albany, NY: State University of New York Press, 2001.

Phillips, Michael. *The Apple Grower: A Guide for the Organic Orchardist.* Rev. ed. White River Junction, VT: Chelsea Green Publishing, 2005.

Pollan, Michael. *A Botany of Desire: A Plant's-Eye View of the World.* New York: Random House, 2001.

Powell, Stephen Russell. *America's Apple.* Hatfield, MA: Brook Hollow Press, 2012.

Ragan, W. H. *Nomenclature of the Apple: A Catalogue of the Known Varieties Referred to in American Publications from 1804 to 1904.* Washington, DC: United States Department of Agriculture, Government Printing Office, 1905.

Sears, Fred. *Productive Orcharding: Modern Methods of Growing and Marketing Fruit.* 2nd ed. Lippincott's Farm Manuals. Philadelphia: Lippincott, 1917.

Shepherd, Geoffrey S., and Gene A. Futrell. *Marketing Farm Products: Economic Analysis.* 7th ed. Ames: Iowa State University Press, 1982.

Souder, William. *On a Farther Shore: The Life and Legacy of Rachel Carson.* New York: Crown Publishers, 2012.

Steingraber, Sandra. *Living Downstream: A Scientist's Personal Investigation of Cancer and the Environment.* New York: Vintage Books, 1998.

Stevenson, G. W., ed. *Food and the Mid-Level Farm.* Cambridge, MA: MIT Press, 2008.

Thoreau, Henry David. "Wild Apples." In *Excursions,* 16th ed. Boston: Houghton, Mifflin, 1863.

Upshall, W. H., ed. *History of Fruit Growing and Handling in United States of America and Canada 1860–1972.* University Park, PA: American Pomological Society, 1976.

Vileisis, Ann. *Kitchen Literacy: How We Lost Knowledge of Where Food Comes From and Why We Need to Get It Back.* Washington, DC: Island Press, 2008.

Waugh, F. A. *Fruit Harvesting, Storing, and Marketing*. New York: Orange Judd, 1901.

Yepson, Roger. *Apples*. New York: W. W. Norton, 1994.

ARTICLES, REPORTS, AND PAPERS

Baker, Brian, Tom Green, Daniel Cooley, Susan Futrell, Lyn Garling, Edwin Rajotte, Grace Gershuny, Jeff Moyer, Abby Seaman, and Stephen Young. *Organic Agriculture and Integrated Pest Management: Synergistic Partnership Needed to Improve the Sustainability of Agriculture and Food Systems*. Madison, WI: IPM Institute of North America, December 2015.

Carroll, J. E., and T. L. Robinson, eds. *New York Integrated Fruit Production Protocol for Apples*. Ithaca, NY: Cornell University, 2006.

Jacobsen, Rowan. "Forgotten Fruit." *Mother Jones*, March/April 2013.

Laskin, David. "A Harvest of Ashes." *Seattle Metropolitan*, December 2014.

Nabhan, Gary, ed. *Forgotten Fruits: Manual and Manifesto*. N.p.: Renewing America's Food Traditions (RAFT) Alliance, 2010.

Pirog, Rich, and Zach Paskiet. *A Geography of Taste: Iowa's Potential for Developing Place-Based and Traditional Foods*. Ames: Leopold Center for Sustainable Agriculture at Iowa State University, 2004.

Pirog, Rich, and John Tyndale. *Comparing Apples to Apples: An Iowa Perspective on Apples and Local Food Systems*. Ames: Leopold Center for Sustainable Agriculture at Iowa State University, 1999.

Seabrook, John. "Crunch." *The New Yorker*, November 21, 2011.

Sewell, Bradford, and Robyn M. Whyatt. *Intolerable Risk: Pesticides in Our Children's Food*. New York: Natural Resources Defense Council, 1989.

DOCUMENTARY FILM

Broken Limbs: Apples, Agriculture, and the New American Farmer. Produced by Jamie Howell and Guy Evans. Oley, PA: Bullfrog Films, 2004.

Seasons in the Valley. Directed by Adam Matalon. Peekskill, NY: Chatsby Films: 2007.

Troublesome Creek: A Midwestern. Produced by Jeanne Jordan and Steven Ascher for *The American Experience*. Boston: West City Films, 1995.

GENERAL RESOURCES

American Fruit Grower. Http://www.growingproduce.com/magazine/american-fruit-grower.

Fruit Growers News. Http://fruitgrowersnews.com.

Good Fruit Grower. Http://www.goodfruit.com.
United States Department of Agriculture Economic Research Service (USDA/ ERS). Https://www.ers.usda.gov.
U.S. Census of Agriculture, 2007 to present. Https://www.agcensus.usda.gov/.
USDA Census of Agriculture Historical Archive, 1840–2002. Http://agcensus .mannlib.cornell.edu/AgCensus/homepage.do.

INDEX

breeding programs, 24–25; GMO apples, 108–9; Iowa State Agricultural College, 93–94; for new varieties, 99–103, 105–9; post–Civil War, 93; at public institutions, 17, 99–101, 105; restricted or trademarked varieties, 97–98, 100–102; rootstocks, 58–59. *See also* research; varieties (cultivars)
Breezy Hill Orchard, 189
Broken Heartland, O. G. Davidson, 123
Brown, Susan, 110
brown marmorated stink bug (BMSB), 178–81
Brunner, Dr. Jay, 170
Budd, J. L., 93–94
Bunker, John (Maine Heritage Orchard), 22, 84, 123–24
Burlington (Iowa), wholesale fruit distribution, 130–34
Burlington Leopold apple, 80, 89, 214
Bussey, Dan, 85–86
Butz, Earl, 122

C&S Wholesale Grocers, 134
Calhoun, Creighton Lee, 24, 84
California, early nurseries, 34
California Fruit Growers Exchange (CFGE), 116
California Winegrowers' Lodi Rules, 192
Cameo apple, 89, 98–99, 101
carbamates, health concerns, 69
carbon dioxide injury, postharvest disorder, 73
carbon sequestration, 70, 209
Carlton Complex fire, 55, 211
Cascade Crest Organics, 53–55,

155–56, 219. *See also* Stennes, Kevin
Cascadian Farm, 187
cedar rust disease, 65
Central State University (Ohio), 37
Chapman, John (Johnny Appleseed), 27–29, 58
Chelan Fresh, 53–55, 101, 125, 135, 198
Chelan Fruit Cooperative, 54, 72, 135, 211–12
Chenango Strawberry apple, 78
Cherokee early orchards, 24
Chilean apples, 12
China: apple production, 96, 139; BMSB origin, 181; exports to, 140; immigrant farmworkers from, 148; juice concentrate from, 96, 139, 217
chlorpyrifos (insecticide), 171–72
chromosomes, number of, 25
citrus scale, vedalia beetles to control, 168–69
Civil War: impact on apple production, 36; impact on farming economy, 115–16; slavery in agriculture, 147
Clark, Aaron, Dana, Brian, Naomi, Silas, and Isaak (Clark Brothers Orchards): Eco Apple certification, 18, 172; Honeycrisp apple, 100, 108; packing and shipping facilities, 71, 72, 113; pest-management strategies, 181–83; planning for future, 213; sales outlets, 134–35; thinning practices, 68–69; wild pollinators, 68
climate change: carbon sequestration, 70, 209; heirloom varieties and, 82; impact on agriculture, 45, 70, 216; locally grown produce and, 13; pests and diseases and, 62

Unsettling of America, The, W. Berry, 174
US Apple, 123
United States Department of Agriculture (USDA), 36, 178

varieties (cultivars): for cider, 138–39; in colonial U.S., 26–27; consumer taste preferences, 92–111; disease resistance, 58, 65; diversity, 17, 22, 40, 81–84, 95–96; GMO, 108–9; in Harold Linder's orchard, 77–81; heirloom varieties, 17, 22, 81–84; "The New England Seven," 94–95, 101; pollination requirements, 67; price-setting for, 114–15; research to develop, 99–103, 109–10; from Russian trees, 93–94; selection criteria, 60; sports, 60; storage attributes, 72–73; topworking established trees, 30, 60. *See also* apple varieties; breeding programs; club apples (restricted or trademarked); *and specific varieties*
Vavilov, Nikolay, 22
vedalia beetle, citrus scale control, 168–69
Vilsack, Tom, 139–40

Washington, George, 23
Washington Apple Commission, 47
Washington Farm Labor Association (WAFLA), 156
Washington State: apple industry, 45–52, 118–19; apple-growing regions, 47; co-ops, 135–36; crop diversity, 118–19; export market, 12, 14, 46, 53, 140; grower statistics, 47–48; H-2A guest worker visas,

155; infrastructure, 45–47; orchard size, 135; University of Washington, 99
Washington State University Decision Aid System, 174
water pollution, from agriculture, 15–16, 199, 210
water projects, in Washington State, 45
Wealthy apple, 84, 85, 95
weather: cold-weather damage, 70, 118; fire blight and, 198; grower preoccupation with, 70; monitoring, 195, 201; rain, 70; varieties for specific climates, 82. *See also* climate change
weed management: herbicides, 65, 167; IPM, 61–62; strategies, 64
Weinreb, Wynne, 18, 48–50, 211; death of, 212; economic concerns, 125–26; innovative practices, 52, 103–4. *See also* Jerzy Boyz Farm
Welch, Jessica and Ryan, 214–15
West Indies, farmworkers from, 152
Whitcomb, Lot, 32
Whole Foods, 134–35, 137
wholesale distributors: apple sales, 13–14; economics of, 125; Lagomarcino-Grupe, 131–33; setting apple prices, 113–15
Winesap apple, 89
Wolf River apple, 78, 84

Xerces Society, 199

Yellow Transparent apple, 21, 84, 94

Zestar! apple, 11, 105, 114